Premature Termination in Psychotherapy

Premature Termination in Psychotherapy

STRATEGIES FOR ENGAGING CLIENTS AND IMPROVING OUTCOMES

Joshua K. Swift and Roger P. Greenberg

American Psychological Association • Washington, DC

Published by
American Psychological Association
750 First Street, NE
Washington, DC 20002
www.apa.org

To order
APA Order Department
P.O. Box 92984
Washington, DC 20090-2984
Tel: (800) 374-2721; Direct: (202) 336-5510
Fax: (202) 336-5502; TDD/TTY: (202) 336-6123
Online: www.apa.org/books/
E-mail: order@apa.org

In the U.K., Europe, Africa, and the Middle East, copies may be ordered from
American Psychological Association
3 Henrietta Street
Covent Garden, London
WC2E 8LU England

Typeset in Goudy by Circle Graphics, Inc., Columbia, MD

Printer: Maple Press, York, PA
Cover Designer: Mercury Publishing Services, Inc., Rockville, MD

The opinions and statements published are the responsibility of the authors, and such opinions and statements do not necessarily represent the policies of the American Psychological Association.

Library of Congress Cataloging-in-Publication Data

Swift, Joshua K., author.
 Premature termination in psychotherapy : strategies for engaging clients and improving outcomes / by Joshua K. Swift and Roger P. Greenberg. — First edition.
     p. ; cm.
 Includes bibliographical references and index.
 ISBN-13: 978-1-4338-1801-1
 ISBN-10: 1-4338-1801-9
 I. Greenberg, Roger P., author. II. American Psychological Association, issuing body.
III. Title.
 [DNLM: 1. Patient Dropouts—psychology. 2. Psychotherapy—methods. 3. Treatment Refusal—psychology. 4. Professional-Patient Relations. WM 420]

 RC480.5
 616.89'14—dc23

                                        2014009044

British Library Cataloguing-in-Publication Data

A CIP record is available from the British Library.

Printed in the United States of America
First Edition
http://dx.doi.org/10.1037/14469-000

This book is dedicated with love and gratitude to our families,
our mentors, our students, and our clients.

For Rebecca, Julia, Ethan, Christian, Elliott, and Agnes
—*Joshua K. Swift*

For Vicki, Michael, Lisa, Hunter, and Spencer
—*Roger P. Greenberg*

CONTENTS

Premature Termination in Psychotherapy

INTRODUCTION

> The secret of a good sermon is to have a good beginning and a good
> ending, then having the two as close together as possible.
> —George Burns

Decades of empirical research have established psychotherapy as a valuable intervention for those suffering from mental health disorders and psychological distress (Lambert, 2013). In addition to the clinical research, countless practitioners have seen the positive effects of various psychological treatments as they have helped their clients recover from their emotional pain and suffering. However, psychotherapy as an intervention is far from perfect. It is disheartening that the same intervention (or the same therapist) can work perfectly for some clients but fail to work for others. Even in carefully controlled clinical trials, only about 60% of clients recover by the end of treatment (Lambert, 2013), and still more conservative outcomes are found in naturalistic settings (Hansen, Lambert, & Forman, 2002). Despite much recent advancement in the field in terms of developing, testing, and refining specific treatment approaches; identifying evidence-based principles of change; and recognizing the important roles of therapist and client variables in

http://dx.doi.org/10.1037/14469-001
Premature Termination in Psychotherapy: Strategies for Engaging Clients and Improving Outcomes,
by J. K. Swift and R. P. Greenberg

treatment processes and outcomes, some clients still end therapy prematurely without having made any significant improvements or gains.

Perhaps the greatest potential for improving the effectiveness of psychotherapy lies in addressing the issue of premature termination. Even the most expert clinicians using treatments with the strongest empirical support cannot be effective if patients drop out of treatment prematurely. Research has clearly demonstrated that patients who do not complete a full course of therapy show poorer outcomes compared with patients who complete treatment (Bjork, Bjorck, Clinton, Sohlberg, & Norring, 2009; Cahill et al., 2003; Klein, Stone, Hicks, & Pritchard, 2003; Knox, Adrians, Everson, Hess, Hill, & Crook-Lyon, 2011; Lampropoulos, 2010). It follows that if we can increase the number of patients who remain in treatment for a full course of therapy, we will, in turn, see improvements in the overall effectiveness of our interventions.

The question that lies before us, then, is how to prevent patients from discontinuing psychotherapy prematurely. This book was written in an attempt to help clinical researchers and practitioners alike find an answer. At the more novice level, the information in this book can help graduate students prepare for their first clients, allowing them to go into their practicum and internship placements with a tool kit already in place for reducing premature termination. Clinical supervisors may find this book useful in helping their supervisees develop the skills necessary to help their patients complete therapy while providing services in a training clinic environment (a setting in which high rates of premature termination are frequently documented). For these readers specifically, we have developed a number of teaching materials (slides, discussion questions, role-plays) that are available for download at http://www.psychotherapyresearchlab.com. Given that even veteran psychologists will experience some premature termination with their clients, this book will also be useful to those more seasoned professionals who are similarly seeking to learn additional ways to decrease patient dropout in their practice. Readers who are interested in psychotherapy research will also find useful the comprehensive yet practice-friendly review of the research on premature termination and the presentation of strategies for reducing its occurrence.

Considering these multiple audiences, we have two main goals for this book. First, we hope readers will gain a better understanding of the problem of premature termination in psychotherapy. Second, we hope readers will learn specific actions that can be taken to reduce the number of patients who drop out. With these goals in mind, the book is split into three parts. Part I includes a discussion of the negative impacts associated with therapy dropout, a review of the frequency of and risk factors for premature discontinuation, and a conceptualization of why some patients choose to drop out of treatment. This section provides a comprehensive, detailed look at the empirical evidence on the topic of premature termination, which then provides a foundation for the strategies we recommend in Part II. Part II presents eight practice recommendations for dealing with the problem of premature discontinuation. Last, Part III describes, in a more concise way, the nature of the problem and our suggested remedies.

PART I: UNDERSTANDING PREMATURE TERMINATION IN PSYCHOTHERAPY

Before one can take steps to reduce premature termination in practice or develop and study strategies for decreasing the occurrence of this negative therapy event, one must understand (a) why some clients choose to drop out and (b) when premature termination is most likely. In addressing these questions, Part I provides a foundation for the rest of the book. Specifically, in Chapter 1, we discuss both a definition (occurring when a client starts an intervention but unilaterally discontinues it before recovering from the problems that led him or her to seek treatment) and a theoretical conceptualization (patients drop out when the perceived or anticipated costs associated with engaging in treatment outweigh the perceived or anticipated benefits) of premature termination in psychotherapy. In Chapter 2, we present the results of a large-scale meta-analysis (including data from 669 studies and more than 84,000 clients) on the topic of dropout. This meta-analysis presents not only findings on the frequency of premature termination but also data on the client, therapist, treatment, and setting variables for which rates of treatment dropout are the highest. Overall, this first section of the book will help readers to better understand the phenomenon of premature termination, thus providing a framework for the strategies to reduce dropout discussed in Part II, and to identify clients and situations that are higher risk for premature discontinuation, providing a road map for situations when the strategies would be of the most benefit.

PART II: STRATEGIES FOR REDUCING PREMATURE TERMINATION

Part II focuses on providing practitioners with specific strategies and techniques that have been empirically demonstrated to reduce the occurrence of premature discontinuation in psychotherapy. Based on the theoretical conception presented in Part I, these strategies are all methods for helping patients perceive and anticipate more benefits and fewer costs with engaging in treatment. The first four strategies are designed to be used in the first few sessions of treatment (although their use may also be warranted in the later stages of therapy as well) and focus on helping patients develop realistic and appropriate expectations and preferences for psychotherapy. With realistic expectations and preferences in place, patients are less likely to be disappointed (a significant cost that often leads to premature termination) once therapy begins. Additionally, discussing expectations and preferences with patients helps build a collaborative relationship—a significant benefit that helps patients become more invested in the therapeutic endeavor. Chapter 3 discusses the strategy of providing role induction, a method for orienting clients to therapy and the roles and behaviors they can expect to occur in treatment. In Chapter 4, we present a rationale for including client preferences and their hopes and desires for therapy in the treatment decision-making process, as well as methods for soliciting, talking about, and addressing these preferences with clients. Chapter 5 presents the strategy of helping clients plan for an appropriate therapy ending right from the start of treatment. Chapter 6 discusses the strategy of providing education about patterns of change in psychotherapy, such as the dose–effect and phase models, and of warning patients that setbacks may occur.

Whereas the first four strategies emphasize efforts providers can make in the first few sessions, the second four focus more on steps that providers can take throughout the course of treatment. Each of these strategies is designed to help patients more readily experience and recognize some of the benefits of psychotherapy, thus increasing the likelihood of continued attendance. In Chapter 7, we discuss methods for strengthening patients' early hope or increasing their belief that change is possible and therapy is an avenue for bringing it about. As patients' level of hope increases, so does their level of motivation for change. Along these lines, Chapter 8 addresses strategies for working with patients to help them make progress based on their level of motivation and readiness to change. Chapter 9 discusses methods for fostering the therapeutic alliance and repairing alliance ruptures. Last, in Chapter 10, we discuss strategies for assessing and discussing treatment progress, both to decrease patients' experience of deterioration or worsening in treatment and to help them more readily recognize the changes that psychotherapy is helping them make. Each of these chapters includes a description of the strategy, a review of the relevant research, and specific instructions for use in practice. By the end of Part II, readers will have developed a tool kit for reducing rates of premature discontinuation in their clinical practice.

Throughout this section of the book, two cases are used to illustrate each of the strategies. The first is Emily, a 24-year-old Caucasian woman who is seeking therapy for relationship difficulties she is having with her boyfriend. In her intake session, she also reveals a childhood history of sexual abuse by a man who was a friend of the family. This is her first time meeting with a therapist. The therapist with whom she is working uses a client-centered approach. The second client is Robert, a 53-year-old Hispanic man who is seeking treatment for long-standing issues with social anxiety. He has been in therapy a number of times throughout his life but has continued to struggle with the same issues. His therapist uses a cognitive–behavioral approach. These two successful cases are contrasted with two similar clients presented in Chapter 1, both of whom drop out of therapy shortly after starting.[1]

PART III: CONCLUSION

Chapter 11 provides a brief review of the main concepts that were presented in the book, including why premature discontinuation is a problem, when it is most likely to occur, how and why it occurs, and what strategies practitioners can use to reduce its occurrence. Limitations of these methods are discussed, as are future research directions. By giving clinical researchers and practitioners a greater understanding of premature discontinuation and specific strategies for preventing dropout, this book is designed to help reduce the rates of premature discontinuation in psychotherapy, leading to improved effectiveness of the interventions we offer.

In conclusion, because premature termination is a significant problem in psychotherapy that limits the effectiveness of the services that we provide to our clients, we hope this book will assist readers (graduate students, seasoned practitioners, clinical supervisors, and psychotherapy researchers alike) to (a) better understand why premature termination sometimes occurs, (b) better recognize the situations (client, therapist, treatment, and setting predictors) in which treatment dropout is most likely to occur, and (c) develop a tool kit of strategies for reducing dropout in psychotherapy. With the increased knowledge that can be gained from this book, we hope that practitioners (graduate students and professionals) will be better able to help their clients complete a full course of treatment. Although some tailoring may be needed, the material in this book has application across clinical settings, and although most of the research reviewed is from adult clients, practitioners who work primarily with children should find many of the strategies useful as well.

---

[1]All of the case examples are composites, and identifying information has been changed to maintain confidentiality.

I

UNDERSTANDING PREMATURE TERMINATION IN PSYCHOTHERAPY

1

WHAT IS PREMATURE TERMINATION, AND WHY DOES IT OCCUR?

Age wrinkles the body; quitting wrinkles the soul.
                                                    —Douglas McArthur

Jane, a 26-year-old woman, started therapy hoping she could get help sorting through her thoughts and emotions after a breakup with her significant other. They had been in a committed relationship for the past 2 years, which started with her moving across the country so that she could live with him. While in the relationship, Jane was repeatedly the victim of emotional and sometimes physical abuse, and she fell into a pattern of trying to win her boyfriend's love and show her worth to him. One month after he broke up with her, Jane still could not make sense of her emotional reaction: She was angry with herself for having stayed in the relationship for so long, yet she missed him and desperately wanted him to take her back.

During the first two sessions of psychodynamic treatment, the therapist sought to understand Jane's experience in this relationship as well as her previous relationship history. The therapist worked hard to develop a therapeutic relationship with Jane during these sessions by displaying empathy,

http://dx.doi.org/10.1037/14469-002
Premature Termination in Psychotherapy: Strategies for Engaging Clients and Improving Outcomes,
by J. K. Swift and R. P. Greenberg

creating a nonjudgmental and safe environment, and validating and processing both her relief and sadness about being out of the relationship. At the end of the second session, Jane stated that she was grateful for the work that had been done so far in therapy and was looking forward to future sessions.

Despite her enthusiasm for therapy, Jane failed to show for her third session. The therapist called to check in with her and left a message on her voicemail. She returned the call 2 days later and scheduled another appointment for the following week. In that session, she indicated that she had missed the last appointment because she had begun spending time with her ex-boyfriend again. However, they had another argument, and she described a new interest in finally being done with the relationship. During the session, the therapist continued to provide support and help her process this decision. At the end of the session, she again expressed enthusiasm for the future work she would do in therapy; however, she failed to show for her next scheduled appointment and made no further contact with her therapist. Unfortunately, she never got to discuss the parallel difficulties she had in maintaining personal relationships and her inability to commit to a relationship with her therapist. Jane had prematurely discontinued therapy.

Michael, a 61-year-old man, called a therapist seeking to join a cognitive–behavioral group for anxiety. The next week, the therapist met with Michael for an initial screening session. During that session, Michael described long-standing symptoms meeting criteria for social phobia. Also during this session, the therapist provided a rationale for the 8-week cognitive–behavioral treatment and answered Michael's questions about the group. Despite his typical avoidance of group settings, Michael indicated that he was ready to take the steps to face his anxiety and expressed excitement about starting the group.

During the first session, the group was focused on providing psycho-education about the development of anxiety from a cognitive–behavioral model. Michael was active in sharing his experience of anxiety with the other group members. At the end of the session, homework was assigned for group members to pay closer attention to their anxiety and take note of their physiological, cognitive, and behavioral reactions to feared situations. Michael completed the homework and arrived for the second group session on time and ready to share. The session focused on identifying and labeling anxiety-provoking thoughts. Again, Michael was an active participant of the group, both opening up to other group members about his experiences and providing helpful support as the other group members shared. At the end of the session, homework for identifying and labeling anxiety-provoking thoughts was given. Michael expressed an understanding of the homework and confirmed that he would be present for the following week's appointment. Yet Michael failed to show, and attempts to call him were unsuccessful. He, like Jane, had dropped out of treatment.

Although the details may not always be the same, unfortunately Jane and Michael's stories are common. Despite the availability of an effective treatment, many clients fail to complete therapy and fully experience its benefits. Thus, practicing clinicians of all types have had or will have clients like Jane and Michael who unilaterally terminate therapy prematurely. At times, practicing clinicians may feel somewhat like Moses in the Old Testament account of the fiery serpents. While he was leading the Israelites out of Egypt, many of the people were bitten by snakes in the wilderness. In consequence, Moses fashioned a brass serpent to be hoisted up on a pole and promised the people that all who simply looked upon it would live. Despite this promise, many who were bitten failed to take advantage of the cure. Similarly, thousands of empirical studies have now clearly demonstrated the effectiveness of psychotherapy when compared with no treatment or with other available treatment options, such as medication (Lambert, 2013). Yet, like Jane and Michael, some clients do not take full advantage of it. Thus, one way for clinical researchers to improve the effectiveness of psychotherapy and clinicians to improve the effectiveness of their practice would be to gain a better understanding of why some clients choose to drop out and to develop ways for reducing its occurrence.

THE PROBLEM OF PREMATURE DISCONTINUATION

Let us begin with a discussion about the issue of premature discontinuation and why it should be considered a major problem in psychotherapy and worthy of our attention. Clients do drop out of therapy, a fact that all therapists have likely experienced. The frequency of its occurrence is discussed in the next chapter. But if a client drops out of treatment, is it really a problem? Should you, as a clinician, be concerned? Or, for those conducting clinical research, is premature termination really important enough that you should exert effort to study it? Given the deleterious effects that premature termination can have on clients, clients' associates, therapists, and clinics and agencies, we believe that focusing on reducing the occurrence of therapy dropout is actually one of the best ways that psychotherapy providers and researchers can use their time.

Problematic Effects on the Client

To determine the priority we should give to focusing on premature termination, let us begin by reviewing what happens to the patient who drops out from therapy. First, patients who prematurely terminate are generally more dissatisfied with the treatment they have received. In one recent qualitative study demonstrating this finding, Knox et al. (2011) conducted in-depth interviews about termination with 12 former psychotherapy patients. These patients were diverse in their demographics and in their reasons for seeking treatment, the type of treatment that they received, and the number of sessions attended. Despite this diversity, patients who had problematic and abrupt terminations almost uniformly reported that they did not benefit from therapy and made statements expressing their dissatisfaction with treatment, particularly with their therapist and the handling of alliance ruptures.

In a quantitative study comparing treatment satisfaction between dropouts and completers, Björk, Bjorck, Clinton, Sohlberg, and Norring (2009) collected follow-up data on 82 clients 2 to 3 years after they ended their eating disorder treatment. Part of the follow-up data collection included a self-report questionnaire on treatment satisfaction. Those clients who ended treatment on their own, before completing the treatment plan, reported much less satisfaction with both their treatment and their therapist's ability to listen and understand compared with clients who had completed therapy. For example, almost half of the dropouts classified themselves as being unsatisfied with treatment, whereas only 17% of the completers described themselves this way.

In another, less recent quantitative study examining satisfaction with treatment, Kokotovic and Tracey (1987) asked patients from a university counseling center to rate their satisfaction with an initial session on a standardized self-report measure. Of the patients for whom therapy was recommended, roughly 22% failed to continue past the intake appointment and were thus classified as dropouts. Kokotovic and Tracey found much greater dissatisfaction among these prematurely terminating patients. Their results indicated that, for their counseling center, level of satisfaction was the best predictor of whether the patient would immediately drop out.

Although it is important to recognize that premature terminators express more dissatisfaction with the treatment they receive, the more valuable question to ask is whether treatment dropouts and completers actually differ in terms of treatment outcomes. Gene Pekarik (1992a) was one of the first psychotherapy researchers to examine this question. In an outpatient clinic located in the Midwestern United States, Pekarik contacted 94 former clients at a 4-month follow-up date. Of these 94 clients, only 26 were classified by their therapists as having completed treatment, whereas the remaining 68 were classified as dropouts. Outcome comparisons were made at the time of termination. On the basis of the therapists' classifications of problem improvement, the clients who had dropped out of treatment were much less likely to be described as having made any progress during therapy. At the 4-month follow-up, the clients were asked to report their current symptoms on a standardized questionnaire and give their opinion about whether they had noticed any decrease in the problems that had brought them into treatment. Most notably, 22% of those clients who dropped out of therapy early (fewer than three sessions) experienced symptoms that were worse than when they had started treatment. Also, on average, the dropouts had lower scores on both the outcome measure and their own rating of change compared with clients who had completed treatment. This finding was true for both adult and child cases.

In a more recent study, Lampropoulos (2010) invited therapists and 85 clients from a university-based training clinic to complete outcome measures at the end of treatment. Of these 85 clients, just slightly more than half ($n = 43$) were categorized by their therapists as treatment dropouts, whereas the remaining 42 were classified as treatment completers. Clients who were classified as dropouts were rated more negatively by their therapists in terms of their posttreatment symptoms and well-being; in addition, the clients who were classified as dropouts rated themselves as having more negative treatment outcomes compared with the treatment completers.

In another study that used a standardized outcome measure (Beck Depression Inventory—II [BDI–II]; Beck, Steer, & Brown, 1996), Cahill and colleagues (2003) compared dropouts and completers from a controlled trial of cognitive therapy. They found that those clients who had completed therapy exhibited almost twice as much improvement on the BDI–II during treatment compared with clients who had prematurely terminated. In fact, although 71.4% of the completers had recovered according to clinically significant change standards, only 13% of the dropouts had achieved such a goal. Similar results indicating that clients who prematurely terminate from therapy have poorer treatment outcomes compared with therapy completers have been demonstrated in a number of other studies (Björk et al., 2009; Klein, Stone, Hicks, & Pritchard, 2003; Lebow, 1982; Pekarik, 1983; Sandell et al., 1993; Swift, Callahan, & Levine, 2009).

Problematic Effects on the Therapist

Clients are not the only ones who experience the deleterious effects of premature discontinuation. Studies have also indicated that therapists are negatively impacted when their clients choose to discontinue prematurely. Service providers experience a loss of revenue and an underutilization of their time associated with dropouts, particularly when the dropout discontinues by not showing up for a scheduled session (Barrett, Chua, Crits-Christoph, Gibbons, & Thompson, 2008; Reis & Brown, 1999). Perhaps the most notable negative effect therapists experience is the sense of failure or demoralization associated with the perception of being rejected by the patient who prematurely terminated. Ogrodniczuk, Joyce, and Piper (2005) described the experience well when they stated that the therapist's sense of self-worth can be threatened by premature terminators, particularly when the therapist's self-esteem is tied to his or her ability to help others. For example, in 1983, Farber administered a questionnaire to 60 psychotherapists asking them to rate the stressfulness of 25 patient behaviors. Of these 25, therapists ranked premature termination of therapy as the third most stressful event, scoring right below patients' suicidal statements and aggression and hostility, but above intense dependency, paranoid delusions, and psychopathy.

In a more in-depth qualitative study, Piselli, Halgin, and MacEwan (2011) interviewed 11 practicing board-certified (American Board of Professional Psychology) psychologists asking about their experience with premature termination. Specifically, the participating therapists were asked to reflect on a former patient who had dropped out of therapy and then discuss the personal and professional impact of the premature termination. The participating therapists identified a number of variables that may have led to the early ending, including patient problems such as lack of motivation or feeling overwhelmed in therapy, as well as mistakes made by the therapists and problems with the therapeutic relationship. Most of the therapists felt at least some responsibility for the patient's premature termination, and the most common feelings were a combination of sadness, disappointment, and frustration. Regret, surprise, confusion, failure, and shame were all also common feelings expressed by these therapists.

Problematic Effects for Others

In addition to the patient and therapist, other individuals and groups can be affected by patient dropout. Just as individual providers experience a financial cost and lost productivity associated with dropouts, mental health clinics and agencies are also faced with the same financial burdens. In fact, one study found that premature terminators are more likely to start and stop treatment on multiple occasions (Carpenter, Del Gaudio, & Morrow, 1979). Because agencies frequently cannot charge for appointments that are not kept, the missed appointment hours associated with dropouts are often wasted. Additionally, the unused appointments take up time that could be used to see other patients in the clinic, resulting in longer waitlists and a decreased ability to help those in need.

Another group that is influenced by premature termination is the dropout's associates. If the premature terminator continues to experience the distress and impairment that led him or her to seek out treatment in the first place (Cahill et al., 2003), the burden of the disorder that is felt by others continues as well. This group may include family members and friends who continue to experience interpersonal strains in their relationships with the client while feeling the need to persist in providing physical and emotional support (Fadden, Bebbington, & Kuipers, 1987; Pai & Kapur, 1982; Winefield & Harvey, 1994). It may also include employers who continue to experience a loss of client productivity due to the impact of the mental health problem. It is important also to note the costs to communities and societies in terms of expenditures on further treatment needs, which can be substantial. In fact, the World Health Organization (2001) indicated that in 2000, mental health disorders accounted for more than 12% of the global burden of disease. Each of these costs remains when individuals who suffer from mental health disorders prematurely terminate from a treatment, which, if completed, could drastically reduce the negative effects. Clearly premature discontinuation has widespread negative consequences, and it is therefore important that we identify ways to reduce its occurrence.

DEFINING THE PROBLEM

If we are going to figure out ways to fix or at least reduce the problem of premature discontinuation in psychotherapy, we must first step back to gain some understanding of what this negative therapy event is. In a previous work (Swift & Greenberg, 2012), we defined it as "occurring when a client starts an intervention but unilaterally discontinues prior to recovering from the problems (symptoms, functional impairment, distress, etc.) that led him or her to seek treatment" (p. 547). Implicit in this definition is the idea that the client has stopped therapy without achieving the therapeutic goals that she or he originally set with the therapist. Also implicit is the idea that the client quit therapy without gaining the full benefits that would have been available if he or she would have continued to attend and be fully invested in the sessions. According to this definition, we mention that premature discontinuation occurs unilaterally on the part of the client—in other words, the client chooses to terminate on his or her own despite the therapist's expectation or recommendation that the client should continue.

Premature discontinuation can be contrasted to a number of other types of therapy endings, including completing therapy, rejecting therapy, and early termination by the therapist. Completing therapy implies a resolution on the part of both the therapist and the client to the therapeutic activity. Rejecting therapy occurs when the client fails to start or show up for the initial appointment. Early termination by the therapist transpires occasionally, due to the life events or needs of a therapist, such as a move, new job, pregnancy, schedule conflict, or newly realized multiple relationship. Additionally, there are times when a therapist may choose to end therapy due to the client's resistance, lack of compliance with treatment, or boundary crossing. Even though these endings occur unilaterally, because the client has not initiated the termination of treatment, we view these endings to be different from premature discontinuation.

Naming and Operationalizing the Construct

Although most would agree with the basic definition that we have provided for premature discontinuation, there is much disagreement in the field with regard to the most appropriate name and operationalization for the construct. Premature discontinuation is referred to by different names in the literature, including attrition, dropout, early termination, premature termination, early withdrawal, and unilateral termination, to name a few. As long as the meaning implies the definition that we have provided, we view these various labels as synonymous and use them interchangeably in the field. We feel that premature discontinuation from psychotherapy, by any other name, is still a significant threat to the effectiveness of treatment.

Although the specific name used to refer to the construct is not all that important, it is essential that a universal operationalization be implemented. Existing research examining the frequency and predictors of premature termination from therapy often produce inconsistent results. It is thought that this is primarily due to the discrepancies in in measurement techniques. Here we review four historically used operationalizations, outlining the strengths and weakness of each, and then reintroduce a newer method for assessing premature termination based on clinically significant change. A summary of each of the operationalizations can be found in Table 1.1.

Duration Based

One of the most frequently used methods for assessing whether a patient has dropped out of therapy is to examine the number of sessions attended. Using duration-based methods of operationalization, any patient who attends less than a specified number of sessions is considered to have dropped out of treatment. Duration-based methods offer a number of advantages. First, they are grounded in the dose–effect literature (Howard, Kopta, Krause, & Orlinsky, 1986; Lambert, Hansen, & Finch, 2001), which indicates that as the number of sessions increases, a patient's likelihood of recovery or treatment success also increases. Second, premature termination is easy to assess with this method—information about treatment duration is readily obtained from any patient's chart, and so a classification can be made without needing an additional rater or questionnaire. Third, ratings based on this method are reliable.

Despite its advantages, the limitations of duration-based measurements preclude their use. First, there is little agreement in the field about the number of sessions that should be used to classify someone as a dropout or a completer.

TABLE 1.1

Strengths and Weaknesses of Existing Operationalizations

Operationalization	Method of measurement	Strengths	Weaknesses
Duration-based	Clients who attend less than a given number of sessions are considered dropouts; most common is median split.	• Grounded in the dose–effect literature • Easy and reliable classification	• Disagreement about required number of sessions • Clients differ widely in the number of sessions needed for recovery.
Failure to complete	Clients who do not complete a specified treatment protocol are considered dropouts.	• Easy and reliable classification	• Decisions are based on protocols and not individual clients. • Does not fit in settings where a specific protocol is not used
Missed appointment	Clients who fail to show for their last scheduled appointment are considered dropouts.	• Easy and reliable classification • Does not presuppose a set number of sessions or a right protocol for every client	• Misclassifies clients who did not progress or are dissatisfied, but informed therapist of ending as well as clients who have recovered but couldn't make an appointment • Does not distinguish between clients who are at different stages in the therapy process (a missed appointment after Session 3 is the same as one after Session 50)
Therapist judgment	After the end of therapy, the therapist makes a determination about whether the client should be considered a dropout.	• Tailored to the individual client (therapist is able to consider individual circumstances, progress, and goals)	• Low between-therapist reliability • Can be biased and flawed
Clinically significant change	Clients who discontinue before making a clinically significant change are considered dropouts.	• Based on actual progress • Tailored to the individual client • Reliable	• May be overly stringent (reliable improvement criteria can be used instead) • May miss some of therapy's nuances (can be combined with therapist judgment)

One such method is the median-split procedure in which all patients from a sample who attend less than the median number of sessions are classified as dropouts (Baekeland & Lundwall, 1975; Hatchett & Park, 2003; Pekarik, 1985). However, this method has little use for practitioners who work with individual patients, not samples. Additionally, using this method, 50% of the sample is always classified as having dropped out regardless of the actual effectiveness of the treatment or therapist. Furthermore, the median for one sample may be six sessions, and the median for another may be 20. In such a situation, a patient who attends 10 sessions would be identified as a dropout in one study and a completer in the other. Various other treatment durations have also been used (e.g., four sessions, six sessions, 10 sessions); however, these vary from one study to the next and depend on the individual researcher's or clinician's theory about what constitutes an adequate dose of treatment.

Even if the field used an agreed-on duration, a crucial limitation with these types of methods is an issue of validity. Although longer durations are generally associated with an increased chance of recovery, there is no set number of sessions that is perfect for every patient. Thus, duration-based methods misclassify as dropouts those patients who end therapy appropriately after a quicker recovery. They also misclassify as completers those patients who attend many sessions without much progress and then discontinue treatment abruptly on their own. Given these limitations, many have argued that duration-based methods for operationalizing premature discontinuation should not be used (Hatchett & Park, 2003; Pekarik, 1985), and we tend to agree with those arguments.

Failure to Complete

A second method for gauging premature discontinuation in psychotherapy is based on treatment completion—namely, any patient who does not complete the full treatment protocol could be categorized as a treatment dropout. Similar to duration-based methods, this operationalization is easy to assess and can be done reliably from one clinician to the next. This method also fits with the idea inherent in the definition of premature discontinuation that the patient has stopped therapy while there was some additional work that was needed or material that should have been covered.

The major limitation with measuring dropout based on failure to complete is that decisions are made based on treatment protocols rather than the needs of individual patients. This definition works well in research settings where empirically supported treatments are applied across patients with fidelity, and each patient is offered a treatment of identical length. However, the conditions that are present in highly controlled research designs are rarely applicable to actual clinical practice. Most practicing clinicians do not simply offer their patients 12 weeks of a manualized protocol for their problems. Instead, treatment length is based on the needs and speed of recovery for each individual patient. Additionally, an operationalization based on failure to complete a specified protocol has the same major limitations as the duration based operationalizations: Some patients will recover and be ready to finish treatment before completing a protocol, and other patients will need many more sessions than a protocol may allow. Those who improve and end early would be classified as dropouts even though recovery has been made, and those who complete the protocol without making any progress would not be classified as dropouts even if they discontinued unilaterally shortly after that.

Missed Appointment

Dropout can also be operationally defined on the basis of missed appointments. With this method, clients would be considered to have dropped out if they miss their last scheduled appointment. Similar to the previously described methods, this means of measurement also shows high reliability and is relatively easy to determine. However, compared with the two previous methods, an appraisal of premature discontinuation based on missed appointments seems to have more applicability to actual clinical practice. This definition does not presuppose that a set number of sessions or a specific treatment protocol is right for each individual client.

However, an operationalization of premature termination based on missed appointments is not without its limitations. The primary limitation with this method is that it has the potential to misclassify some types of clients. For example, according to this type of measurement, a client would automatically be classified as a dropout no matter what the reason for missing the appointment. Errors in classification could then occur when clients have recovered but miss their last appointment because extra-therapeutic events (such as a move) prevented them from attending the final session. Additionally, clients who have recovered but didn't realize the need for a final session would also be classified as dropouts. Furthermore, this operationalization does not distinguish between clients who may be at different stages in the therapy process. For example, a client who attends two sessions and then does not show up for a third and a client who attends 50 sessions and then does not show up for the very last one would both be classified as premature terminators. This method also has the potential to misclassify some clients as completers. For example, a client who has not made any progress in therapy and who is dissatisfied with the therapeutic work may stop treatment by failing to schedule another appointment rather than no-showing. Despite the lack of progress and a therapist's belief that the client should continue, because no appointment was missed, the client would be considered a treatment completer according to this method. Although limitations with the missed appointment method are present, it has been argued to be preferable to duration-based methods (Hatchett & Park, 2003; Pekarik, 1985).

Therapist Judgment

Another popular method for assessing premature termination in therapy is to base the classification on therapist judgment. Two ways of surveying therapist judgment are observed in the literature. The first, and by far the more commonly used, is simply to ask therapists to make a categorical rating of their clients as dropouts or completers after the end of treatment. For example, a therapist could be asked, "In your opinion, did your client drop out of treatment?" The second is to have therapists complete a quantitative measure assessing the client's level of dropout. For example, Reis and Brown (2006) developed the Termination Status Questionnaire for such a purpose. Using a measure to assess dropout is thought to better recognize that clients may be at different degrees of dropping out or completing therapy; however, research has yet to demonstrate the superiority or applicability of such measures.

Regardless of the exact questions asked, therapist judgment has historically been regarded as the most accurate and preferable method for assessing treatment dropout (Pekarik, 1985). Using this method, instead of just being based on a number of sessions or whether a session was missed, dropout classifications can be based on the individual client's reasons for seeking treatment. This allows the therapist to make a more fine-tuned determination of whether the therapy goals have been met and the therapy process completed. The therapist, with his or her personal involvement in the therapy process, is able to account for nuances when making a dropout decision that the methods described earlier would miss.

Therapist judgment is not without its shortcomings, however. First, this method has the potential for low reliability because different therapists may have different ideas about the purpose of therapy and the meaning of dropout. Second, therapists' expectations for therapy do not always match their clients' expectations, particularly when it comes to the necessary treatment length (Mueller & Pekarik, 2000). Thus, clients may sometimes feel like therapy has been successful and are ready to end treatment, even though their therapists feel like more work is needed. Third, therapists may be hesitant to recognize or report their clients as premature terminators, perceiving a sense of blame or possible failure. Last, research has indicated that therapist judgments in general are often not accurate when compared with statistically based methods of judgment (Garb, 2005; Grove, Zald, Lebow, Snitz, & Nelson, 2000), particularly in judgments of client outcome and recovery (Hannan et al., 2005).

A New Method Based on Change

Hatchett and Park (2003) first proposed and then Swift et al. (2009) further refined and tested a new way to gauge premature termination in psychotherapy based on clinically significant change. Clinically significant change is a construct that was introduced by Jacobson and colleagues as a method for assessing improvement in therapy (Jacobson, Follette, & Resvenstorf, 1984; Jacobson & Truax, 1991). It is obtained when (a) the patient moves from scoring in the clinical to the nonclinical range on a standardized outcome measure and (b) the change in score reflects a reliable improvement (an improvement that exceeds fluctuations in scores that might be due to measurement error). Clinically significant change is now commonly used to assess treatment outcomes; however, it can also be used to determine whether a patient has dropped out of psychotherapy.

According to this method, any patient who discontinues therapy before making a clinically significant improvement would be considered a treatment dropout. In contrast, any patient who discontinues treatment having already made a clinically significant improvement would be considered a treatment completer. We believe that this operationalization of dropout best fits the definition for the construct because it is based on patient change. This definition does not require patients to attend a certain number of sessions like the duration-based and failure to complete methods, recognizing that some patients may recover after only one or two sessions and some patients may require many months of treatment. In contrast to the missed appointment method, this method does not require a formal termination session for patients to count as therapy completers. Also, in contrast to therapist judgment, this method is based on the patient's self-report of his or her symptoms, which may be less prone to the biases that are inherent in basing dropout classifications on therapist opinion alone.

Empirical Research Comparing the Methods

Not surprisingly, it has been found that using different methods of operationalization results in different dropout prevalence rates. Pekarik (1985) conducted one of the earliest studies comparing dropout measures. In this study, 152 patients were classified using two methods (therapist judgment and duration-based) as either dropouts or completers after their termination of treatment. Whereas 53% of the patients were classified as premature discontinuers based on therapist judgment, 67% were classified as dropouts based on treatment duration. Two major reviews of premature discontinuation in therapy have also found differences in prevalence rates between the existing operationalizations. In a review of 125 studies, Wierzbicki and Pekarik (1993) found a 48% dropout rate for studies that assessed premature discontinuation based on therapist judgment or a set number of sessions. In contrast, a 36% dropout rate was found for studies that used the missed appointment method. This difference was statistically significant. In a more recent review with 669 studies, Swift and Greenberg (2012) found a dropout rate of 18.4% for studies using the failure to complete measure, 18.3% for duration-based studies, 24.4% for missed appointment, and 37.6% when dropout was assessed by therapist judgment.

Although these studies provide evidence for different dropout prevalence rates depending on the operationalization that is used, a more important question to ask is whether the methods match in their classification of individual patients. For example, one would want to know how often therapist judgment indicates a patient has dropped out when the duration-based method (or one of the others) indicates a patient has completed therapy. If the methods match in their classification of patients, then it makes little difference which operationalization is used. If, however, the methods do not match in their classifications, it becomes important for the field to adopt a universal method for assessing the construct.

Pekarik's (1985) previously mentioned study gives us some initial idea about whether the methods match up in their classifications. Obviously, if 53% of Pekarik's 152 patients were classified as dropouts by therapist judgment and 67% were classified as dropouts by the duration-based method, then these two methods differed in their classification for at least 21 of the patients. However, the methods for classification may have differed for even more patients. Although unlikely, it is possible that the entire 33% who attended enough sessions to be deemed completers were classified as dropouts by their therapists. In this case, instead of differing in classification for 21 patients, there would have been a discrepancy between the methods for 122 of the 152 patients. What a difference! However, Pekarik did not provide enough data to allow us to calculate how often a mismatch in classification occurred. Fortunately, two more recent studies have made these types of comparisons.

In the first study, Hatchett and Park (2003) compared three methods for classifying clients as premature terminators: therapist judgment, failure to attend the last scheduled appointment, and the median-split duration-based procedure. For this study, 85 clients from their university counseling center were classified as dropouts or completers by each of the three methods. Whereas 40.8% of the clients were classified as premature terminators by both the therapist judgment and the failure to attend methods, 53.1% were classified as dropouts by the median-split duration-based method. So already we see that, at least for some clients, there must have been differences in findings due to the classification methods. But how different were they? Hatchett and Park calculated kappa coefficients to statistically assess the level of agreement. A kappa coefficient is a statistical procedure that is typically used to represent the level of agreement between two raters (in this case, two methods of measurement). Rather than just examining the frequency of agreement, calculation of a kappa coefficient takes into account the agreement that occurs by chance. Like a correlation, if there is a complete agreement between the two raters (or methods), the kappa value will equal 1.0. In contrast, no agreement between the raters would result in a kappa value of 0.0. Hatchett and Park found that the therapist judgment and failure to attend methods had a kappa of .62, therapist judgment and median-split had a kappa of .31, and failure to attend and median-split had a kappa .36. These results suggest some convergence on the construct by therapist judgment and failure to attend, but little convergence of either of those two methods with the duration-based method. One may interpret these results by concluding that therapists often make their judgments about who dropped out of treatment based on whether the client failed to attend the last scheduled session. The results also suggest that, according to therapists, some clients may successfully complete therapy even after only a few sessions, and other clients may drop out even after attending many sessions.

In a second study to directly compare operationalizations for premature discontinuation, Swift et al. (2009) took it a step further and examined how often the existing classification systems converged with the newer measure of dropout based on change. For their study, 135 clients from a psychology department training clinic were coded as either dropouts or completers by the missed appointment, median-split, therapist judgment, and clinically significant change methods. Although 48.1% of the clients were classified as dropouts by the missed-appointment method and 50% by the median-split method, almost three quarters of the clients (74.1%) were classified as dropouts by their therapists and 77% by clinically significant change criteria (77% discontinued therapy before making a clinically significant change). Feeling that the standard of clinically significant change may be a little too stringent, Swift and colleagues also classified clients on the basis of whether a reliable improvement had been made. With this less stringent criterion, 63% of the clients were still labeled as premature terminators; in other words, 63% had quit therapy before their self-reported distress levels had improved. The high rates of dropout found are notable. Admittedly, these percentages are somewhat higher than findings from other studies, but they seem to more closely match findings from other training settings.

In looking at Swift et al.'s (2009) results, one can easily see that different measurement systems did not match just based on the percentages. Similar to Hatchett and Park (2003), Swift et al. also calculated the kappa coefficients between all of the pairs of operationalizations. These can be found in Table 1.2. First, the kappa coefficients indicate a significant degree of convergence

TABLE 1.2
Kappa Coefficients Comparing Five Dropout
Operationalizations

Method of classification	2	3	4	5
1. CSC method	.67*	.13	.00	.04
2. RC method		.14	.06	.07
3. Median-split method			.01	.10
4. Missed-appointment method				.48*
5. Therapist-judgment method				

Note. CSC = clinically significant change; RC = reliable change. Reprinted from "Using Clinically Significant Change to Identify Premature Termination," by J. K. Swift, J. L. Callahan, and J. C. Levine, 2009, *Psychotherapy, 46,* p. 332. Copyright 2009 by the American Psychological Association.
*p < .001.

between the clinically significant change and reliable change methods; this is not surprising given that clinically significant change subsumes reliable change. Consistent with Hatchett and Park's findings, one will also notice that there was a significant degree of convergence between therapist judgment and the missed appointment methods. Again, this convergence suggests that therapists are making their judgments at least partially based on whether the client failed to attend the last scheduled session. However, the kappa values do indicate that categorizing clients as dropouts or completers based on the median-split method, missed-appointment method, and therapist judgment method did not match at all with whether the clients had improved or made a clinically significant change.

Table 1.3 provides another illustration of these findings. In this table, the median-split, missed-appointment, and therapist judgment methods are each compared with patient recovery based on clinically significant change definitions. For each method comparison, the numbers in the upper right corners represent the frequency of a classification of dropout when recovery has occurred, or a false negative. The numbers in the lower left corners of each method comparison represent the frequency of a classification of completion when recovery has not occurred, or a false positive. Clearly, the three historically used methods lead to a significant number of errors in labeling patients as dropouts or completers. For example, based on therapist judgment, 22 patients were classified as having dropped out of therapy even though they had made a significant change. Even perhaps more disturbing, based on missed-appointment criteria, 54 of the 135 patients were classified as having completed therapy even though they failed to make a significant improvement.

So which method for operationalizing dropout should be used? Although they are by far the simplest, many have argued against the use of duration-based methods (Hatchett & Park, 2003; Pekarik, 1985), and we would suggest the

TABLE 1.3

Comparisons of Patient Recovery to Dropout Classifications
by Three Other Popularly Used Methods

Dropout classification	Patient recovery as classified by CSC	
	Not recovered	Recovered
Median split		
Dropout	56	11[a]
Completer	48[b]	20
Missed appointment		
Dropout	50	15[a]
Completer	54[b]	16
Therapist judgment		
Dropout	78	22[a]
Completer	26[b]	9

Note. CSC = clinically significant change. Reprinted from "Using Clinically Significant Change to Identify Premature Termination," by J. K. Swift, J. L. Callahan, and J. C. Levine, 2009, *Psychotherapy, 46*, p. 332. Copyright 2009 by the American Psychological Association. [a]Represents a classification of dropout when recovery had occurred. [b]Represents a classification of completion when recovery had not occurred.

same. Based on Hatchett and Park's (2003) and Swift et al.'s (2009) findings, it appears that therapist judgment and missed appointment are converging on the same construct. However, is the construct on which they are converging premature termination? It seems like both are at least occasionally missing the mark. Both methods label some patients as having dropped out even though they recovered from the distress for which they sought treatment. Both also classify some patients as having completed therapy even though they have failed to make a positive change. For these reasons, we recommend that clinical researchers and practitioners base their decisions about patient dropout on either clinically significant change or reliable improvement criteria. We believe that these operationalizations best fit with the definition of dropout as discontinuing therapy before improving from the problems that led one to seek treatment.

CONCEPTUALIZING THE PROBLEM

Although it is important, particularly for psychotherapy researchers, to identify and adopt a universal definition and operationalization for premature discontinuation of therapy, it is of even more importance, particularly for practitioners, to gain an understanding of why some patients choose to drop out. With a deeper understanding of patients' motivations and reasons for dropping out, therapists will be in a better place to implement interventions and techniques to help their patients complete therapy. To build a framework for understanding why some patients drop out of therapy, let us start by identifying some of the reasons patients give for their early terminations.

In the first study to contact and directly ask premature terminators their reasons for dropping out, Garfield (1963) contacted 11 clients who had discontinued therapy before the seventh session. Six of the 11 clients gave an external difficulty (e.g., transportation difficulties, work schedule time limitations) as their primary reason for quitting, three did not feel that therapy or the therapist was helping, and two stated that they had improved. When compared with the reasons for terminating for a matched sample of completers, the terminators were much more likely to state external difficulties or dissatisfaction with therapy as the problem.

In a more recent and much larger study, Acosta (1980) interviewed 74 prematurely terminating clients about their reasons for ending therapy. Specifically, Acosta was interested in examining whether Mexican American, African American, and Anglo American dropouts differed in the reasons that they provided. Surprisingly, there were no significant differences between the three groups. Instead, Acosta found that regardless of ethnicity, participating clients primarily stated that negative attitudes toward the therapist or a lack of perceived benefits were their main reasons for ending therapy early. However, similar to Garfield, Acosta found that a small minority of premature terminators (18%) did report improvement as their reason for terminating.

A few years later, Pekarik (1992b) conducted a similar study with 86 prematurely terminating clients (49 adults, 37 parents of child clients) from an outpatient mental health clinic. These therapy dropouts were all contacted 4 months after their intake appointment and asked why they had chosen to terminate treatment. Thirty-three percent of the adult clients and 22% of the parents of child clients reported dissatisfaction with therapy or the therapist as their main reason for terminating. An additional 31% of the adult clients and 46% of the child clients' parents reported environmental obstacles as getting in the way. In contrast to the two earlier studies, Pekarik reported that a significant percentage of both adult and parents of child clients reported improvement as their reason for terminating (37% and 32%, respectively). Although slightly different from Garfield's (1963) and Acosta's (1980) findings, these results match the percentages found by Pekarik (1983) almost a decade earlier.

Several other, more recent studies have also found similar results. In 1995, Manthei asked 13 prematurely discontinuing clients why they had decided not to continue with counseling. In this study, 23% of the clients stated that they had improved sufficiently, whereas another 23% reported dissatisfaction, 47% reported that the cost was excessive, and 38% reported that they sought help elsewhere without stating the reason why they had done so. Thunnissen, Remans, and Trijsburg (2006) assessed reasons for prematurely terminating from a 3-month inpatient treatment program. More than half of their participants reported overwhelming anxiety resulting from the inpatient program as their reason for dropping out, whereas a smaller group of clients reported improvement and an even smaller group reported dissatisfaction. External factors were also mentioned by more than a third of the dropouts. Finally, Bados, Balaguer, and Saldana (2007) interviewed 89 dropouts after the end of their treatment. Of these clients, 46.7% expressed dissatisfaction with the treatment or therapist, external difficulties were cited by 40%, and improvement for 13.3%.

Some commonalities in these studies can be observed. First, across studies, the reasons clients gave for prematurely terminating generally fell into one of three categories. The first, which was reported between 22% and 46.7% of the time, was dissatisfaction with the therapist or treatment. These were clients who began therapy, but, due to some unmet expectations regarding the therapy encounter, they decided it was best to stop attending. The second, which was reported between 40% and 55% of the time, was external or environmental obstacles that had gotten in the way of therapy. The last, which was reported only 13% to 37% of the time, was discontinuing because of sufficient improvement. On the basis of our definition of premature discontinuation, we would not classify these clients as therapy dropouts. Rather, we view these improved clients as false positives, or clients who were mistakenly classified as premature terminators by their therapists. One reason that does not seem to fall into the previous categories was reported by Thunnissen et al. (2006) for the majority of their clients: anxiety about the treatment. These clients were not necessarily dissatisfied with the way treatment was going but displayed a lack of motivation to face the painful or risky aspects of therapy.

Although patients' reasons for prematurely terminating can be generally classified into these broad categories, from the studies that have been reviewed, it is evident that dropouts are not a homogenous group when it comes to their motives for ending therapy early. Instead of simply having a classification system for categorizing patients' reasons for prematurely terminating, it is important that we have an overarching framework for conceptualizing why some patients choose to drop out of psychotherapy. In a previous article (Swift, Greenberg, Whipple, & Kominiak, 2012), we conceptualized premature discontinuation as being more likely to occur when the patient's perceived or anticipated costs associated with therapy attendance outweigh the perceived or anticipated benefits. Figure 1.1 provides a simple diagram illustrating this conceptualization of premature discontinuation.

As helping professionals, we are all aware of the benefits associated with therapy attendance. These benefits may include just having someone to listen, enhanced well-being, decreased symptoms, improved work or school performance, better social relationships, an increased understanding of oneself,

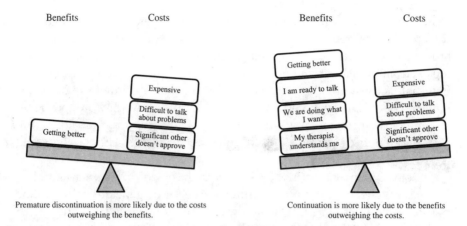

Benefits   Costs   Benefits   Costs

Premature discontinuation is more likely due to the costs outweighing the benefits.

Continuation is more likely due to the benefits outweighing the costs.

Figure 1.1. A conceptualization of why clients choose to terminate prematurely based on perceived and anticipated costs and benefits associated with attending and engaging in psychotherapy.

and maybe even improved physical health, to name a few. However, attending and engaging in therapy can also be a difficult task for many patients, one that is associated with a number of perceived costs. These costs include extra burdens associated with therapy fees, scheduling conflicts, arranging transportation, and the like. Additionally, some of these costs may include facing the stigma and negative opinions from family and friends that may accompany therapy attendance. Finally, the process of self-disclosure and approaching painful and sometimes embarrassing topics in therapy is not an easy task and should also be considered a cost that may contribute to a patient's choice to drop out.

Thus, premature termination can be understood in terms of a balance of costs and benefits. If a patient perceives or anticipates little benefit from therapy, he or she is at an increased risk of dropping out. Even if benefits are perceived, if the costs or burdens are too heavy, patients are not likely to continue and finish the therapy process. This conceptualization provides us with a framework not only for understanding why some patients choose to dropout but also for guiding the strategies that we can take to reduce its occurrence. Our job as clinicians and researchers, and the focus of the second section of the book, is to increase our patients' perception of benefits and minimize their experience of costs associated with attending therapy. At first glance this sounds simple: By providing an effective treatment, most practitioners would argue that they are trying to help clients experience the benefits of psychotherapy. Although receiving a treatment that works is effective for some clients, it may not be that simple for others. For example, although the treatment may be working, for clients with erroneous expectations, it may not be working fast enough. Also, although the treatment may be effective from the therapist's point of view, the client may not notice as readily the benefits and progress he or she is experiencing. On top of that, progress in psychotherapy is not an easy and immediate thing for every client, and some may experience setbacks, deterioration, or ruptures in the therapeutic alliance. Additionally, even if progress is being made, if the client finds a particular treatment aversive or simply not well-suited to his or her values and beliefs, he or she will not likely continue with it for long. For these clients and others who are at a higher risk of dropping out of treatment prematurely, it is important that steps be taken to help them more fully perceive and anticipate the benefits of psychotherapy and discount the costs associated with continued attendance.

2

PREDICTORS OF PREMATURE TERMINATION IN PSYCHOTHERAPY

It's always too soon to quit.

—Norman Vincent Peale

In Chapter 1, we described some of the deleterious effects of premature termination in psychotherapy and introduced a conceptualization for why this negative therapy event occurs. That conceptualization sets the stage for implementing strategies to reduce the occurrence of premature termination in practice. However, to efficiently take these steps, it is also important to be able to identify how often premature termination occurs in therapy and recognize which patients and which situations are associated with a higher dropout risk. A number of reviews have been conducted with these goals in mind. These reviews have focused primarily on identifying which patient characteristics predict premature termination, including both demographic characteristics (e.g., age, ethnicity, education level, gender) and psychological variables (e.g., diagnosis, psychological mindedness, readiness to change). However, treatment (e.g., theoretical orientation, individual vs. group, manualization), setting (e.g., type of clinic), and therapist (e.g., experience level, gender, age) variables have also received some attention in the literature.

http://dx.doi.org/10.1037/14469-003
Premature Termination in Psychotherapy: Strategies for Engaging Clients and Improving Outcomes,
by J. K. Swift and R. P. Greenberg

NARRATIVE REVIEWS

The first review of premature discontinuation in psychotherapy was conducted by Baekeland and Lundwall and was published in 1975. Although Baekeland and Lundwall's review included studies covering a number of topic areas (e.g., internal medical conditions), the results for approximately 60 studies pertaining to psychotherapy with adults were summarized. In general, they estimated that between 20% and 60% of all patients drop out of therapy by either not returning after the first visit or by attending no more than four times. Age and gender were related to dropout, with younger patients and females more likely to discontinue prematurely in a handful of studies. Socioeconomic status (SES) was also correlated with dropout, with lower income patients being more likely to terminate prematurely. In terms of diagnosis, there were mixed results, with some studies finding higher dropout rates among certain disorders and other studies failing to find an association. Additionally, patients who dropped out were found to be less motivated for therapy and to have a lower level of psychological minded-ness. Finally, those with lower IQs were suggested to be at a higher risk of dropping out. Baekeland and Lundwall also reviewed the relationship between a number of non-patient-related variables and the likelihood of dropping out of treatment. Higher dropout rates were suggested to be associated with lengthier wait-list times, more negative therapist attitudes and expectations toward patients, lower levels of therapist experience, therapy interruption, male therapists, and lower patient–therapist similarity. In the end, Baekeland and Lundwall were careful to point out that none of these associations were found universally across studies, and they suggested further research in this area.

The next comprehensive review of premature discontinuation in psychotherapy was conducted by Garfield (1994) as part of the fourth edition of the *Bergin and Garfield's Handbook of Psychotherapy and Behavior Change* (Bergin & Garfield, 1994). Although Garfield never provided an estimated dropout rate for psychotherapy in this review, he did point out that across studies, the median number of therapy sessions attended by clients was some-where between five and eight. Garfield argued that this number is typically insufficient for successful therapy, and thus the majority of psychotherapy clients could be described as treatment dropouts. In reviewing the variables associated with dropout rates, Garfield reported that there was at least some evidence of a relationship between dropout and client SES (lower economic status associated with higher rates), ethnicity (higher rates among ethnic minorities), and education level (lower education level was linked to higher rates). In contrast, Garfield concluded that no relationship existed between premature termination and clients' gender, age, and diagnosis.

Just a few years later, Reis and Brown (1999) completed the next review of premature termination in psychotherapy. They estimated, largely based on Baekeland and Lundwall's (1975) earlier findings, that roughly between 30% and 60% of clients drop out of therapy. In their review of the client variables that predict premature termination, they concluded that although a significant relationship with SES and ethnicity does exist, there is no consistent support for a relationship between client dropout and age, gender, marital status, and diagnosis.

Most recently, Barrett, Chua, Crits-Christoph, Gibbons, and Thompson (2008) estimated that roughly 50% of clients drop out by the third session of psychotherapy, with approximately 32% ending after a single session. They stated that the existing research generally indicates a relationship between premature termination and ethnic minority status and SES but no relationship with client age. However, they also specifically mentioned that even where significant relationships have been found, the results are far from consistent for any of the client demographic variables.

Some consistent findings from these narrative reviews are apparent. First, they all suggest that roughly half of all clients drop out of treatment prematurely. Second, most of them suggest that belonging to an ethnic minority and having a lower SES are associated with a higher likelihood of dropping out. However, all of the reviews emphasize that even for these two variables, the results are inconsistent, and caution should be used when attempting to link premature termination to any client demographic variable. Although the information gained from these reviews is valuable, it is limited given that they were all subjective narratives without any description of a systematic set of procedures for identifying studies or comparing the results between studies. Given the lack of a systematic approach, it is difficult to tell the degree to which the reviewers' biases may have influenced the results that were found and the conclusions that were made.

WIERZBICKI AND PEKARIK'S META-ANALYSIS

In contrast to the many narrative reviews that have been conducted examining premature discontinuation from psychotherapy, to date only two systematic, statistical, and comprehensive reviews of this negative therapy event have been performed. The first to use meta-analytic techniques to broadly examine premature termination was Wierzbicki and Pekarik (1993). For their meta-analysis, they identified 125 studies on psychotherapy dropout that had been conducted between 1974 and 1990. Studies were included if they were published in English, reported a dropout rate, included a clinical sample, and were not limited exclusively to clients seeking treatment for a drug or alcohol problem. In pulling together the data from these studies, they first were interested in calculating an average rate of premature termination for the field. Second, they were interested in identifying the study, demographic, psychological, and therapist variables that were associated with higher rates of dropout.

In terms of their first goal, Wierzbicki and Pekarik (1993) simply calculated an average dropout rate across all 125 studies. They found that on average almost half of all clients (M = 46.86%, SD = 22.25%) discontinue therapy prematurely. Although studies varied in the individual dropout rates that were reported, given the large number of studies that were included, the 95% confidence interval (CI) around their average was relatively small, ranging from 42.9% to 50.82%. Wierzbicki and Pekarik concluded by saying that this dropout rate should generalize to many clinical contexts. However, to make such a claim, it is important to examine the degree of heterogeneity between studies as well as test potential moderators. Although they did not report a test of heterogeneity, Wierzbicki and Pekarik did test potential moderators by conducting multiple analyses of variance (ANOVAs), correlations, and meta-analyses.

For the ANOVAs, Wierzbicki and Pekarik (1993) tested whether dropout rates differed depending on four study variables: mode of treatment (individual vs. group), study setting (university, private clinic, public clinic, or other), type of client (adults, mixed, or children), and definition of dropout (failure to attend, therapist judgment, or duration-based). They found no differences in the rates of premature termination as a function of the treatment mode, $F(1, 123) = 0.19$, the setting, $F(1, 115) = 1.04$, or type of client, $F(1, 131) = 0.00$. In contrast, the dropout rates did differ significantly depending on the way that it was measured, $F(1, 118) = 3.22$, $p < .05$. Specifically, the rate of premature termination hovered at 48% when it was assessed through therapist judgment or by a duration-based method. However, when it was defined as failure to attend, the rate of premature termination was only 35.87%. This finding illustrates the need for a universal operationalization of premature discontinuation as discussed in Chapter 1 of this book.

Wierzbicki and Pekarik (1993) next tested whether rates of premature discontinuation were associated with a number of study variables that could be continuously coded within the studies. These continuously coded variables included the average age of patients; percent male patients; percent Caucasian; average years of education; average SES; percent of patients married; percent of patients with an emotional disorder, behavioral disorder, psychotic disorder, substance abuse disorder, and health or developmental disorder; percent having received previous treatment; average length of wait for treatment; average number of sessions; percent of self-referred patients; percent of Caucasian therapists; average number of years of experience for the therapists; and percent of therapists with a PhD, MD, MSW, or MA. Among all of these correlational tests, not one indicated a significant relationship.

Last, for studies that reported data separately for dropouts and completers, Wierzbicki and Pekarik (1993) were able to calculate an effect size for the difference between groups for gender, ethnicity, age, education, SES, and marital status. Of these six patient demographic variables, significant but small effects were found for ethnicity ($d = 0.23$), education level ($d = 0.28$), and SES ($d = 0.37$). These results indicate an increased risk of dropping out of therapy associated with ethnic minority status, lower levels of education, and lower SES. However, Wiezbicki and Pekarik's results are somewhat contradictory. Although significance was found for these three variables in terms of effect size differences between dropouts and completers, the correlational tests failed to find significant relationships for any of them. This discrepancy may be due to the number of studies that were included in each type of analysis: The correlational tests could include data from all 125 studies, whereas the meta-analyses only included data from 19 to 36 studies. Additionally, the meta-analyses included actual data from dropouts and completers, whereas the correlational analyses only included aggregate, study-level data. Regardless of the reason, the discrepancies in the results are evident.

Although limitations were present, Wierzbicki and Pekarik's (1993) meta-analysis represented a major step forward compared with the narrative reviews that had been conducted previously. Namely, Wierzbicki and Pekarik used a systematic set of procedures for identifying and coding studies and statistical techniques for pooling the results. The major finding from their meta-analysis was that dropout is a significant problem for psychotherapy, occurring with almost 50% of all patients. This value is similar to the ranges that had been reported by other reviews; however, their meta-analysis provided a more precise estimate. Despite the significant advantages, Wierzbicki and Pekarik's meta-analysis did not shed much light on the patient risk factors associated with dropping out. Although three demographic variables were identified through one set of analyses (ethnicity, education level, and SES), the same variables were found to be nonsignificant predictors in another set of analyses. This inconsistency matches the inconsistencies from the narrative reviews, and thus we are still no closer to identifying which types of patients are at a higher risk for premature discontinuation from psychotherapy.

AN UPDATED META-ANALYSIS

Although Wierzbicki and Pekarik's (1993) review furthered the field's understanding of the occurrence of psychotherapy dropout, it was conducted almost 2 decades ago, and thus the results may not accurately represent current findings of premature discontinuation in therapy. Three major changes have occurred in the field since Wierzbicki and Pekarik conducted their original review, each of which may date their results. First, changes have occurred in the way treatments are provided. Some of these changes include an increased number of providers, managed care, an acceptance of mental health and psychological treatment options as equal to physical health treatments, a continued emphasis on treating patients in the least restrictive or intensive environment, the offering of services in locations and through formats that are accessible to a greater number of patients, the increase in services that are covered and offered to low-income patients, and the strong emphasis now placed on using well-defined, brief, time-limited interventions (DeLeon, Kenkel, Garcia-Shelton, & VandenBos, 2011). These changes in the makeup of interventions and the way that they are provided may have had an influence on therapy dropout.

Second, Wierzbicki and Pekarik's (1993) results may be dated because of changes in the practice of reporting dropout rates. In contrast to much of the time period covered by the original review, reporting of dropout rates has now become standard practice for treatment outcome studies. Given that in the past reporting of dropout rates was not standard, it is possible that previous studies only reported dropout rates when the study was specifically designed to examine dropout or when dropout was a significant or noteworthy problem. A number of treatment outcome studies may not have reported dropout rates because rates were low, rates were unusually high and the clinician or researcher invested in the treatment did not want to disclose that fact, or reporting the rates did not seem relevant to the clinician or researcher. Reporting of dropout rates is now standard for all outcome studies (American Psychological Association Publications and Communications Board Working Group on Journal Article Reporting Standards, 2008). Reviewing results from the greater number and percentage of studies that now report dropout rates may give us a clearer and more accurate picture of premature discontinuation across the field.

Third, Wierzbicki and Pekarik's (1993) results may be dated due to advancements that have been made in the data-analytic techniques for meta-analyses. For the overall dropout rate, Wierzbicki and Pekarik simply averaged the rates reported by the 125 studies. Additionally, when examining moderators, they conducted simple ANOVAs and correlations. According to today's standards, these strategies are seen as flawed because they do not assign weights for studies depending on sample size or follow the appropriate rules for assigning degrees of freedom (Borenstein, Hedges, Higgins, & Rothstein, 2009). Current strategies and programs are available that allow the calculation of weighted averages, allow more appropriate testing for moderators, and allow the use of meta-regression instead of simple correlations.

Given the limitations of Wierzbicki and Pekarik's (1993) meta-analysis and the changes that have occurred in the field over the past 20 years, we undertook the task of conducting an updated meta-analytic review of premature termination. It was our hope that this updated meta-analysis would provide an overall estimate of dropout that could serve as a broad evaluation of psychotherapy and a benchmark for future treatment studies. Additionally, we hoped that through this meta-analysis we could further evaluate the patient, treatment, setting, and therapist variables that are associated with higher rates of premature discontinuation, thus allowing clinicians and researchers to identify risk factors for when dropout might be more likely.

Method

We recognize that not all readers will be interested in the specific details of how this meta-analysis was conducted. However, we feel that some of the details are necessary to fully consider the implications of the results. As a result, here we summarize some of the main points from our literature search and study coding. Interested readers are referred to our paper published in the *Journal of Consulting and Clinical Psychology* (Swift & Greenberg, 2012) for additional details.

Given that Wierzbicki and Pekarik (1993) reviewed studies through June 1990, our review of the literature only covered articles published from July 1990 through June 2010. In conducting this search, we wanted to be broad and identify any study that reported a treatment dropout rate, not just those whose main focus was the study of premature termination. Although we wanted to be broad, we did want to place some limits to the scope of this review. These limits led us to decide to not include studies with child patients, studies that were limited exclusively to drug or alcohol patients, studies that were limited entirely to patients being seen for a health concern (e.g., diabetes, weight management), studies of only self-help or technology-based interventions, and studies of couples or family therapy. Finally, we only included studies with actual patients and not therapy analogues. The overall flow of studies can be found in Figure 2.1.

We used three primary search strategies to identify articles to be included in this meta-analysis. First, we searched the database PsycINFO using the terms *attrition, patient variables, continuance, dropout, psychotherapy dropout, termination,* or *therapist variables.* Using these terms, 13,191 citations were identified and reviewed, of which 198 studies met all inclusion and exclusion criteria for this meta-analysis. Although this search identified a large number of studies for inclusion, we were concerned that many outcome studies that may have reported dropout rates were not identified because dropout or some derivation of the word was not included in the title, abstract, or as

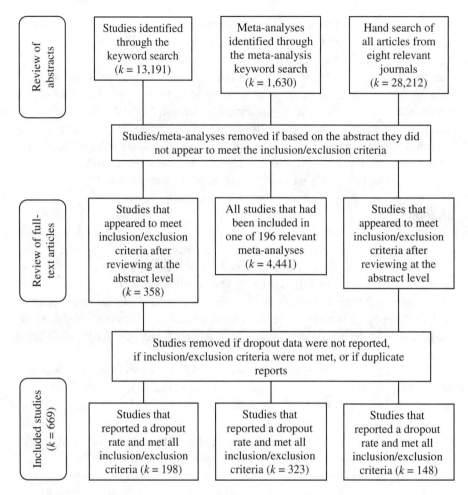

Figure 2.1. Study flow chart for identification of studies to be included in this review. Reprinted from "Premature Discontinuation in Adult Psychotherapy: A Meta-Analysis," by J. K. Swift and R. P. Greenberg, 2012, *Journal of Consulting and Clinical Psychology, 80*, p. 550. Copyright 2012 by the American Psychological Association.

a keyword. To be more inclusive, we conducted a second search by looking for treatment outcome studies that have been included in previously conducted meta-analyses of treatment effects. We searched PsycINFO using the terms *meta-analysis* and *psychotherapy* or *therapy* or *psychological treatment* or *psychological intervention*. This search resulted in 1,630 meta-analysis citations, which resulted in 196 relevant meta-analyses. All of the studies that were included in one of the 196 meta-analyses were then reviewed. From this search, 323 additional studies met all inclusion and exclusion criteria for the meta-analysis. Through conducting the first two search strategies, we noticed that articles published in certain journals were more likely to report dropout rates. We thus conducted a third search by hand searching these journals (*American Journal of Psychiatry*, *Archives of General Psychiatry*, *Behavior Therapy*, *Behaviour Research and Therapy*, *British Journal of Psychiatry*, *Journal of Consulting and Clinical Psychology*, *Psychotherapy*, and *Psychotherapy Research*). Also included in this hand search were any studies that were referenced by other identified studies. This hand search resulted in an additional 148 studies that met all inclusion and exclusion criteria.

A total of 669 studies were found to meet all inclusion and exclusion criteria and were included in this meta-analysis. Although we tried to find and review as many studies as possible, we recognize that our search likely missed some studies that reported dropout rates. Given the search strategies that were used, the large number of studies that were reviewed, and the large number of studies that were included in this meta-analysis, we believe that our included studies are a good representation of any studies that may have been missed.

Each of the 669 included studies was then coded, including an identification of the study dropout rate and data for 20 other treatment, client, therapist, and study variables that were to be tested as moderators and covariates. The study dropout rate was coded as the percentage of clients who started the intervention and were identified as dropouts according to each author's method of operationalization.

Seven client variables were coded. Client *diagnosis* was coded as anxiety disorder, eating disorder, mood disorder, personality disorder, psychotic disorder, trauma, or other. Client *age* was coded as a study average. *Race* was coded for each study as the percent of Caucasian clients. Client *gender* was coded as percent female for each study. *Marital status* was coded as the percent of clients married or in a committed relationship. *Employment* was coded as the percent of clients in full- or part-time employment. *Education* was coded both as the average number of years of education and as the percent of clients with at least some college-level education. When studies reported the data, averages and percentages between dropouts and completers on each of these client variables was coded.

Five treatment variables were coded. Treatment *orientation* was coded as cognitive–behavioral (including cognitive–behavioral therapies, cognitive therapies, and behavioral therapies), integrative, psychodynamic, solution-focused, supportive/client-centered, and other. Separate dropout rates were recorded as subgroups in studies that compared two or more treatment options. Treatment *format* was coded as group, individual, or combination (group and individual). The *time limitations* of treatment were coded as none, low (time limited and 20 or fewer sessions offered), and high (time limited and more than 20 sessions offered). Treatment *manualization* was coded as yes or no depending on whether the interventions were offered in a manualized format. Last, treatment *setting* was coded as outpatient clinic affiliated with a hospital or medical school, private outpatient clinic or practice, public outpatient clinic, research/specialty clinic, university affiliated clinic (psychology department training clinic and university counseling center), or inpatient.

Four provider variables were coded. Provider *experience* level was coded as trainees (before degree attainment), experienced (after degree attainment), and mixed (studies with both trainees and experienced clinicians serving as providers). Provider *gender* was coded as the percent of female providers. Provider *race* was coded as the percent of Caucasian providers. Last, the average provider *age* was coded for each study that reported these data.

Four study or design variables were also coded. *Definition of dropout* was coded as failed to complete a treatment protocol, attended less than a given number of sessions, stopped attending, or therapist judgment. This coding was based on the method of operationalization used by the original authors. Study *type* was coded as either efficacy or effectiveness. Efficacy studies are those that emphasize internal validity and typically take place in a laboratory or controlled setting, and effectiveness studies are those that emphasize external validity and take place in applied real-world clinical settings (Lambert & Ogles, 2004). To best get at this distinction, we coded a study as being an efficacy study if (a) participants were recruited for participation, (b) strict exclusion criteria were used to screen participants for inclusion, and/or (c) the study procedures followed a strict protocol. *Year of publication* was also coded as was the *type of search strategy* that had been used to identify the study (original keyword search, treatment outcome meta-analysis search, or hand search).

Given the wide range of studies that were included in this meta-analysis (e.g., the way the studies were conducted, the interventions used, the clients treated), a random effects model was used in the calculation of the overall dropout rate and all testing of moderators and covariates. All data-analyses were conducted using the computer program Comprehensive Meta-analysis (Version 2), developed by Borenstein, Hedges, Higgins, and Rothstein (2005). First, a weighted average dropout rate (number of clients who prematurely terminated out of the total number of clients who started the intervention) for the 669 included studies was calculated. Homogeneity in study dropout rates was examined using the Q statistic; a significant Q value indicates heterogeneity in the dropout rates reported among the studies. The I^2 statistic was also calculated, which illustrates the degree of heterogeneity using a percentage. For the categorical variables (treatment orientation, format, setting, time limits, manualization, client diagnosis, provider experience level, study type, dropout definition, and search criteria), a Q statistic was used to test between-group differences. With these between-group analyses, a significant Q value indicates a difference between groups in reported dropout rates. For the continuous variables (client average age, percent female, percent Caucasian, percent in a committed relationship, percent employed, average years of education, percent with some college education, provider average age, provider percent female, provider percent Caucasian, and year of study publication), several meta-regression analyses were conducted. A regression coefficient was calculated for each predictor separately and was then tested for significance using a Z test. Finally, many of the studies made comparisons between dropouts and completers for client demographic variables, including client age, race, gender, marital status, employment status, and level of education. Separate meta-analyses were run for each of these variables to further examine differences between dropouts and completers. Effect sizes (Cohen's d) were calculated for each variable and study in which sufficient data were present (i.e., means, SDs, proportion of cases, or results from statistical tests comparing dropouts to completers). The weighted effect size was tested for statistical significance using a Z test, and a fail-safe N was calculated for each comparison. Although all of the studies were included in the calculation of the overall average dropout rate, some studies were not included in the various tests of the moderators and covariates because details, data, or both were missing from the original articles.

The meta-analysis included 83,834 adult patients from 669 studies. A reference list of the included studies can be found at http://www.psycho therapyresearchlab.com. In summary, the majority of studies were of anxiety ($k = 201$) and mood disorder ($k = 148$) treatments, were provided in an individual format ($k = 438$), tested a cognitive-behavioral intervention ($k = 439$), were time limited with the duration specified at less than 20 sessions ($k = 449$), were delivered in research or specialty clinic ($k = 124$), and were of treatments delivered by experienced clinicians ($k = 285$). Failure to complete was the most frequent definition of dropout used ($k = 314$), followed by attending less than a given number of sessions ($k = 131$) and therapist judgment ($k = 63$). The majority of the studies were coded as efficacy-type studies ($k = 398$) compared with effectiveness studies ($k = 235$).

Frequency of Premature Discontinuation

Across all studies, the weighted mean dropout rate was only 19.7%. The 95% CIs (18.7%, 20.7%) indicate a high level of precision around this average rate of premature termination. Although this dropout rate indicates that one in five therapy patients discontinues treatment prematurely, this rate is significantly lower than the dropout rate found by Wierzbicki and Pekarik (1993) 2 decades ago (47%). This is excellent news. Instead of half of all patients finding treatment to be unacceptable, these findings suggest that the large majority of patients are willing to continue in treatment until the therapy work is completed.

However, one may wonder why there is such a big difference between our findings and those from Wierzbicki and Pekarik's (1993) meta-analysis. One hypothesis is that over the past 20 years, therapists and treatments have been improving and the field is now better at meeting patients' wants and needs. If this were the case, the improvement would likely have occurred linearly, with dropout rates being close to 50% in the early 1990s and then gradually decreasing to where they are currently, 20%. We failed to find any relationship between the year the study was published and the reported dropout rate, $Z = 0.30$, $p = .76$, $B = -0.002$, 95% CI [−0.135, 0.010], so it is not likely that therapists and treatments have actually been improving, at least in terms of dropout.

Another possible explanation for the differing dropout rates between the two reviews is the difference in the included studies. Where Wierzbicki and Pekarik (1993) analyzed 125 studies from 1974 to 1990 (almost a 30-year span), we included data from 669 studies published over the past 20 years. The comprehensive nature of our review likely resulted in including types of studies that were not included in their earlier review. Our keyword search matching Wierzbicki and Pekarik's resulted in only 198 studies, whereas our additional search strategies (meta-analysis and hand search) resulted in 471 studies. Analyses indicated that studies found through the second two searches yielded significantly lower average dropout rates compared with the first. Additionally, at the time of Wierzbicki and Pekarik's review, outcome studies infrequently reported dropout rates. Thus, their meta-analysis likely included only studies in which dropout had been a significant problem and deemed worthy of reporting or studying. In contrast, many journals now require the reporting of dropout rates even if only one or two patients prematurely ended treatment. Including all of these studies in our meta-analysis would provide a lower estimate of the occurrence of this negative therapy event.

Although the average dropout rate across all studies was only 20%, individual studies varied greatly in the rates that were reported. In fact, whereas about 75 studies reported a dropout rate of 5% or less, five studies reported that more than 70% of their patients had prematurely terminated. Calculations of the Q statistic did find the studies to be highly heterogeneous in their dropout estimates, $Q(668) = 7694.74$, $p < .001$, $I^2 = 93.32$. Given the lack of uniformity in the rates that were reported it is important to look closer at the potential patient, treatment, provider, setting, and study moderators and correlates that may be able to predict when patients are more likely to discontinue treatment prematurely.

Patient Predictors

It is important to be able to recognize the types of patients who are at a higher risk of dropping out of therapy prematurely so that they can be given special attention early on in therapy. The relationship between premature discontinuation and the patient variables was tested through three types of analyses: subgroup analysis for patient diagnosis; separate meta-analyses for patient age, gender, race, marital status, employment, and education; and separate meta-regressions for patient age, gender, race, marital status, employment, and education. Results of the subgroup analysis for patient diagnosis can be found in Table 2.1. Patient diagnosis was found to significantly moderate the overall dropout rate, with the highest dropout rates for studies that either did not specify one particular disorder as the focus of treatment or that treated a disorder that did not fall into one of the other diagnostic categories, followed by treatments for personality (25.6%) and eating disorders (23.9%). It makes sense that the highest rates of premature termination would be found for both of these groups of patients. These two types of disorders are characterized by their rigidity, and treatment progress with both is often slow. Given the slow progress that is often seen with both, patients could easily become discouraged and drop out after losing hope that treatment could be of some help. Additionally, working with these types of patients is difficult work for therapists who may also become discouraged and as a result act in a way that contributes to patients' decisions to discontinue prematurely.

Six separate meta-analyses were conducted for the patient variables in which studies reported data for both dropouts and completers (see Table 2.2

TABLE 2.1
Results From the Subgroup Analysis of Patient Diagnosis

Diagnostic category	No. of included studies (k)	Dropout rate	95% CI	Q value	p value
Anxiety disorder	201	16.2%	15.0%, 17.5%		
Eating disorder	52	23.9%	20.5%, 27.6%		
Mood disorder	148	17.4%	15.6%, 19.4%		
Personality disorder	50	25.6%	22.3%, 29.1%		
Psychotic disorder	26	16.1%	12.4%, 20.7%		
Trauma	71	20.5%	17.5%, 23.7%		
Other	119	27.3%	24.8%, 30.0%		
				93.58	<.001

Note. CI = confidence interval. Adapted from "Premature Discontinuation in Adult Psychotherapy: A Meta-Analysis," by J. K. Swift and R. P. Greenberg, 2012, *Journal of Consulting and Clinical Psychology, 80,* p. 553. Copyright 2012 by the American Psychological Association.

TABLE 2.2
Results From the Meta-Analyses (Weighted Mean Effect Size)
for the Client Variables

Variable (k)	d	95% CI	Z value	Direction	Fail-safe N
Age (52)	0.16	0.07, 0.24	3.58*	Dropouts younger	297
Gender (38)	0.01	−0.09, 0.11	0.15	—	—
Race (11)	0.16	0.00, 0.32	2.01	—	—
Marital status (15)	0.14	−0.02, 0.30	1.76	—	—
Employment (13)	0.20	−0.03, 0.43	1.71	—	—
Education (17)	0.29	0.11, 0.47	3.10*	Dropouts ↓ educated	69

Note. CI = confidence interval. Reprinted from "Premature Discontinuation in Adult Psychotherapy:
A Meta-Analysis," by J. K. Swift and R. P. Greenberg, 2012, *Journal of Consulting and Clinical Psychology,*
80, p. 554. Copyright 2012 by the American Psychological Association.
*$p < .008$.

for results). Significant effect sizes were found for patient age ($d = 0.16$, dropouts on average were younger) and education ($d = 0.29$, dropouts on average were less educated). However, effect sizes comparing dropouts to completers were not significant for gender, race, marital status, or employment.

Seven separate meta-regressions were also conducted for each of the client variables that could be continuously coded across studies (see Table 2.3 for results). Significant prediction was found between the study rates of premature discontinuation and average study age (higher dropout rates were associated with younger samples), percent of female participants in a study (higher dropout rates were associated with fewer female participants), and percent of participants in a married or committed relationship (higher dropout rates were associated with fewer participants in a committed relationship). The percentages of clients who were Caucasian, employed, having attended some college, and participants' average years of education were not found to be significantly related to rates of premature discontinuation in the meta-regression analyses.

In summary, of the client variables that were examined, results between the various tests were consistent for only three: client age, ethnicity, and employment status. In both tests, client age was a significant predictor of dropout with younger clients being more likely to prematurely terminate across studies. This finding does match with what has been reported in previous reviews (Baekeland & Lundwall, 1975; Barrett et al., 2008). Thus, therapists should pay particular attention to the possibility of premature termination with their younger adult clients. In both sets of tests client ethnicity and employment status were found to be unrelated to rates of premature termination. This result, particularly for client ethnicity, contradicts a conclusion that has been made in previous reviews—namely, that ethnic minority

TABLE 2.3
Results From the Meta-Regressions (Method of Moments)
for the Client Variables

Variable (*k*)	Point estimate (*B*)	95% CI	*Z* value
Age (515)			
Slope	−0.014	−0.021, −0.007	3.95*
Intercept	−0.882	−1.154, −0.610	
Gender—percent female (521)			
Slope	0.480	0.157, 0.802	2.92*
Intercept	−1.717	−1.948, −1.487	
Race—percent Caucasian (243)			
Slope	−0.226	−0.752, 0.300	0.84
Intercept	−1.115	−1.537, −0.693	
Marital—percent committed (298)			
Slope	−0.985	−1.436, −0.533	4.28*
Intercept	−0.987	−1.199, −0.774	
Employment—percent employed (164)			
Slope	−0.447	−0.969, 0.075	1.68
Intercept	−1.226	−1.536, −0.916	
Education—average years (101)			
Slope	−0.034	−0.137, 0.068	0.66
Intercept	−0.861	−2.264, 0.542	
Education—percent some college (131)			
Slope	0.187	−0.345, 0.718	0.69
Intercept	−1.450	−1.803, −1.097	

Note. CI = confidence interval. Reprinted from "Premature Discontinuation in Adult Psychotherapy: A Meta-Analysis," by J. K. Swift and R. P. Greenberg, 2012, *Journal of Consulting and Clinical Psychology, 80,* p. 554. Copyright 2012 by the American Psychological Association.
* $p < .0045$.

clients are more likely to discontinue treatment prematurely. In the past decade or two, there has been an increased focus on developing culturally adapted treatments (DeLeon et al., 2011), and perhaps these adaptations have resulted in lower dropout rates for ethnic minority clients.

Among the various tests that we conducted, results were inconsistent for the client variables of gender, marital status, and education. The meta-analyses indicated that dropouts and completers differed in terms of education, but not gender, race, marital status, or employment. The meta-regressions indicated that gender and marital status predicted therapy dropout, but race, employment, and education did not. These differences may be due to the way the data were examined. In the meta-analyses, only studies that reported data for both dropouts and completers on the given variable could be included. However, the vast majority of studies did not include this type of data. The finding of educational differences between dropouts and completers was based on only 17 of the 669 studies. Many studies could not be included in the demographic analyses because they did not report data, even though they stated that dropouts and completers did not differ on any of the demographic variables. Many more studies could be included in the meta-regressions because these analyses were based on the averages for all study participants. However, these analyses do not tell us whether there are actual differences between dropouts and completers, only that across studies, the variable is or is not associated with rates of premature discontinuation. The lack of consistency in findings for these client demographic variables fits with the inconsistencies that have also been pointed out in previous reviews (Barrett et al., 2008; Garfield, 1994; Reis & Brown, 1999).

Treatment Predictors

Certain interventions and intervention variables may also be associated with rates of premature termination from therapy. One way to evaluate the effectiveness or efficacy of an intervention is to examine the number of clients who are able and willing to complete the treatment. Comparisons between treatments provide information that can be useful to providers in making decisions about which interventions would be most appropriate for their clients. Additionally, these types of comparisons allow clinical researchers and providers to identify interventions that may need adjusting to be seen as more acceptable to clients. Finally, regardless of theoretical orientation, certain intervention characteristics may be associated with lower rates of premature termination. If these characteristics can be identified, then providers can seek to include them in their therapy approach, regardless of orientation. With these goals in mind, comparisons were made to test differences in dropout rates when studies were grouped by the five treatment moderators, including treatment orientation, treatment format (individual vs. group), time limits, manualization, and treatment setting. Results for each of these subgroup moderator analyses are reported in Table 2.4.

Perhaps the most important of these findings is that dropout rates did not differ significantly between theoretical orientations. In fact, there was a difference of less than 3 percentage points between the orientations with the highest (psychodynamic psychotherapy) and lowest (humanistic, existential, and supportive psychotherapies) rates of dropout. It appears that the famous "dodo bird verdict" that was originally postulated for treatment outcomes (Rosenzweig, 1936) applies to premature discontinuation as well. After a race in Lewis Carroll's *Alice's Adventures in Wonderland*, the contestants approached the dodo bird and asked who had won the race. The dodo responded, "All have won and all must have prizes." Applied to premature termination, all of the orientations have won in that the dropout rates for each are much lower than previous dropout estimates for the field and one

TABLE 2.4
Results From the Subgroup Analysis of
Treatment Moderators on Therapy Dropout

Moderator (k)	Dropout rate	95% CI	Q value	P value
Treatment orientation			1.59	.90
Cognitive–behavioral (439)	18.4%	17.4%, 19.5%		
Psychodynamic (69)	20.0%	16.7%, 23.8%		
Solution-focused (12)	19.2%	14.2%, 25.3%		
Supportive (55)	17.3%	14.7%, 20.3%		
Integrative (47)	19.1%	15.7%, 22.9%		
Other (32)	18.0%	13.8%, 23.2%		
Treatment format			6.15	.05
Individual (438)	18.7%	17.5%, 20.0%		
Group (169)	19.7%	18.0%, 21.6%		
Combination (27)	24.6%	19.9%, 29.9%		
Time limited			85.19	< .001
No time limit (131)	29.0%	26.6%, 31.6%		
Low time limit (449)	17.8%	16.8%, 18.7%		
High time limit (64)	20.7%	17.8%, 24.1%		
Manualized			65.86	< .001
Yes (392)	18.3%	25.9%, 30.7%		
No (138)	28.3%	17.2%, 19.3%		
Setting			47.18	< .001
Inpatient (34)	20.8%	16.8%, 25.5%		
Outpatient—hospital (99)	20.4%	18.3%, 22.8%		
Outpatient—private (72)	17.4%	13.9%, 21.5%		
Outpatient—public (59)	23.4%	20.3%, 26.8%		
University-based clinic (53)	30.4%	26.6%, 34.4%		
Research/specialty clinic (124)	17.3%	15.3%, 19.5%		

Note. CI = confidence interval. Reprinted from "Premature Discontinuation in Adult Psychotherapy:
A Meta-Analysis," by J. K. Swift and R. P. Greenberg, 2012, *Journal of Consulting and Clinical Psychology, 80,*
p. 553. Copyright 2012 by the American Psychological Association.

orientation does not show to be superior to another. This finding suggests that the specific treatment itself does not necessarily explain why a client would choose to end therapy prematurely. In contrast, we believe that this finding illustrates the important role of the common factors in clients' decisions about continuing with treatment. Rather than basing decisions to drop out on the specific techniques (one type of technique is not more abrasive than another), clients likely base their decisions on whether the techniques fit with their expectations and preferences and whether they are able to connect with their therapists.

The lack of difference in dropout rates between theoretical orientations also suggests that there may be some other treatment variables that moderate clients' decisions to end therapy prematurely. Dropout was not moderated by treatment format. Individual and group therapy produced very similar rates of premature discontinuation. However, the studies that included a combination of individual and group resulted in higher rates of dropout. Although combination treatments may be highly effective in approaching clients' problems from multiple angles, providers should be aware that some clients may have a hard time keeping up with the increased level of time commitment.

Significant differences in dropout rates were found for whether the intervention was time limited and whether the intervention was manualized. In terms of time limits, it is important to note that the length of treatment was not the important factor (treatments with more than 20 planned sessions had similar rates to those with fewer than 20 planned sessions). Instead, the mere act of specifying duration was associated with lower dropout rates. This seems to speak to the importance of patients' expectations for treatment length. In general, research has indicated that patients only expect to attend a few appointments (Mueller & Pekarik, 2000; Pekarik, 1991; Swift & Callahan, 2008); however, if they are made aware that a greater number of sessions are involved in the treatment, they know what to expect and are more likely to follow through with that expectation. Similarly, manualized interventions had lower rates of premature termination. We hypothesize that this is because the treatment rationale is provided early on for most manualized treatments. Thus, we suggest that regardless of theoretical orientation, providers offer early role and duration education to all of their patients. The treatment setting (university-based clinics, including psychology department training clinics and university counseling centers, experienced the highest average rates of premature discontinuation) is also a significant moderator of patient dropout. This may be due to the type of patient that is typically seen in these types of settings (younger adults) or to the type of clinician who typically provides the services (trainees). It could also be that patient investment and perceived credibility for the services provided in these settings can be low due to the minimal or absent fees charged. Either way, clinicians who work in these settings should be particularly aware of this problem and should exert extra effort to use dropout-reducing strategies with all of their patients.

Treatment by Disorder Effects: "What Works for Whom" or "All Have Won"?

Earlier, we stated that the findings when testing treatment moderators supported the dodo bird verdict in that dropout rates were highly similar across theoretical orientations. However, the comparisons just discussed were made across all types of patients. Almost half a century ago Gordon Paul (1967) suggested that the field seek to answer the now famous question: "*What* treatment, by *whom*, is most effective for *this* individual with *that* specific problem, and under *which* set of circumstances?" (p. 111). On the basis of this suggestion, it would also be important to examine whether a treatment by disorder interaction exists. In other words, do treatments differ in their rates of therapy dropout when applied to specific disorders?

To test the treatment-by-disorder interaction, we separated the studies out into 12 disorder groups. Then, within each group, we compared the dropout rates between the existing treatments using the same subgroup meta-analytic techniques described earlier. Table 2.5 reports the results from these subgroup analyses.

In summary, dropout rates did not differ significantly between the included treatment approaches for nine of the studied disorder categories: bereavement, borderline personality disorder, generalized anxiety disorder, obsessive–compulsive disorder, other personality disorders, panic disorder, psychotic disorders, social phobia, and somatoform disorders. In contrast, significant differences in treatment dropout rates were found for depression, eating disorders, and posttraumatic stress disorder (PTSD). For depression, integrative approaches had the lowest average dropout rate (10.9%), whereas the highest dropout rates were observed in cognitive–behavioral analysis system of psychotherapy (CBASP; 23.0%). For the eating disorders, dialectical behavior therapy (DBT) was found to have the lowest average dropout rate (5.9%). Last, for PTSD, the lowest average dropout rate was found for the integrative approaches (8.8%), and the highest average dropout rate was found for full cognitive behavior therapy (CBT; 28.5%).

For those three disorder categories, we further examined the treatment conditions to see whether there was some systematic reason for the differences that were found. For each of the three disorder categories (depression, PTSD, and eating disorders), we conducted pairwise comparisons between the treatments that were identified. For depression, the integrative category was found to be significantly lower in their average dropout rates compared with the CBASP, cognitive therapy, full CBT, interpersonal psychotherapy, solution-focused therapy, and supportive psychotherapy approaches. In addition, CBASP was found to have significantly higher dropout rates than both the integrative treatments and cognitive therapy. Given the dropout rate differences and the general absence of systematic differences in study characteristics, it can be assumed that depressed patients find an integrative approach to be more acceptable or easier to complete than CBASP or the other treatment approaches for depression. This finding seems to suggest that openness in the techniques and approaches used might be the best fit when working with depressed patients.

For the eating disorders, DBT was found to have significantly lower rates of premature termination compared with all other treatment groups. Although DBT does integrate ideas and techniques from other treatment

TABLE 2.5
Results From the Treatment-by-Disorder Dropout Analyses

Disorder category	Treatment approach	k	Dropout rate	95% CI	Between-group Q value	df (Q)	P value
Bereavement	Average	9	24.9%	20.7%, 29.7%	1.93	1	.17
	Psychodynamic	4	26.2%	21.5%, 31.5%			
	Supportive	5	17.5%	9.7%, 29.5%			
BPD	Average	25	24.0%	20.1%, 28.4%	1.55	2	.46
	Cognitive therapy	5	21.5%	14.2%, 31.2%			
	DBT	12	23.5%	18.8%, 28.9%			
	Psychodynamic	8	30.5%	19.6%, 44.1%			
Depression	Average	161	19.2%	17.8%, 20.8%	22.69	9	<.01
	Behavioral therapy	7	15.5%	7.5%, 29.2%			
	CBASP	4	23.0%	20.4%, 25.9%			
	Cognitive therapy	27	17.2%	14.1%, 20.8%			
	DBT	4	13.3%	6.7%, 24.6%			
	Full CBT	46	20.4%	16.3%, 25.2%			
	Integrative	8	10.9%	7.5%, 15.7%			
	IPT	23	18.2%	13.1%, 24.7%			
	Psychodynamic	15	15.2%	9.2%, 24.2%			
	Solution-focused	6	17.8%	13.6%, 22.9%			
	Supportive	21	18.6%	14.2%, 24.0%			
Eating disorders	Average	60	24.2%	21.7%, 26.9%	14.63	7	<.05
	Behavior therapy	4	22.2%	12.1%, 37.2%			
	Cognitive therapy	4	25.1%	15.7%, 37.6%			
	DBT	4	5.9%	2.5%, 13.4%			
	Full CBT	29	23.7%	20.2%, 27.6%			
	Integrative	3	28.4%	18.8%, 40.4%			
	IPT	4	22.8%	12.8%, 37.4%			
	Psychodynamic	7	27.1%	20.4%, 35.0%			
	Supportive	5	27.6%	20.1%, 36.7%			

		N	%	95% CI		df	
GAD	Average	47	15.2%	12.9%, 18.0%	4.82	6	.57
	Behavior therapy (AR)	7	16.4%	10.6%, 24.5%			
	Behavior therapy (other)	5	15.0%	0.10%, 22.1%			
	Cognitive therapy	6	13.9%	9.0%, 21.0%			
	Full CBT	20	15.2%	11.4%, 19.9%			
	Integrative	3	10.5%	5.1%, 20.5%			
	Psychodynamic	3	11.3%	3.9%, 28.7%			
	Supportive	3	26.4%	14.2%, 43.7%			
OCD	Average	45	16.3%	14.0%, 19.0%	3.02	2	.22
	Behavior therapy (exposure)	21	18.7%	14.9%, 23.1%			
	Cognitive therapy	4	17.2%	10.0%, 28.1%			
	Full CBT	20	14.0%	11.0%, 17.7%			
Other personality	Average	15	20.3%	12.6%, 30.9%	1.90	1	.17
	CBT	6	13.1%	5.6%, 27.7%			
	Psychodynamic	9	25.6%	14.5%, 41.1%			
Panic disorder	Average	80	15.4%	13.7%, 17.3%	4.62	4	.33
	Behavior therapy (AR)	8	11.4%	6.1%, 20.0%			
	Behavior therapy (exposure)	13	14.0%	11.3%, 17.1%			
	Cognitive therapy	16	14.9%	10.8%, 20.1%			
	Full CBT	38	17.5%	14.7%, 20.7%			
	Supportive	5	11.5%	4.9%, 24.4%			
Psychotic disorders	Average	27	16.5%	13.5%, 20.1%	4.02	3	.26
	Behavior therapy	3	14.8%	10.4%, 20.8%			
	Cognitive therapy	3	24.9%	15.3%, 37.7%			
	Full CBT	17	16.2%	11.9%, 21.8%			
	Supportive	4	11.2%	4.7%, 24.5%			

(continues)

TABLE 2.5
Results From the Treatment-by-Disorder Dropout Analyses *(Continued)*

Disorder category	Treatment approach	k	Dropout rate	95% CI	Between-group Q value	df (Q)	P value
PTSD	Average	92	21.0%	18.8%, 23.5%	20.20	7	<.01
	Behavior therapy (AR)	4	12.1%	5.5%, 24.6%			
	Behavior therapy (exposure)	25	23.2%	19.3%, 27.6%			
	Cognitive therapy	8	15.2%	9.6%, 23.3%			
	CPT	5	23.7%	16.3%, 33.1%			
	EMDR	10	16.9%	10.0%, 27.2%			
	Full CBT	27	28.5%	22.4%, 35.6%			
	Integrative	4	8.8%	2.9%, 23.7%			
	Supportive	9	15.2%	11.1%, 20.5%			
Social phobia	Average	52	18.0%	15.5%, 20.7%	0.59	3	.90
	Behavior therapy (exposure)	14	17.5%	12.4%, 24.0%			
	Cognitive therapy	5	14.5%	7.3%, 26.8%			
	Full CBT	30	18.3%	15.4%, 21.6%			
	Integrative	3	20.3%	8.8%, 40.2%			
Somatoform disorders	Average	7	11.1%	4.1%, 26.4%	0.00	1	.97
	Behavior therapy	3	10.9%	2.7%, 34.7%			
	Full CBT	4	11.3%	2.7%, 36.9%			

Note. AR = applied relaxation; BPD = borderline personality disorder; CBASP = cognitive–behavioral analysis system of psychotherapy; CBT = cognitive–behavior therapy; CI = confidence interval; CPT = cognitive processing therapy; DBT = dialectical behavior therapy; EMDR = eye movement desensitization reprocessing; GAD = generalized anxiety disorder; IPT = interpersonal psychotherapy; PTSD = posttraumatic stress disorder; OCD = obsessive–compulsive disorder.

approaches, it is a structured manualized treatment with a set duration, both of which are factors that have been linked to lower rates of premature discontinuation. Additional components of DBT, such as the strict behavioral guidelines, the availability of phone consultation, and the four skills modules (mindfulness, distress tolerance, emotion regulation, and interpersonal effectiveness), may be particularly useful in helping patients with eating disorders complete treatment.

Last, for PTSD, full CBT was found to have significantly higher rates of premature termination than applied relaxation, cognitive therapy, the integrative treatments, and supportive psychotherapy; supportive psychotherapy was found to have significantly lower rates than exposure-based interventions. The three treatments for PTSD that were found to have the highest dropout rates were CBT (28.5%), exposure (23.2%), and cognitive processing therapy (23.2%). Each of these three treatments has a strong exposure component. Although exposure has been found to be highly beneficial in reducing PTSD symptoms (Foa et al., 2005; Resick, Nishith, Weaver, Astin, & Feuer, 2002), clinicians should be aware that jumping too quickly into this technique might raise anxieties in patients, potentially leading them to drop out prematurely.

In general, the results from this set of analyses suggest that although outcome differences may or may not exist between the treatment approaches for these disorders, clients primarily found the treatments that were included in this review to be equally acceptable. The lack of differences found here provides some further support for the dodo bird verdict that "all must have prizes" (Rosenzweig, 1936) rather than the idea that some treatments are better suited for certain disorders (Roth & Fonagy, 2004; Task Force on Promotion and Dissemination of Psychological Procedures, 1995). Even where significant differences between treatments were found (depression, PTSD, and eating disorders), it was the integrative treatments that exhibited the lowest rates of premature termination (it should be noted that DBT could also be considered an integrative approach given the multiple theories, techniques, and worldviews that are used in the treatment). This finding suggests that for these disorders at least, perhaps the common factors (i.e., the therapeutic alliance, having a rationale for the problem and a believed-in method for treating it) rather than the specific techniques are enough to keep clients in therapy (Greenberg, 2012).

A few other recommendations from these findings can be made. First, therapists may want to consider adopting, to some degree, an integrative approach to their work. Bringing positive elements from other treatment approaches has the potential to make treatment more pleasant for clients (e.g., focus on the common factors, adding mindfulness or centering components) and thus reduce rates of premature termination. The exact techniques that can be incorporated can be based on the clinician's judgment of the client's needs as well as the client's expectations and preferences. Second, clinicians who frequently use one of the treatments that have been identified as having a higher dropout rate (e.g., CBASP for depression, full CBT for PTSD) may want to pay particular attention to this higher risk and work to thoughtfully include in their practice many of the dropout-reducing strategies that are presented later in this book. These findings can also serve as a benchmark for those developing or testing new treatment approaches. For example, a developer of a new treatment approach for social phobia should be aware that dropout rates for the existing approaches that were included here ranged from roughly 15% to 20%. If a higher dropout rate is found for the newly developed treatment, the developer may want to work to alter the approach so that it is more acceptable to clients.

Provider Predictors

Premature termination from psychotherapy is a complex phenomenon. Not only is it possible for patient and treatment variables to predict or influence its occurrence, but the characteristics of the treatment provider may also play a significant role. Thus, we examined four provider variables as potential moderators. First, we used a subgroup analysis to examine whether dropout rates differed depending on the experience level of the therapist. Those studies with trainees as the providers ($k = 59$) had an average dropout rate of 26.6%. In contrast, those studies with experienced therapists as the providers ($k = 285$) had a dropout rate of only 17.3%, and those studies with both trainees and experienced therapists ($k = 99$) had an average dropout right in the middle at 22.0%. Clearly, clinicians who are in training have greater difficulty keeping their patients in treatment. There may be a number of reasons for this finding, including the fact that trainees often work in university-based clinics and in general see a younger clientele group, both of which are associated with higher rates of premature termination. However, we would speculate, based on the literature, that therapists become more responsive and focused on the relationship as they move beyond their years of basic training, skills that have been found to have a strong influence on treatment outcomes (Hardy, Stiles, Barkham, & Startup, 1998; Norcross, 2011; Stiles, Honos-Webb, & Surko, 1998). This observation harks back to studies published more than 60 years ago showing that senior clinicians embracing different orientations were more similar in their views of the ideal therapy relationship than were novice and less experienced therapists proclaiming allegiance to the same therapy model (Fiedler, 1950a, 1950b)! The treatment gains associated with experience may also reflect the positive impact that has

TABLE 2.6
Results From the Meta-Regressions (Method of Moments)
for the Provider and Study Variables

Variable (k)	Point estimate	95% CI	Z value
Provider age (31)			
Slope	−0.053	−0.090, −0.016	2.79
Intercept	0.684	−0.697, 2.065	
Provider gender—percent female (147)			
Slope	0.348	−0.117, 0.812	1.47
Intercept	−1.651	−1.955, −1.346	
Provider race—percent Caucasian (20)			
Slope	0.793	−0.079, 1.666	1.78
Intercept	−1.541	−2.285, −0.796	

Note. CI = confidence interval. Adapted from "Premature Discontinuation in Adult Psychotherapy: A Meta-Analysis," by J. K. Swift and R. P. Greenberg, 2012, *Journal of Consulting and Clinical Psychology, 80,* p. 555. Copyright 2012 by the American Psychological Association.

resulted from the growing awareness of the importance of common factors that cut across all brands of therapy (Greenberg, 2012; Wampold, 2001).

The association between three provider demographic variables and premature discontinuation was also tested through meta-regression analyses. The provider variables included average age, gender, and ethnicity. The results from these three analyses can be seen in Table 2.6. In summary, none of these three provider variables significantly (at the Bonferroni-corrected alpha level) predicted the study dropout rates. These findings suggest that regardless of demographics, providers of all types should be concerned about the possibility of their patients dropping out of therapy.

Study Predictors

Let us also briefly mention the results from our examination of three additional study and design variables, the results of which can be found in Table 2.7. First, the results indicated that rates of premature discontinuation were significantly moderated by dropout definition. This finding matches that reported by Wierzbicki and Pekarik (1993) and others (Hatchett & Park, 2003; Swift, Callahan, & Levine, 2009). In our review, we found that dropout rates were significantly higher when determined by therapist judgment compared with the other methods of classification. Of particular note is the fact that therapists report that almost 40% of their patients are dropping out prematurely. This difference may be due to the type of studies that used therapist judgment (more frequently effectiveness studies), but this finding may also be due to differences in the assumptions that are made about dropouts

TABLE 2.7
Results From the Subgroup Analysis of Client, Provider, and Study Moderators on Therapy Dropout

Moderator (k)	Dropout rate	95% CI	Q value	p value
Dropout definition			94.40	< .001
Failed to complete (314)	18.4%	17.3%, 19.6%		
< # of sessions (131)	18.3%	16.4%, 20.3%		
Stopped attending (45)	24.4%	20.9%, 28.2%		
Therapist judgment (63)	37.6%	33.2%, 42.3%		
Study type			81.85	< .001
Efficacy (398)	17.0%	16.0%, 17.9%		
Effectiveness (235)	26.0%	24.2%, 27.9%		
Search strategy			115.13	< .001
Key-word search (198)	28.1%	26.1%, 30.2%		
Meta-analysis search (322)	16.4%	15.4%, 17.5%		
Hand search (149)	17.0%	15.2%, 19.1%		

Note. CI = confidence interval. Adapted from "Premature Discontinuation in Adult Psychotherapy: A Meta-Analysis," by J. K. Swift and R. P. Greenberg, 2012, *Journal of Consulting and Clinical Psychology, 80,* p. 550. Copyright 2012 by the American Psychological Association.

depending on the classification method. To further the field's understanding of therapy dropout, it is important that a consistent operationalization, such as the one presented in the previous chapter, be adopted.

In this review, we found that rates of premature discontinuation were lower for efficacy-type studies (17%) than for effectiveness studies (26%). The difference in dropout rates between these two types of studies may be due to differences in the degree of control over variables such as the types of clients served, what problems are worked on, who administers the treatment, and how the intervention is delivered. Indeed, this review also found that time-limited interventions and manualized treatments, which were most often paired with efficacy studies, also had lower dropout rates. While efficacy-type studies focus on controlling these conditions in an effort to increase internal consistency, control over all of these conditions is not typical for many real-world clients and settings. Hansen, Lambert, and Forman (2002) pointed out the discrepancy in treatment durations between efficacy studies and actual practice, with clients in actual clinical settings attending fewer sessions and being less likely to recover by the end of treatment. Because of differences in the level of control over variables such as the types of clients served, one might conclude that results from clinical trials are not relevant to practice. Although efficacy studies do not always mirror what typically happens in clinical practice, and differences in the levels of control may explain most of the differences in dropout rates, it might still be beneficial for clinical settings to adopt some of the procedures that could be decreasing the rates of premature discontinuation. For example, efficacy studies and treatment protocols often begin with information about what the therapy will look like and how long it will last. Given this fact, practicing clinicians may benefit from addressing role and duration expectations at the start of therapy even if a specific protocol is not used (Garfield, 1994; Reis & Brown, 2006; Swift & Callahan, 2011). Differences in dropout rates between efficacy and effectiveness studies and time-limited and open-ended duration treatments could also be due to the brevity of the interventions. Although clients might be more likely to complete briefer interventions, treatments with a small number of allowable sessions are typically focused on addressing specific problems, which may not fit with many clients' goals for therapy.

Limitations of the Meta-Analysis

Two limitations of this meta-analysis should be considered when interpreting the findings. First, although we tried to be comprehensive in our review, we recognize that many studies that reported dropout rates likely were not included. Some of these may have been missed by our search of the literature; others may have never been published. We chose not to include unpublished studies in order to match more closely the procedures of Wierzbicki and Pekarik (1993); however, this does somewhat limit the comprehensiveness of our results. Additionally, many studies conducted over the time period of the review examined the efficacy or effectiveness of psychological interventions but did not report dropout rates. Given the large number of studies that we searched and the large number of studies that we included in the analyses, we believe that our results represent those studies that have been missed to the best degree possible. Some studies were not included in the various tests of the moderators and covariates due to missing details or data in the original articles, including some studies that stated, without reporting the actual data, that significant differences between dropouts and completers were not found. Rather than assign a zero value for the comparisons in these studies, which, taken across studies, might underestimate differences, studies that did not include sufficient data on a specific variable were not included in the analyses for that variable, which, in turn, could have led to an overestimate of true effects for the six meta-analyses conducted for the client variables (Table 2.3). Given the smaller fail-safe N for educational differences, this result should be interpreted with extreme caution.

A second limitation of this study can be found in the variables that were examined. The set of variables we analyzed were chosen on the basis of the list of variables originally studied by Wierzbicki and Pekarik (1993), with some additional variables included that we believed were important (i.e., treatment orientation, efficacy vs. effectiveness, study design). However, the results of this meta-analysis are limited because a number of other variables that may play a significant role in therapy dropout were not included—variables such as the therapeutic alliance, client expectations and preferences, and collaboration, to name a few. The decision was made to not include these variables in this meta-analysis because the relationship between therapy dropout and some of these process variables has been recently reviewed by others (e.g., Sharf, Primavera, & Diener, 2010; Swift, Callahan, & Vollmer, 2011; Tryon & Winograd, 2011). However, future research should continue to investigate the roles that these types of variables play in preventing clients from prematurely terminating.

SUMMARY AND CONCLUSIONS FROM THE META-ANALYSIS

To take efficient steps to reduce premature discontinuation, it is important for psychotherapy providers and researchers to be able to recognize how often premature discontinuation occurs in therapy and identify which clients and situations are associated with a higher dropout risk. Previous reviews have estimated that approximately 50% of all clients end therapy prematurely; however, our findings indicated that currently only about 20% of clients are therapy dropouts. Previous reviews have been inconsistent in identifying the client, treatment, and setting—variables that predict premature termination. From our large-scale comprehensive review that included data from 669 studies, we found that rates of premature termination are moderated by client diagnosis (higher in personality and eating disorders), client age (higher with younger clients), provider experience level (higher for trainees), and the setting in which the intervention was provided (higher in university-based clinics). In contrast, dropout rates were not moderated by treatment orientation, whether the treatment was provided in individual or group format, and rates were not consistently associated with the client demographic variables of gender, ethnicity, marital status, employment status, and education level.

Although a lower rate of dropout was found in this meta-analysis compared with previous reviews, premature discontinuation from therapy is still a significant problem that needs to be addressed: One in five clients still discontinues therapy prematurely. It is important to increase efforts to help these clients stay in therapy for the full duration, and some recommendations based on the findings from this review can be made for researchers and practicing clinicians. In terms of future research, as previously mentioned, it is important that the field adopt a consistent definition of *dropout*. Without a consistent definition, it is difficult to compare results from one study to the next. If the previously mentioned method that combines therapist judgment with the other operationalizations (failure to complete and reliable improvement or clinically significant change) were to be adopted, researchers in both efficacy and effectiveness studies would need to administer standardized outcome scales at each session. Session-by-session administration of outcome measures also has the advantage of providing end-state data for clients who drop out prematurely. Therapists could then use this end-state information to make a decision about whether each of their clients has dropped out. Also, it is important that treatment outcome and process outcome studies not only report data on rates of premature discontinuation but also provide demographic information for both dropout and completer groups.

Additionally, those studying dropout may want to focus their research efforts on the settings (university-based clinics), patients (younger patients, those with personality and eating disorders), and situations (effectiveness research) where dropout rates are the highest. Furthermore, this review focused on providing a broad and generalized analysis of premature discontinuation in psychological treatments for adults. Future reviews are needed to study dropout in the areas not covered by this review, including examining the influence of process variables on dropout, studying dropout in substance abuse treatments, reviewing dropout for children or family therapy (or both), and so on.

In terms of clinical implications, the results from this review point to a number of patient, setting, clinician, and treatment variables associated with an increased likelihood of dropout. By paying attention to these variables and making adaptations where needed, clinicians may be able to reduce rates of premature discontinuation in their work with patients. For example, the findings from this review suggest that clinicians should work particularly on retention with younger patients and those with a personality or eating disorder diagnosis. Extra efforts to prevent dropout should also be emphasized for trainees and in university-based clinic settings, variables also found to be associated with higher rates of premature termination.

II

STRATEGIES FOR REDUCING PREMATURE TERMINATION

3

PROVIDE ROLE INDUCTION

Before anything else, preparation is the key to success.
—Alexander Graham Bell

Although often exciting and full of promise, beginnings are also frequently overwhelming and sometimes even scary. J. R. R. Tolkien's *Lord of the Rings* tells the story of two hobbits, Frodo Baggins and Samwise Gamgee, who set off on a journey to—unbeknownst to them at the time—save their world. As they begin their voyage, Sam hesitates, looking back at his familiar homeland and forward across lands he has never seen before. Frodo notices this trepidation and shares with Sam something his uncle Bilbo Baggins used to say to him: "It's a dangerous business, Frodo, going out of your door. You step into the road, and if you don't keep your feet, there is no telling where you might be swept off to." We have all likely experienced a comparable sense of apprehension and anxiety at times when beginning a new journey in life.

Similarly, starting therapy can be a daunting and intimidating process for patients. For novice patients, everything is uncertain. They may have questions that range from where to sit and how to pay, to what topics are appropriate for discussion in session. Even those patients who have had

http://dx.doi.org/10.1037/14469-004
Premature Termination in Psychotherapy: Strategies for Engaging Clients and Improving Outcomes,
by J. K. Swift and R. P. Greenberg

previous therapy experience may be uncertain about how everything will work with their new therapist. These feelings of anxiety and uncertainty are one potential cost of seeking psychotherapy that, for some patients, may result in a decision to drop out. Other patients may not have as much difficulty with the uncertainty associated with therapy. In fact, based on previous therapy experience or information from other sources (media, friends, the Internet), some patients begin therapy with certain role expectations in mind. The term *role expectations* refers to the patient and therapist behaviors that the patient believes will be present in treatment. These may be beliefs about whether the therapist will offer advice or who will be doing most of the talking in session. Although they may not have to face uncertainty when starting therapy, patients with preexisting role expectations may also be at risk for dropping out. Specifically, some of these patients may hold role expectations that are inappropriate for psychotherapy altogether or role expectations that are appropriate but do not fit with the behaviors and expectations of their particular therapist. When framed as a cost, expectations that are not met may be interpreted as an error or inadequacy in the therapist and/or treatment, and the patient may quickly drop out as a result.

Indeed, a large body of research has found a link between unmet role expectations and premature discontinuation from psychotherapy (Aubuchon-Endsley & Callahan, 2009; Callahan, Aubuchon-Endsley, Borja, & Swift, 2009; Constantino, Glass, Arnkoff, Ametrano, & Smith, 2011; Garfield, 1994; Greenberg, Constantino, & Bruce, 2006; Reis & Brown, 1999). For example, Aubuchon-Endsley and Callahan (2009) had 53 consecutive adult patients in a training clinic setting complete a measure of role expectations before starting treatment. On the basis of the participating patients' scores, they were able to calculate a "normative reference range" for role expectations on the measure (within 1 SD from the mean). They found that patients who expressed role expectations outside of the "normative reference range" (higher or lower) were over 7 times more likely to terminate prematurely than were patients whose expectations fell in the normal range. Given the link between unmet and unrealistic role expectations and premature termination in psychotherapy, our first recommendation is for providers to assess and seek to correct patients' role expectations early in treatment.

DEFINITION AND DESCRIPTION

For both clients who are largely uncertain about therapy and clients with inaccurate role expectations, role induction is a potential way to reduce the occurrence of dropout. *Role induction* is the process of educating clients about appropriate therapy behaviors early on in treatment. Orne and Wender

(1968) were among the first to talk about this type of pretherapy preparation. In that seminal work, they stated that a client can benefit from psychotherapy only if he or she is first familiar with "certain ground rules, including the purpose of the enterprise and the roles to be played by the participants" (p. 1202). They argued that a client's understanding does not have to be too detailed or specific, but he or she must at least have a general idea of the activities that go on in this type of social interaction before it begins. In socializing the client to psychotherapy, Orne and Wender suggested that the therapist provide an explanation of psychotherapy and describe the roles of the participants. On the basis of Orne and Wender's early recommendations and the decades of research in this topic area that have followed, we believe that role induction is best accomplished when all of three domains are covered: (a) the general behaviors of an ideal client; (b) the general behaviors the client can expect from the therapist; and (c) the specific nature, purpose, and behaviors associated with the particular treatment approach.

First, clients need to know what is expected of them. Rather than facing uncertainty and fear that they may be doing things wrong, clients who have information about what is expected of them can engage more easily in the activities that will help them recover. The client should be taught that although the therapist plays an important role, progress in therapy is largely dependent on the efforts of the client. Clients can be instructed to talk openly and honestly about problems, thoughts, and feelings, regardless of how personal or painful they may be. They can also be encouraged to fully invest and engage in the in-session and out-of-session activities that they and their therapists come up with as part of their treatment. Finally, clients can also be told that their regular feedback, positive or negative, regarding the therapist, techniques, and therapy progress is strongly desired.

Second, clients need to know what they can expect from their therapist. This may differ from one theoretical orientation to the next, but in general, clients should be told that the therapist's primary job is not to solve the problems but to assist the client in the journey of finding solutions. Each therapist may go about this in a different way and so the therapist's exact approach should be communicated to the client. This communication should include whether the therapist or client is going to direct the session, whether the therapist will give advice, ask questions, use challenges, and provide interpretations. Regardless of the specific behaviors, during the socialization phase the client also needs to get a sense that he or she can trust the therapist, that the therapist will be accepting and understanding, not judgmental or condemning, of the client's problems. Conveying these later characteristics is often better done through actions than words.

Third, patients need to be provided a credible treatment rationale. Most therapy approaches suggest that sometime during the initial phase of therapy the therapist should provide the patient with a treatment rationale, which first includes a theoretically sound causal explanation of the patient's problems and, second, a description of the techniques and procedures that will be used to treat those problems. It is essential that the procedures and techniques fit theoretically with the causal explanation. A treatment rationale should also include specific details about the appropriate patient and therapist behaviors. Earlier, we mentioned that the patient and therapist roles should be discussed generally (e.g., the patient should be open in his or her communication). In the treatment rationale, a more detailed description of the roles should be provided, such as the content area of the communication or the type of homework that may be assigned. Understandably, the treatment rationale provided is going to vary depending on the patient's problems and the therapist's theoretical approach. However, the specific details of the rationale are not of consequence as long as they are shared with and make sense to the patient. In their article, Orne and Wender (1968) stated, "In the context of the interview, it matters little what rationale is given to help the patient understand psychotherapy. It is important, however, that some rationale be given" (p. 1208). Along the same lines, Jerome Frank described all theories of psychotherapy as "myth." He indicated that the content of the particular myth is largely based on the worldview of a given culture and generally irrelevant in producing patient change compared with the power of the patient's belief in that myth (Frank & Frank, 1991).

EMPIRICAL RESEARCH

One of the first studies to test a role induction procedure was conducted by Hoehn-Saric, Frank, Imber, Nash, Stone, and Battle (1964). In this study, 40 outpatient patients were randomly assigned to role induction and control groups. Those assigned to the role induction condition met with a clinician briefly before being assigned a therapist (therapists were blind to the experimental condition). The role induction included teaching the patient the general purpose of psychotherapy (i.e., psychotherapy was explained as a learning processes that takes time but that would help patients learn how to better handle their problems), behaviors that could be expected from the therapist (i.e., not to give advice or talk too much, but instead to try to listen, understand, and clarify problems), and expected patient behaviors (i.e., talk freely to the therapist even when it is difficult and share feelings, particularly those toward the therapist). Those patients who had received the role induction on average attended more therapy sessions, more easily developed a therapeutic relationship with their therapist, displayed more positive and less negative therapy behaviors during therapy, and evidenced greater therapy improvements. Additionally, those who did not receive the role induction had a dropout rate that was twice as high as the role induction patients by the fourth therapy session.

Another noteworthy study examining the effects of role induction was conducted by Warren and Rice (1972) with 55 low-prognosis patients at the University of Chicago Counseling and Psychotherapy Research Center. In this study, patients were assigned to one of three conditions, which included a control group that received 20 sessions of patient-centered therapy, a semicontrol group that received the 20 sessions plus four additional 30 minute preappointment sessions in which they could discuss any problems they were having in therapy, and an experimental group that received the 20 sessions plus four additional 30 minute preappointment sessions in which they were trained how to participate productively in therapy in addition to being able to discuss any problems with therapy. The control group had a 28% treatment dropout rate with almost half of these patients (47%) failing to stay for at least 18 sessions. In contrast, the semicontrol group had only a 10% dropout rate, but 40% of the patients still failed to remain for at least 18 of the 20 planned sessions. The experimental group far outperformed the other two groups with 0% dropout and only 11% of the patients failing to attend at least 18 sessions. Additionally, observer ratings of sessions found that those patients who received the role induction more actively engaged in the therapy process.

Another much more recent study examining the effects of role induction on premature discontinuation was conducted by Reis and Brown (2006) with adult outpatients. For their study, Reis and Brown randomly assigned 125 patients to role induction and control groups. Before the intake appointment those in the role induction group watched a 12-minute therapy orientation video and those in the control group watched a 17-minute video about the development of a managed care system. Therapy then proceeded as usual for all patients, and at the end of treatment, therapists rated each patient as either a treatment dropout or completer on the Termination Status Questionnaire (Reis & Brown, 2006). A significant difference between groups was found with patients who watched the therapy orientation video being rated lower on the dropout questionnaire compared with control patients.

Over the past half century, dozens of similar studies have likewise found role induction to be an effective strategy for orienting patients to therapy (see Strassle, Borckardt, Handler, & Nash, 2011, for a narrative review). However, to date, only one empirical review has attempted to pool the findings from the various studies. In a 1996 meta-analysis, Monks examined the influence of role induction on attendance, premature termination, therapy behaviors, and treatment outcomes. On the basis of data from 28 studies, Monks (1996) found that those who received some type of pretherapy education attended a significantly greater number of sessions ($d = 0.32$), were less likely to drop out of treatment ($d = 0.23$), showed more positive therapy behaviors ($d = 0.20$), and displayed greater improvements while in treatment ($d = 0.34$). Although this meta-analysis was not published, the results clearly display the positive benefits that can come from role induction.

Although we place it in the same category as role induction, a somewhat separate line of research has examined the usefulness of presenting clients with a credible treatment rationale. Only a handful of studies have experimentally examined the influence of the treatment rationale. In one interesting study, Oliveau, Agras, Leitenberg, Moore, and Wright (1969) treated 30 female college students who had a fear of snakes with systematic desensitization. A treatment rationale preceded the systematic desensitization for only half of the participants. Those who received the rationale showed significantly greater levels of fear reduction. Other studies in this area have also generally found that increased expectations follow more thorough rationales (Ahmed & Westra, 2009; Horvath, 1990; Kazdin & Krouse, 1983). However, most of these studies have been analogue in nature, with college students as participants and expectations representing treatment outcomes.

The importance of a credible treatment rationale has also been suggested by findings from other types of studies. For example, Ilardi and Craighead (1994) pointed out that most of the benefits from cognitive–behavioral treatments are observed in the first few sessions before the implementation of any specific techniques. They suggested that these early changes are at least partially due to the client's faith in a credible treatment rationale. Also, although not experimental in nature, a plethora of research has found a link between treatment credibility and treatment outcomes. In one review that included data from 30 studies, Weaver (1998) found a significant correlation ($r = .38$) between perceived credibility and outcome. This same review found that the included treatments were no more effective than control conditions once credibility was controlled. In two other more recent meta-analyses, outcome expectations have been found to significantly predict treatment outcomes (Arnkoff, Glass, & Shapiro, 2002; Constantino et al., 2011). Although outcome expectations may be the result of many variables, it is not likely that a client will have positive treatment expectations unless a coherent and credible treatment rationale is presented.

PUTTING IT INTO PRACTICE

When thinking about providing clients with role induction, the first question that may come to mind is what should be included. We mentioned earlier that role induction is best accomplished when all of three domains are covered: (a) the general behaviors of an ideal client; (b) the general behaviors the client can expect from the therapist; and (c) the specific nature, purpose, and behaviors associated with the particular treatment approach (i.e., the treatment rationale). There is perhaps a fourth category of information that if provided could also help to alleviate some of the client's worries about coming in to treatment: logistical information. Simple things such as telling clients when and where to pay, how early they should show up for their session, who they will interact with in the clinic, how long the session will last, whether they will need to complete routine measures and/or paperwork, for example, can go a long way to relieve anxieties about being in a new situation. More detailed role induction should take place with clients who are new to therapy. However, some role induction should occur with all clients to correct for inappropriate role expectations as needed. Our specific content suggestions for each of these four categories are provided in Exhibit 3.1.

EXHIBIT 3.1
Topic Areas for Inclusion in Role Induction

Logistical information
- Clinic/site overview (goals of site, clinic staff, layout)
- General paperwork needs (e.g., intake paperwork, billing)
- Procedures and goals of the intake session
- Setup for therapy sessions
  - Session length and frequency
  - Pre- and postsession measures (instructions and purpose)
  - Any regular session structure (e.g., who starts, where to start)

Desired client roles and behaviors
- Progress is primarily dependent on client's efforts
  - Importance of engagement/efforts in and out of session
- Importance of open and honest communication about problems, thoughts, and feelings
- Encouragement to freely share feelings regarding the therapist, techniques, and therapy progress

Therapist roles and behaviors
- Will focus on listening, understanding, and earning the client's trust
- Goal is to assist the client in solving his or her own problems
- Depending on the therapist's approach, should also inform the client of stances on
  - who should direct or lead the session
  - whether advice will be given
  - whether questions, challenges, interpretations, etc. will be used

Treatment rationale
- A theoretically sound causal explanation of the client's problems
- A description of the procedures that will be used to treat those problems
  - Specific techniques
  - Specific client behaviors and jobs
  - Specific therapist behaviors and jobs

A number of other examples of role induction and treatment rationales are also available in the literature. For example, Orne and Wender's 1968 article contains an appendix with two lengthy excerpts of their socialization interview. Their full interview is about 15 minutes in length, and it primarily focuses on the general roles and behaviors for clients and therapists. Although they conceded that it is in monologue form, they do recommend that it be tailored to the situation and be made more interactive with questions and discussion. More recently, Strassle and colleagues adapted Orne and Wender's original interview, and a complete text of their role induction can be found in an appendix to their 2011 article. Their adaptations were to make the induction more educational and less interactive, use more updated language, and include a small amount of additional logistical and treatment rationale information.

Another commonly used example of role induction is *Tell It Like It Is*, a 12-minute video presentation developed by Acosta, Evans, Yamamoto, and Wilcox in 1980. This program describes seven types of desirable client behaviors (share your problems, be open and honest with how you feel, share if you think therapy is taking too long to work, tell if you don't plan on coming back, be open if you are unhappy with your therapist, be willing to talk about uncomfortable things, share even small problems with your therapist) with the overall goal to help clients

(1) better understand the process of seeing a therapist; (2) more clearly express problems, needs, and therapy expectations to the therapist; (3) be more open, direct, assertive, and self-disclosing with the therapist; and (4) take a more active role in the therapy process. (Acosta, Yamamoto, Evans, & Skilbeck, 1983, p. 874)

The program was specifically developed for ethnic minority and low-income clients; however, it has been shown to be effective with other client groups as well. A more detailed description of the video can be found in Acosta et al. (1980).

Detailed examples of treatment rationales are also readily available in the literature. They can be found at the start of most treatment manuals. Although these examples can provide a general example of the content that can be covered with clients, we strongly recommend that clinicians tailor the rationale to the individual client. Tailoring in this manner will help the client see how a particular treatment approach will fit his or her problems and needs.

In addition to considering what information to share with clients, it is important to identify an appropriate method for providing role induction. Perhaps the easiest to implement is a simple discussion between the therapist and the client. Providing role induction in this manner allows clients to ask questions and allows therapists to personalize the message to the individual client's situation. To save time in session, many have used video, audio, and text formats for role induction. Presentation in one of these formats may seem more official to clients and help them recognize that there is a consensus on the importance of the behaviors and roles that are discussed instead of it simply being based on the opinion of their individual therapist. Additionally, these standard formats guarantee that all essential information will be covered, and they can easily be administered to all clients without much effort from the therapist. However, not all of the information presented will be relevant to each client and, as a result, some clients may pay less attention to the information or dismiss it all together. With either a discussion between the client and therapist or a standard video presentation, much of the induction will be presented as information shared with the client. The discussion has the obvious advantage of being interactive and allowing client questions to be answered. However, video presentations have another advantage in that demonstrations of the behaviors can be incorporated. Thus, not only are clients being told what to do or not to do in therapy, they also can watch an example of these behaviors taking place. Part of the decision about which type of role induction format should be used depends on the content being shared. Although a video presentation may be useful to orient a client to the clinic or describe the general therapy process and general roles and behaviors of clients and therapists, the treatment rationale needs to be specific to the client's presenting concerns. Thus, we recommend the treatment rationale always be presented in person, possibly using handouts to supplement.

The last practical concern for role induction is the appropriate timing of the procedure. In general, it is important to start treatment off on the right foot, so we would recommend that it be included early in therapy. However, the exact timing again depends on the content of the socialization. Some information on logistics should be provided before the patient ever comes in to the clinic. This can occur over the phone in the initial contact, or through video/instructions on a website. Similarly, general information about therapy and the patient and therapist roles can also be shared before the intake appointment, possibly through a video that is posted on a clinic website or that can be watched in the waiting room. Given that the treatment rationale needs to be tailored to the patient's individual presenting concerns, it should wait until the end or after the intake appointment when the therapist has a better conceptualization of the problems. This might be a good time for therapists to provide the other role induction information or review it if it was previously presented in video or text format.

Finally, role induction may best be accomplished when therapists first gain an understanding of what role expectations their patients hold for therapy. Therapists can then choose to reinforce those role expectations if they are reasonable and fit with the particular therapist's style, or they can spend time helping patients adjust their expectations if the initial ones are not entirely appropriate. One occasionally used measure for patient role expectations is the Psychotherapy Expectancy Inventory—Revised (PEI–R; Berzins, Herron, & Seidman, 1971; Rickers-Ovsiankina, Geller, Berzins, & Rogers, 1971). This self-report questionnaire includes 30 items assessing role expectations in four domains: expectations for the therapist to give advice, to provide approval, to simply focus on listening to the patient, or to work on developing the therapeutic relationship. Another measure that is sometimes used to evaluate role expectations is the Milwaukee Psychotherapy Expectations Questionnaire (MPEQ; Norberg, Wetterneck, Sass, & Kanter, 2011). The MPEQ includes nine items that assess expectations for process-related variables. The majority of these items assess expectations for the therapist (e.g., he or she will provide support, will be sincere, will be interested in me), but some also assess expectations for the patient (e.g., I will come to every appointment, express my true thoughts and feelings, share concerns with the therapist). Therapists can also simply assess patients' role expectations by asking questions such as, "Before coming in, did you have any thoughts about what therapy would be like?" "What types of things were you hoping that I, as a therapist, would do?" and "As a patient, what do you think is your role in therapy?"

CLINICAL EXAMPLES

The following dialogue is an excerpt from the role induction that was conducted with Emily. This was her first time seeking services, so the role induction focused primarily on the general patient and therapist behaviors that she could expect. This conversation took place at the end of her intake session.

Therapist: Emily, I really appreciate everything you have shared with me today and how open you have been in talking about the struggles you have been going through. It has really helped me gain a better understanding of what you have been facing. How did it feel, sharing these things with me?

Emily: Well I was really nervous at first—I didn't even know if I was going to make it in. But once I got going, it wasn't that bad. Actually, I can't believe I shared so much.

Therapist: I am glad that you did have the courage to come in and share what you did. Since this is your first time talking with a therapist, I thought I would take a moment and share with you what therapy is typically like. Is that OK?

Emily:	Sure, that would be really helpful.
Therapist:	Psychotherapy is primarily an opportunity for you to work on some of the struggles you shared with me today in a safe environment. It is a chance for you to explore some of your experiences, thoughts, and feelings, as well as some of the actions you might want to take. For it to work, it is important for you continue to try to talk freely about these things with me, even if it is painful or you are worried about what I might think. As you talk, you don't have to worry that it all makes sense, just share whatever it is that you are thinking and feeling. Throughout this process I am going to be trying hard to understand your experience. I am going to try to understand, not so I can give you lots of advice or tell you exactly what to do, but so I can reflect back to you what I am hearing and help you explore and process it all at a deeper level. Now it might take some time, but through this process, we will both come to better understand the problems and start to see some possible solutions. Those solutions might be some new ways of thinking about things, new ways of acting, or maybe just finally being able to let go of some of the painful things you have been holding on to. Again, my job won't be to tell you exactly how to fix the problems, but I will help guide you through the journey to find solutions. How does that all sound?
Emily:	Good; I mean it would be great to have someone just fix things for me, but I realize that wouldn't really work. It will be nice, though, to have someone help as I sort it all out.

Although it was important in Emily's role induction, given that she is a novice to therapy, to focus on the general behaviors of the patient and therapist, Robert has had much more experience with treatment, and so more attention was given in his role induction to the behaviors that fit with the specific approach to be used. The following dialogue is an excerpt from the start of the first treatment session.

Therapist:	Last time we talked some about tackling your social anxiety from a cognitive–behavioral perspective. You mentioned that none of your previous therapists have worked with you using this type of approach, so I wanted to briefly mention again some of the things that you can expect as we work together. How does that sound?
Robert:	Good.
Therapist:	OK. Well, from a cognitive–behavioral model, your current social anxiety can be seen as a result of both your thoughts

and behaviors. Now there may have been some things in your past that have led to where you are at now—things that you told me about last time we met, like getting bullied while growing up. Although that is important and we may address it some, we are going to focus more on your current thoughts and behaviors that perpetuate the anxiety problem. In general, we find that people with your type of anxiety tend to evaluate and make predictions about social situations in a certain way that leads to worry and fear. Typically they either overestimate the threatening aspects of the situation or they overestimate the negative consequences that will follow social mistakes. Many people with social anxiety even end up having some of these types of thoughts about the anxiety itself and what people will think of it.

Robert: Yeah, all the time.

Therapist: What ends up happening is the worries and negative thoughts stop you from doing the things that you might otherwise want to do.

Robert: Like what I mentioned last time when I was so worried that I skipped out on the office party?

Therapist: Right. So in treatment we are going to focus on those current thoughts and behaviors. At first, your job is going to be to try to identify and share with me the worry thoughts that seem to haunt you. I will have some worksheets and exercises to help you do this. My job will be to try to help you identify some of the errors in those thoughts. As we do that, we will practice challenging them to try to look at things in a non-anxiety-provoking way. As we work together it will be important for you to practice out of session the things that we talk about in here—that is, take time to identify and continually challenge your thoughts whenever you are experiencing anxiety. Then we will start to develop a plan for approaching your anxiety. This might be the hard part, but instead of avoiding things when they seem threatening, we are actually going to work on approaching social situations that might seem scary.

Robert: You mean you might want me to speak in public . . . I don't think I can do that.

Therapist: Well, we are going to take it nice and slow and approach things at a gradual level, nothing too hard at first. With this, my job is going to be to help you develop a good plan for approaching the anxiety-provoking situations and to problem solve any barriers that might get in the way. Although it may be hard, your job is going to be to put a lot of effort into the approaching exercises and not let the fear or worry get in your way. Again, I will be here with you throughout the process to look at what worked, what didn't work, and to help you figure out what the next step is. What do you think?

Robert: Sounds a lot different than anything I have done in the past, but after 53 years, maybe different is what I need.

With both Robert and Emily the therapists sought to address role expectations by providing education about the appropriate and desired behaviors for treatment. Although the cases differed slightly, in both situations the education included a description of what was expected of the client (e.g., talking openly, actively facing fears), what the client could expect of the therapist (e.g., listen and look for patterns, help identify thinking errors), and how those client and therapist behaviors fit with the goals of the treatment. In these cases, the role induction focused primarily on providing education, and Robert and Emily were receptive to the education that was given.

In contrast to Robert and Emily's cases, there may be instances when therapists need to spend more time correcting the unrealistic role expectations their clients hold. Clients may hold unrealistic expectations based on previous experiences with therapy or beliefs they have obtained about therapy from television, movies, and other portrayals in pop culture. In these situations, therapists should first take the time to fully assess what the erroneous beliefs are, where they came from, and how the client feels about them. They can then seek to normalize the mistaken beliefs so that clients do not feel as challenged when the therapist tries to correct them. Therapists should then share their views about the appropriate roles and behaviors for therapy, giving a solid rationale for these ideas. Some clients may readily accept the new ideas; others may be somewhat hesitant about the education presented. For the latter, it is important for therapists to work collaboratively with their clients to find a set of roles and behaviors they can both accept.

CONCLUSION

In this chapter, we presented role induction as the first strategy that providers can use to reduce the occurrence of premature termination in their practice. *Role induction* is a process for (a) assessing clients existing role expectations for treatment, (b) providing education about appropriate and desired roles and behaviors for therapy, and (c) correcting unrealistic role expectations when needed. A large body of research has found evidence linking unmet role expectations to premature termination in therapy (Aubuchon-Endsley & Callahan, 2009; Callahan et al., 2009; Constantino et al., 2011; Garfield, 1994; Greenberg et al., 2006; Reis & Brown, 1999) and supporting role induction as a potential tool for reducing treatment dropout (Monks, 1996; Strassle et al., 2011). Although a large body of research on role induction exists, much of it is dated. For example, although the principles in Acosta et al.'s (1980) role induction video are still relevant, clients may not find it credible given the format in which the information is presented. Current research is needed to develop and test more up-to-date methods for educating clients about the appropriate roles and behaviors for psychotherapy.

In terms of clinical practice, we recommend that providers start with routinely assessing their clients' preexisting role expectations for treatment. Therapists may want to use a standard measure such as the PEI–R or the MPEQ in addition to informal inquiries regarding the client's beliefs about what should happen in treatment. We recommend that, in providing education about appropriate and desired roles and behaviors, therapists share information about the general behaviors of the ideal client, the general behaviors that clients can expect from them as therapists, the specific client and therapist behaviors that fit with the particular treatment approach that will be used, and a rationale for how these behaviors fit with the goals and aims of therapy. For those clients who hold unrealistic role expectations, it is important that therapists validate and normalize the beliefs clients have before attempting to correct them. Finally, in making efforts to correct mistaken beliefs about therapy, rather than directly confronting clients, therapists should seek to work with them so a collaborative agreement can be made. This type of collaboration fits with the research on accommodating client preferences in therapy, a strategy that is discussed in Chapter 4.

In conclusion, we recommend that therapists seek to provide role induction in the first meeting so that clients can avoid the cost of beginning therapy with the anxiety that uncertainty can bring. However, we also recommend that therapists revisit the topic of role expectations periodically with their clients, given that their beliefs and preferences about therapy will likely evolve as they engage in the therapy process.

4

INCORPORATE PREFERENCES INTO THE TREATMENT DECISION-MAKING PROCESS

To know what you prefer instead of humbly saying Amen to what the world tells you ought to prefer, is to have kept your soul alive.
—Robert Louis Stevenson

In the previous chapter, we discussed the value of addressing clients' role expectations for psychotherapy. By addressing role expectations, clients can have a better idea about what is likely to happen in treatment, thus avoiding the worries that often accompany uncertainty and the dissatisfaction that is often associated with unmet beliefs. Similar to holding beliefs about what is likely to occur in psychotherapy, most clients have specific desires regarding what they hope will happen. These hopes and desires for treatment are referred to as *client preferences*, and addressing them is another way for therapists to reduce premature discontinuation in their practice.

Although most therapists would say that they care about their clients' opinions and desires for treatment, actually taking steps to accommodate client preferences doesn't often occur. Frequently, therapists fall into the trap of believing that they know best what treatment and conditions their clients ought to prefer—the doctor-knows-best model. However, this is not

http://dx.doi.org/10.1037/14469-007
Premature Termination in Psychotherapy: Strategies for Engaging Clients and Improving Outcomes, by J. K. Swift and R. P. Greenberg

always the case. Therapists often base their treatment approach solely on their clinical experience and judgment, going with the treatment that they always use, or the empirical research, choosing a treatment based on the results from the latest clinical trial. However, there is now ample evidence that psychotherapy is most effective when treatment decisions are tailored to the individual characteristics of the client (Norcross, 2011), client preferences being one of them (Swift, Callahan, & Vollmer, 2011). Indeed, the American Psychological Association (2006) statement on evidence-based practice in psychology clearly states that all three (empirical research, clinical judgment, and client values and preferences) should be considered equally when making treatment decisions.

Based on the cost–benefit conceptualization of premature termination, the strategy of incorporating client preferences into the treatment decision-making process can lead to a number of perceived and anticipated benefits that have the potential to help clients continue to attend. When therapists allow their clients to express their preferences and be fully involved in the treatment decision-making process, clients become more invested in the choices that they make, and thus more motivated to continue therapy through to the end. Additionally, discussing preferences can provide an opportunity for the therapist to enhance the alliance and sense of collaboration that will take place in therapy (a dropout-reducing strategy that is discussed more fully in Chapter 9). In contrast, ignoring clients' preferences often leads to significant perceived and anticipated costs by clients, which in turn often results in treatment dropout. For example, therapists who make treatment decisions on their own have the potential to choose treatments that some of their clients will simply be unwilling to try. Additionally, when making this choice for them, therapists can rob their clients of their right to self-determination, one of the guiding principles of the ethics code of the American Psychological Association (2002).

DEFINITION AND DESCRIPTION

Client preferences are defined as the specific variables or attributes clients desire in the therapy encounter. In other words, they represent the behaviors, treatments, and therapist characteristics that clients would choose if they were allowed to make the treatment decisions. Although similar, client preferences can be contrasted with *client expectations*. Whereas preferences represent desires and values, expectations reflect what clients actually believe should or will happen in therapy. For example, growing up in Seattle, one might expect it to rain more days than not; however, one can still prefer a clear, sunny day to a cloudy, wet one.

Patient preferences for therapy generally fall under one of three main categories: role, therapist, or treatment-type preferences. *Role preferences* consist of the behaviors and activities patients desire themselves and their therapists to engage in while in therapy. Examples of role preferences include desires for the therapist to take an advice-giving or a listening role, inclination for or against the inclusion of between-session homework, and preferring treatment to be offered in an individual or group format.

Therapist preferences consist of the characteristics and attributes that patients hope their therapist possesses. Therapist preferences can focus on demographic characteristics, such as desires for a therapist of a particular ethnicity, gender, or age. Although these characteristics may not seem to be all that important in determining treatment outcomes, for some clients, they are critical. For example, a female client who has experienced a significant amount of abuse by males in her past may not be ready to work with a male therapist, or an ethnic minority client who is struggling with conflicting values between his or her minority culture and the majority culture may have a strong desire to work with someone who has navigated the same issues. Preferences for therapist demographic characteristics most likely play the largest role in decisions about starting therapy. However, once the therapist and client have started working together, preferences about therapist interpersonal characteristics may play a larger role in clients' decisions to drop out. Examples of these types of preferences include desires between a therapist who is more professional or one who is more casual in his or her interpersonal style or between a therapist who is going to be more empathic and understanding of clients' difficulties or one who is going to challenge clients to face their problems head on. A unique instance of this type of preference occurred in two studies, separated by a 3-decade interval, examining male and female college students' preferences for the personality characteristics they would want in their ideal psychotherapist (DeGeorge, Constantino, Greenberg, Swift, & Smith Hansen, 2013; Greenberg & Zeldow, 1980). In general, the studies revealed some enduring sex differences, with men preferring a therapist with more historically stereotypical feminine gender-role traits and women favoring a therapist with more historically stereotypical masculine gender-role traits.

Last, *treatment-type preferences* refer to the kind of intervention that is hoped for. The most evident treatment-type preference would be a preference between psychotherapy and medication. Although some clients are open to either form of treatment, other potential clients will refuse to engage in one or the other if it is offered to them against their preferences. For those clients who are willing to engage in psychotherapy, some prefer a specific type of treatment orientation (e.g., patient-centered, cognitive–behavioral, psychodynamic). These preferences may come from previous successful or unsuccessful experiences in treatment as well as other sources (e.g., discussions with friends, treatments that have been mentioned in the news, research that they have done on the Internet). Although clients may not know the "brand names" of all of the various treatment orientations, most likely have some idea whether they would like a more action-oriented or insight-oriented approach.

Integrating patient preferences into the treatment decision-making process reduces the likelihood of premature termination by addressing both costs and benefits that might lead a patient to choose to either drop out or continue in psychotherapy. In general, patients often seek therapy feeling stuck or lost with regard to the methods for reducing their distress or fixing their problems. It can thus be easy for therapists, as experts in psychopathology and treatment techniques, to assume responsibility for helping their patients get unstuck by providing solutions. However, patients, as experts in their own lives, may still be able to contribute to the decision-making process. Most of the time people have some idea about how their problems developed, they know what interventions have worked in the past, and they know what interventions they are willing and motivated to try now.

When individuals are given a choice, they will benefit twofold. First, according to cognitive dissonance theory (Cooper, 2012; Draycott & Dabbs, 1998; Festinger, 1957), allowing a patient to choose an option results in a stronger motivation to make the chosen option look like it was the right choice. In other words, in choosing Treatment A over Treatment B, she or he will become motivated to make Treatment A look like it is superior to Treatment B. That investment translates into the patient being more fully engaged in the chosen treatment and, in turn, being less likely to drop out. A demonstration of this effect can be found in a simple study by Rose, Geers, Rasinski, and Fowler (2012). Participants were told that in a moment they would be asked to place their hand into a container of water and crushed ice, but before doing so, they would be able to apply one of two novel pain-relieving treatments. Both treatments were then described to participants as ointments, one that warms the hand, protecting it like a glove, and one that blocks pain receptors in the hand. In reality, both ointments were identical and inert. Half of the participants were given 2 minutes to think about the product and make a choice; the other half were also given 2 minutes to think, but then the experimenter made the choice for them. All participants were then asked to hold their hand under water and report the amount of pain that they were experiencing every 15 seconds. Those who were given a choice in their treatment consistently reported less pain than those who were not given the choice, particularly as time increased. This study is one of many that demonstrates that allowing patients to choose their own treatment results in greater perceived benefits in their chosen treatment option, which as a result increases their likelihood of continuing with that treatment.

Second, integrating patient preferences into the treatment decision-making process has the potential to reduce the likelihood of premature discontinuation because it creates an opportunity to build the patient's hope. In allowing a patient to make a choice about therapy, the therapist is essentially telling the patient that he or she is an expert about himself or herself and capable of making a reasonable decision. This expression of confidence may strengthen the hope that the patient has for himself or herself. Those who are given a choice are more likely to think, "If my therapist trusts me to make good decisions, maybe I can trust myself in figuring out a solution to my problems." Strengthening early hope as a method for reducing premature discontinuation is discussed more fully in the next chapter.

In contrast to the benefits that come with integrating client preferences and allowing a client to make a choice among treatment options, not accommodating preferences and not giving choices can actually be seen as a cost in therapy. According to psychological reactance theory (Brehm, 1966), not allowing an individual to choose between options leads to a devaluing of the option that was assigned and negative feelings toward the decision maker. In Rose et al.'s (2012) cold-water experiment mentioned earlier, a third group of participants were simply told that the ointment was a cleansing solution that needed to be applied before submerging one's hand in the water. Although those in the choice condition reported less pain then those in this control condition, those in the no-choice condition actually reported more pain than those who knew the ointment was inert. Applied to therapy, removing clients' freedom to choose or ignoring their preferences can result in negative feelings and disappointment, which in turn may lead to a lack of motivation to engage in treatment and eventual drop out of therapy. This very finding has been demonstrated in several empirical studies of psychotherapy, as the following section details.

EMPIRICAL RESEARCH

A growing body of research has found evidence supporting the integration of client preferences as a method for reducing premature termination in psychotherapy. Studies in the area of preferences usually take one of three design formats. The first includes studies that assign clients to preference match or preference nonmatch conditions. For example, Manthei, Vitalo, and Ivey (1982) allowed clients to listen to audio recordings of eight potential therapists. Some of their participants were then allowed to choose their therapist, whereas others were informed that they would be randomly assigned to one. The second format includes studies that assign clients to treatment conditions, and by chance some clients are assigned to a treatment that matches their preferences and others are given a treatment that does not match. An example of this type of study was conducted by Kocsis et al. (2009), who assessed treatment preferences at the start of the study but then randomly assigned all their participants to either pharmacotherapy, psychotherapy, or a combination treatment. Because treatment assignment was done randomly, some clients who preferred pharmacotherapy received it, whereas others received psychotherapy. Likewise, some clients who preferred psychotherapy received it, whereas others received pharmacotherapy. The third category of studies is referred to as *partially randomized preference trials* (PRPTs). In this type of study, clients who refuse to be randomized to a treatment condition are given their treatment of choice. Their outcomes are then compared with those of clients who agreed to randomization. Bedi et al. (2000) conducted a PRPT when they randomized some clients to antidepressants or psychotherapy, but then allowed those clients who refused randomization to choose between the two treatment options. Table 4.1 lists the strengths and limitations of each type of study design.

TABLE 4.1
Comparison of Designs Used to Measure Preference Effects

Design type	Method of treatment allocation	Strengths (+) and weaknesses (−)
Assignment to preference conditions (match/no match)	Clients are randomized/assigned to have their preferences matched, or are given a choice of their preferred condition, or are randomized/assigned to receive a nonpreferred condition or no choice.	(+) Study was explicitly designed to measure preference effects (−). Little can be inferred about the treatment effects.
Assignment to treatment conditions (randomized controlled trials)	Clients are randomized/assigned to a type of treatment (e.g., cognitive behavior therapy, pharmacotherapy) that, by chance, may or may not match their preferences.	(+) Gold standard for evaluating treatments (−) Although treatment conditions are equal because of randomization, preference conditions may not be (−). Preferences may not be as strong because some clients refuse randomization.
Partially randomized preference trial	Clients who refuse randomization are given their preferred treatment condition, and the remaining clients are randomized to a treatment.	(+) Includes clients who refuse randomization (−) Compares clients who receive their preferred treatment to clients who have no preference (no clients get a nonpreferred treatment)

Note. From "The Impact of Client Treatment Preferences on Outcome: A Meta-Analysis," by J. K. Swift and J. L. Callahan, 2009, *Journal of Clinical Psychology, 65*, p. 370. Copyright 2009 by Wiley Periodicals, Inc. Adapted with permission.

Although not particularly addressing the influence of preferences on dropout, a significant body of research has demonstrated their influence on the development of the therapeutic alliance and treatment outcomes. For example, in a review of options and evidence for treating depression, Greenberg and Goldman (2009) highlighted, among other things, the benefits that taking client preferences into consideration might provide. For example, one cited study (Iacoviello et al., 2007) found that therapeutic alliance increased over time for depressed clients who preferred and received psychotherapy. In contrast, the treatment alliance decreased over time for depressed clients who preferred psychotherapy but received medication instead. For clients expressing a preference for medication, the alliance did not change over time no matter which treatment they received. Similarly, in the large National Institute of Mental Health depression study, matching clients to their preferred treatment resulted in a more positive alliance and better treatment retention (Elkin et al., 1999). Another instance of benefits was shown in a depression study in which matched participants had more rapid symptom improvement than nonmatched clients had (Lin et al., 2005). Further, in a comprehensive review of the influence of matching preferences on treatment outcomes, Swift et al. (2011) aggregated data from 33 studies and found an outcome effect size of $d = 0.31$ in favor of those clients whose preferences were matched in therapy.

Specific to the topic of dropout, Swift et al. (2011) identified 18 studies that compared dropout rates for clients who were given a treatment condition (role, therapist, or treatment type) that matched their preferences to clients who were either not given a choice or who were given a condition that directly contradicted their preferences. For each study, an odds ratio effect size was calculated to represent the likelihood of a client dropping out in one condition over the other. For this meta-analysis, the data were set up so that an odds ratio of 1.00 meant that clients were equally likely to drop out of both groups, an odds ratio less than 1.00 meant that clients were less likely to drop out when their preferences were matched, and an odds ratio greater than 1.00 meant that clients were more likely to drop out when their preferences were matched. A forest plot of the odds ratio effect sizes for each study and the aggregate effect can be found in Figure 4.1. Across studies, the aggregated odds ratio was 0.59, 95% confidence interval [0.44, 0.78]. This result indicates that clients who receive their preferred conditions were between one half and one third less likely to drop out of therapy prematurely compared with clients who did not receive their preferred therapy conditions, or for every five nonmatched clients who drop out prematurely, only three preference-matched clients will drop out.

Swift et al. (2011) and Swift, Callahan, Ivanovic, and Kominiak (2013) followed their main analysis by examining whether accommodating client preferences resulted in greater or fewer dropouts depending on the type of condition, treatment, setting, or client. Only one of the moderators they

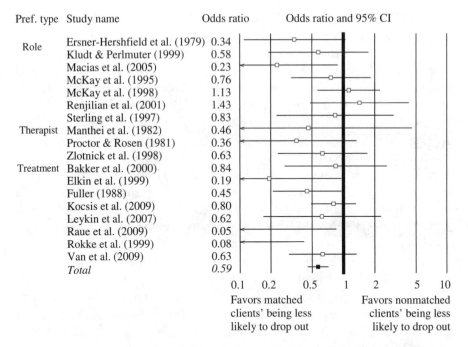

Pref. type	Study name	Odds ratio	Odds ratio and 95% CI
Role	Ersner-Hershfield et al. (1979)	0.34	
	Kludt & Perlmuter (1999)	0.58	
	Macias et al. (2005)	0.23	
	McKay et al. (1995)	0.76	
	McKay et al. (1998)	1.13	
	Renjilian et al. (2001)	1.43	
	Sterling et al. (1997)	0.83	
Therapist	Manthei et al. (1982)	0.46	
	Proctor & Rosen (1981)	0.36	
	Zlotnick et al. (1998)	0.63	
Treatment	Bakker et al. (2000)	0.84	
	Elkin et al. (1999)	0.19	
	Fuller (1988)	0.45	
	Kocsis et al. (2009)	0.80	
	Leykin et al. (2007)	0.62	
	Raue et al. (2009)	0.05	
	Rokke et al. (1999)	0.08	
	Van et al. (2009)	0.63	
	Total	*0.59*	

0.1   0.2   0.5   1   2   5   10

Favors matched   Favors nonmatched
clients' being less   clients' being less
likely to drop out   likely to drop out

Figure 4.1. Dropout effect sizes (odds ratios) for preference match versus nonmatch groups. Squares in the figure represent the odds ratio effect sizes; lines represent the 95% confidence intervals (CIs). As can be seen in the figure, 16 of the 18 studies found that matched clients were less likely to drop out. From "The Impact of Client Treatment Preferences on Outcome: A Meta-Analysis," by J. K. Swift and J. L. Callahan, 2009, *Journal of Clinical Psychology, 65*, p. 370. Copyright 2009 by Wiley Periodicals, Inc. Reprinted with permission.

tested was found to be significant: treatment duration. In briefer treatments, preference nonmatched clients were much more likely to drop out than were preference-matched clients; however, in treatments of a longer duration, clients who received a nonpreferred treatment were only slightly more likely to drop out than were preference-matched clients. Swift et al. (2013) provided a few hypotheses for why treatment duration would correlate with the preference effect, including the possibilities (a) that as clients continue in therapy for longer durations, other variables such as the therapeutic alliance play a larger role in determining whether one drops out prematurely; (b) that as treatment continues, clients may experience a shift in preferences to more closely match the treatment conditions they have been given; and (c) that clients who seek brief treatments may have specific ideas about whom or what might be able to help them get through their problems quickly and thus may be less willing to stick with therapy if it does not match those ideas right from the start. Although this result is interesting, the more important results were those that failed to find significance. These null results indicate that there is no evidence that matching clients to their preferred conditions has a differential effect for different types of clients, regardless of client diagnosis, age, gender, ethnicity, marital status, and education level. In other words, the results suggest that preference accommodation reduces dropout for all types of clients.

PUTTING IT INTO PRACTICE

Integrating patient preferences into the treatment decision-making process is a multistep collaborative endeavor that can occur at many time points during therapy. It begins with a discussion of preferences early on in the therapy encounter. In many private practice situations, patients make initial decisions based on their preferences before even contacting a therapist. For example, a patient who would like to work with a female therapist is not likely even to call a male therapist to schedule an appointment. Similarly, a patient who prefers medication over talk therapy will probably begin by contacting his or her medical doctor or a psychiatrist. However, in many settings, patients contact a clinic not knowing with whom they might be assigned to work or the exact nature of the services they are likely to receive. In these settings, patient preferences can be queried over the phone or through some initial paperwork. Vollmer, Grote, Lange, and Walker (2009) developed the Treatment Preference Interview as a paper method for assessing preferences from each domain (role, therapist, and treatment) in the initial encounter. A copy of this interview can be found in the chapter on preferences (Swift et al., 2011) in the book *Psychotherapy Relationships That Work* (Norcross, 2011). Additional paper measures for assessing role preferences include the Psychotherapy Expectancy Inventory-Revised (Berzins, Herron, & Seidman, 1971; Rickers-Ovsiankina, Geller, Berzins, & Rogers, 1971), which can be adapted to measure the strength of preferences (instead of expectations) for approval-seeking, advice-seeking, audience-seeking, and relationship-seeking; and the preference version of the Treatment Preferences and Experience questionnaire (Berg, Sandahl, & Clinton, 2008), which measures preferences for outward- versus inward-oriented treatments, support, and catharsis. Rather than simply assessing which option is most preferred, these measures assess the strength of preference for each of the options presented. Information regarding preference strength can allow a clinician to see when using a combination of roles might be most appropriate.

However, simply performing an initial inquiry of preferences, although useful, may not be adequate to fully integrate preferences into the treatment decision-making process. For starters, many patients may be hesitant about expressing their preferences. A current stereotype across health care settings is that the "doctor knows best." Patients may see therapists as experts or authority figures and thus may be uncertain whether it is appropriate for them to share their own opinions. Therapists should take time to help patients acknowledge their own expertise and help them bring their voice to the decision-making table.

A second reason many patients may be hesitant about expressing their preferences is that they do not know what the treatment options are or do not have enough information to make an informed decision. This is particularly true when making decisions about which type of treatment approach might be most appropriate. It is essential for therapists to take time to describe their case conceptualization to their patients and then teach them about each of the available treatment options. When providing an overview of these options, therapists should highlight some of the potential strengths and limitations of each, describing to the patient what benefits or costs might lead one to choose one option over another.

Although most preference discussions occur early on in therapy, therapists may want to revisit their patients' preferences occasionally as sessions progress. The process of revisiting preferences is helpful for several reasons. First, patient preferences for treatment can change over time. Changes in life circumstances and experiences can lead to a desire for a different treatment approach or emphasis. Additionally, preferences may shift as patients gain experience with a therapist and a more trusting relationship is developed or as they gain experience with a treatment and see that it is not exactly what they had expected when indicating their initial preference. Second, despite the therapist's best attempts, the patient's preferences might not be met. Patients sometimes have difficulty articulating what they want early on in treatment, and therapists sometimes have difficulty understanding exactly what their patients' preferences are. Regularly checking in with the patient concerning his or her preferences helps the therapist ensure that there is continued agreement on the appropriate goals and tasks for therapy. Checking in on preferences fits nicely with outcome monitoring and patient–therapist discussions of treatment progress, which is discussed as a method for reducing premature discontinuation in Chapter 10.

Even though the existing empirical research clearly demonstrates the benefits in reducing premature termination that come with accommodating client preference (Swift et al., 2011), there may be times when a client's preferences cannot or should not be met. As examples, a client may strongly desire a female therapist, but there are no female therapists with openings in the area; or a client may express a desire for advice, but the therapist has strong beliefs against offering advice in treatment; or a client might come to therapy wanting a specific treatment that the therapist believes would be contraindicated for that particular person. One simple solution for situations when preferences cannot be met is to refer the client to another provider who might be able to better accommodate his or her preferences. However, this solution is not always possible and may frequently not be the best course of action. Instead, when initial preferences cannot or should not be met, the therapist can first attempt to gain a better understanding of the reasons for the client's preference. Once these reasons are understood, the therapist may be able to help the client see other ways in which those underlying preferences can be met or help the client better understand why his or her preferences would be contraindicated. The therapist and client can then decide together whether they want to try one of the other therapy options or whether a referral to another provider or clinic is needed. The goal throughout this process is to help clients feel like they are equal partners with a legitimate opinion and stake in deciding what is going to happen in their treatment.

CLINICAL EXAMPLES

In her initial screening documents, Emily expressed a preference for a female therapist; however, no female therapists had openings at the time. The following is an excerpt from a phone call between Emily and a male therapist who had been assigned to work with her.

Therapist:	Emily, I noticed in your paperwork that you indicated a desire to work with a female therapist. Unfortunately, none of our female clinicians currently have openings in their schedule. I was wondering if you could help me understand your preference for a female therapist a little more.
Emily:	Oh . . . um. I don't have anything against you or other guy therapists, I am sure you are all very good. Given my past, I was just thinking that I would have an easier time talking to another woman.
Therapist:	Sounds like you think you would be a bit more comfortable opening up to a female, like she would understand you more?
Emily:	Yeah, understand, but also really be able to listen and not judge me or blame me for anything. My relationship with my boyfriend is really rocky right now, and I have been hurt by other men in the past. I just think it might be hard for me to trust another guy right now.
Therapist:	I see. It sounds like you have had a rough time with males and it is difficult for you to imagine that you could trust

another one, even if he is a therapist, enough to talk about the difficulties you are experiencing. Maybe you even have some worry that I might take your boyfriend's side rather than listen to and accept your thoughts and feelings.

Emily: Yeah, but talking to you now, it seems like you are really understanding.

Therapist: Emily, I want you to know that if we were to work together, I would try my best to listen to you and understand everything that you are going through. Building that trust in therapy is really important to me, and so I would focus on being nonjudgmental and accepting. At the same time, though, I think your preferences are very important—I believe that you probably have the best idea about what might or might not work in helping you face the distress you are experiencing. If you would like, I can put your name on the wait-list, and as soon as a female therapist has an opening, she will give you a call. It may be a couple of weeks, but I will make sure one of them contacts you as soon as possible. Or we can try meeting together now and see if it works out, see if you end up feeling comfortable with me even though I am a male.

Emily: Let's go ahead and give it a try.

The following interaction between Robert and his therapist took place after his therapist provided a treatment rationale for a cognitive–behavioral approach. His therapist knew he wanted to use a cognitive–behavioral approach with Robert, and so he did not offer him other treatment options. Instead, the therapist let him decide some of the specifics about treatment.

Therapist: You have a couple of options within this cognitive–behavioral framework for addressing your anxiety. First, you can choose between group and individual sessions. I regularly offer a 12-session group using the techniques that we have discussed, and the next one actually starts next week. Or I would be happy to continue to meet with you on a one-on-one basis.

Robert: Individual for sure!

Therapist: Sounds like you are pretty set with that, but let me just briefly mention to you some of the benefits of each. Some people really like the groups because they get a chance to hear from people who are facing similar problems with anxiety. It is often nice to see that you are not alone in what you are experiencing and to have a few more people to cheer you on as we work through some of those exposures that we have discussed. Also, group members can often provide a different perspective or have a way of saying things that might really sink in for you as we work on challenging some of your anxiety-provoking thoughts. In addition, because it's a group setting, it provides a live experience for you to practice facing your social anxiety. Last, the fee that I charge for group therapy is substantially lower than what I charge for individual appointments. Other people really like individual therapy better because of the individual attention that they get. In individual therapy you usually get more time to explore all of the factors that are contributing to your anxiety as well as the stressors that you face each week. We also will get to tailor your treatment a little more with regard to the timing of the techniques that we will use.

Robert: I hadn't thought of all those benefits for group therapy before, but I still think meeting with you individually would be the better option for me.

Therapist: OK, sounds good. With our individual appointments, we also have options for how often you would like to meet. Sometimes it is beneficial to meet twice per week in the beginning to really get a lot of practice with challenging anxiety-provoking thoughts and to have more frequent check-ins once we get to the exposures. But, for a lot of people, once per week is adequate, and meeting twice per week doesn't fit with their schedules. Which would you prefer?

Robert: Can we start with twice per week and move to weekly sessions after a little while?

Therapist: Alright, what days work best for you?

In both of these case examples, the clients had relatively few options for treatment. With Emily, despite her preference for a female therapist, no female therapists were available at the time. This vignette provides a good example of how to discuss treatment options with clients when preferences cannot be met. The therapist first sought to better understand the reasons underlying Emily's preference for a female therapist. Then, the therapist attempted to present a different option (a male therapist) that might still be able to meet the underlying reasons. Finally, the therapist offered Emily a few additional options, in case she still did not want to work with a male therapist. Using this strategy, the therapist still allowed her to make a choice. The same steps could be applied when working with a client whose preferences are contraindicated. Robert's therapist was unwilling to use an alternative treatment approach with him, believing that cognitive behavior therapy was necessary for him to successfully overcome his anxieties. As a result, the therapist sought to include the element of choice into the decision-making process by asking about preferences for individual versus group and the frequency of visits.

CONCLUSION

In this chapter, accommodating client preferences was presented as a second strategy for reducing premature termination in psychotherapy. *Client preferences* refer to clients' hopes and desires for treatment, including hopes for therapy roles and behaviors, therapist characteristics, and types of treatment. The existing empirical research has found that clients whose preferences are matched are almost half as likely to drop out of treatment prematurely compared with clients whose preferences are mismatched or ignored (Swift et al., 2011). Although the evidence for preference accommodation is there, this is a relatively young area of research in the field. What research does exist has largely focused on investigating the effects of accommodating preferences for treatment type, particularly preferences for medication or psychotherapy. Further research is needed to identify how client preferences are developed as well as to identify the more nuanced preferences for therapy roles and therapist interpersonal characteristics. Additionally, researchers should study how preferences change and develop over the course of therapy and directly examine whether preferences should still be accommodated when they are contraindicated.

On the basis of the body of research that does exist, however, we feel confident in making the general recommendation of preference accommodation as a method for reducing treatment dropout. Incorporating preferences into the treatment decision-making process should begin with an assessment of preferences early in therapy, perhaps in the first session. Therapist should work to elicit these preferences by first providing information to clients, given that they do not often know much about the options that do exist. Once clients know the pros and cons of the various treatment options and therapists know clients' values and beliefs, they are in a position in which they can work collaboratively to come up with treatment decisions. This collaboration will help clients build a strong therapeutic relationship with their therapist (see Chapter 9) as well as help motivate them to be more invested in the treatment (see Chapter 8), and both benefits will help them remain engaged in the therapeutic process. Similar to role expectations, as clients gain experience in therapy, their preferences may shift or change. Thus, it is important for therapists to occasionally revisit the topic of expectations and preferences with their clients and ask whether their beliefs and desires are still being met. If client preferences have changed, therapists may want to remind clients of the original treatment plan and the reasons for the plan that they developed collaboratively but then talk about what a change would entail and decide whether it is still desired. As preferences are discussed and accommodated throughout therapy, clients will be in a better place to think about and plan for a full course of treatment.

5

ASSIST IN PLANNING FOR APPROPRIATE TERMINATION

If I see an ending, I can work backward.

—Arthur Miller

Patients often begin treatment focused only on the present moment. They can sometimes be so worried about what types of things will or should happen in therapy and whether their therapist will respect their values and opinions that they forget to look at the big picture. However, once patients have developed clear and appropriate expectations through role induction (Chapter 3), and they know that their preferences will be considered (Chapter 4), they will be ready, and willing, to start thinking about the end of psychotherapy and what it is that they are trying to achieve while in treatment. In the poem "East Coker," T. S. Eliot starts with the line "In my beginning is my end." He repeats this line a number of times throughout the poem and goes on to describe how although for many thinking about death leads to despair, recognizing the finiteness of life can actually lead to inspiration to start off on the right foot and to maximize each moment that life contains. Eliot ends his poem with the line "In my end is my beginning."

http://dx.doi.org/10.1037/14469-005
Premature Termination in Psychotherapy: Strategies for Engaging Clients and Improving Outcomes,
by J. K. Swift and R. P. Greenberg

Similarly, by talking about and planning for the end of therapy early on, patients are better able to commit to a full course of treatment and make the most of each and every session. By having this type of discussion with their therapists at the beginning of therapy, they will have a goal to look forward to and will know what to anticipate in the end. Talking with patients about appropriate termination includes (a) providing them with education about typical treatment durations, (b) developing a plan for recognizing and talking about desires to end therapy once progress has been made, and (c) discussing what to do if desires to end therapy prematurely do arise. By having patients talk about the end of treatment, they are better able to anticipate all of the potential benefits that can come through engaging in therapy. Additionally, by having a specific end goal in mind, patients may be more willing to push through the costs that may come up during treatment and thus be less likely to drop out prematurely.

DEFINITION AND DESCRIPTION

The first step in discussing appropriate termination with patients is to help them develop realistic expectations about treatment duration. It is important to acknowledge that most patients expect therapy to work quickly (Mueller & Pekarik, 2000; Pekarik, 1991; Pekarik & Wierzbicki, 1986). For example, Pekarik (1991) conducted a study in which 131 outpatients were asked to endorse how many sessions they expected to attend among the following options: one or two, three to five, six to 10, nine to 12, 13 to 17, 18 to 25, and 26 or more. Eleven percent expected to attend just one or two sessions, 30% expected three to five sessions, and a full 74% expected 10 sessions or fewer. In our own research, we similarly asked patients about their expected duration, only without the response options. As part of one larger study (Swift & Callahan, 2011), 30 patients seeking services in a psychology department clinic were asked to write in how many sessions they expected to attend. Of these 30 patients, 10 either filled in the space with question marks or wrote, "I don't know." The average response for the remaining 20 patients was just six sessions. In another study (Swift & Callahan, 2008), 417 participants were asked about their duration expectations in terms of likelihood of treatment success. Participants in this study expected approximately 25% of patients to recover in just two sessions, 44% by the end of four sessions, and 61% by the end of eight sessions.

The problem lies in the disagreement between clients' low duration expectations and the more realistic figures reported by therapists and demonstrated by the dose–effect literature as necessary for successful therapy

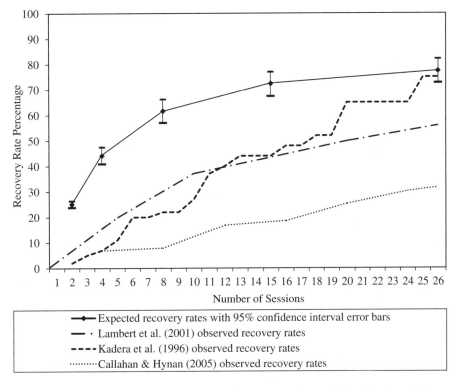

Figure 5.1. Comparison of client-expected recovery rates and duration to actual recovery rates in psychotherapy. At each of the given sessions (2, 4, 8, 15, and 26), participant expectations for recovery were much higher than recovery rates that have been demonstrated in the literature. For example, participants expected approximately 45% of clients to recover by four sessions, but actual recovery rates were between 5% and 17%. Reprinted from "A Delay Discounting Measure of Great Expectations and the Effectiveness of Psychotherapy," by J. K. Swift and J. L. Callahan, 2008, *Professional Psychology: Research and Practice, 39,* p. 584. Copyright 2008 by the American Psychological Association.

outcomes. Figure 5.1 illustrates the differences between expectations found by Swift and Callahan (2008) and actual recovery rates from three other dose–effect studies, each with hundreds to thousands of clients. Specifically, it demonstrates that whereas 60% of clients expect to recover by eight sessions of treatment, the literature indicates that only between 10% and 30% of clients do recover in this short amount of time.

A number of studies have linked these low duration estimates to premature termination (Aubuchon-Endsley & Callahan, 2009; Callahan, Aubuchon-Endsley, Borja, & Swift, 2009; Garfield, 1994; Mueller & Pekarik,

2000; Pekarik & Wierzbicki, 1986; Scamardo, Bobele, & Biever, 2004). The link between low duration expectations and premature termination may differ depending on the type of client and the amount of progress made early on in therapy. Most clients will fail to meet their expectations of recovery in so few sessions; consequently, they will likely experience some disappointment and frustration, perhaps believing that therapy is not working for them like it should. According to the costs–benefits conceptualization of premature termination presented in Chapter 1, this disappointment results in a failure to see the potential benefits that psychotherapy might bring. With the costs outweighing the benefits, the client is likely to drop out prematurely.

In contrast, a number of other clients will show some early improvements in terms of their general sense of hope and well-being. Ken Howard, who first presented the phase model of psychotherapy, indicated that many clients will see initial improvements in these areas within two to four sessions (Howard, Lueger, Maling, & Martinovich, 1993). For clients with low duration expectations, early improvement may mistakenly be viewed as recovery. However, according to data on the phase model, true recovery in terms of significantly decreased symptoms or improved functioning takes much longer (Callahan, Swift, & Hynan, 2006; Haase et al., 2008; Howard et al., 1993; Stulz & Lutz, 2007). Consequently, clients with low duration expectations and who make early progress may also drop out, mistakenly thinking they have completed the therapy endeavor, although real, stable change has not yet been made.

So what can be done to help clients avoid disappointment at slower-than-expected progress or avoid mistaking initial improvements for full recovery? In both situations, education about appropriate treatment duration is likely to be helpful. Simply informing clients about how long treatment might last can go a long way in reducing dropout. Remember, the results from the meta-analysis reported in Chapter 2 indicated that time-limited treatments (regardless of what those time limits were) had much lower dropout rates compared with treatments that were provided with no set duration. If therapists provide clients with a duration estimate, clients can better formulate their expectations for how soon they may see progress and how long it may take for full recovery or lasting change.

Although there is good evidence that brief psychotherapies may be helpful for some (Dewan, Steenbarger, & Greenberg, 2012), giving reasonable information regarding the possible length of psychotherapy needs to be handled with care. Although there is adequate evidence indicating that different clients need different lengths of treatment (Baldwin, Berkeljon, Atkins, Olsen, Nielsen, 2009; Barkham et al., 2006), in general an increased number of sessions is typically related to better and more long-standing outcomes (Cuijpers et al., 2010; Cuijpers, Van Straten, Warmerdam, & Smits,

2008), and with a greater number of sessions, a greater number of clients are likely to recover. For example, as Lambert (2013) has pointed out, only about 10% of clients will have recovered by the end of a single session, 50% by the end of about 20 sessions, and 75% by the end of about 40 sessions. Similarly, evidence derived from psychodynamic psychotherapies of clients with complex or chronic emotional problems has revealed that longer term therapies produce outcomes that are superior to shorter term methods (Leichsenring & Rabung, 2008; Shedler, 2010).

Patients can be informed about some of the reasons for having psychotherapy sessions extend over a period of several months and told that added benefits may flow from a treatment that is not overly abbreviated. For instance, it can be noted that psychotherapy is often usefully extended when discussion reveals that there are more issues to be dealt with after the initial complaint is resolved. Relatedly, over time, interactions with a therapist may lead to extending the goals of therapy. As Shedler (2010) suggested, treatment that is successful may be aimed at something beyond only symptom relief, including goals such as enhancing the capacity to have more fulfilling relationships, making more effective use of one's abilities and talents, developing a realistically enhanced sense of self-esteem, and facing challenges in life with more freedom and flexibility.

After helping patients develop realistic expectations for treatment duration, providers can also help their patients plan for appropriate termination by developing a strategy for recognizing and talking about patient desires to end therapy once progress has been made. Endings can often be just as intimidating as beginnings, particularly if the patient does not know what to expect from the ending. Even if clients feel like they are ready for treatment to end, they may be hesitant about bringing up this possibility with their therapists because they worry that their therapists might disapprove or that they might hurt their therapists' feelings. Rather than face these possibilities, some patients may simply choose to end therapy abruptly when they feel it is time. Although such patients may have made significant progress and may actually be ready to end therapy, if they discontinue on their own, they miss the opportunity for gaining closure and experiencing the benefits that an appropriate termination can provide. Providing role induction—specifically teaching patients how to appropriately terminate therapy—is one possible way to avoid these types of early treatment endings.

The third part to early discussions about appropriate termination is to develop a plan for handling thoughts of premature termination when they do occur. Given that 20% of clients do prematurely terminate from treatment, one might guess that an even greater percentage have some thoughts of dropping out at some point during therapy. These thoughts could be due to building frustration with treatment or the therapist, or they may simply occur because the costs associated with continued attendance are starting to outweigh the perceived therapeutic benefits. If they have not been warned that thoughts like this may occur, clients are more likely to act on them without ever discussing them with the therapist. In contrast, if thoughts of this type are normalized and clients are instructed on what to do with them, they will be more likely to talk about them with their therapists. Together the therapist and client can then work on a plan for making changes to treatment if needed or making a plan for collaboratively ending therapy.

EMPIRICAL RESEARCH

Although not a true empirical test of the recommendation to discuss appropriate termination with clients early on in therapy, results from our dropout meta-analysis reported in Chapter 2 do support this technique. Specifically, in the meta-analysis, we found that time-limited interventions result in lower dropout rates compared with treatments with an open duration. For that analysis, we separated 644 treatments into one of three groups: those with no time limit ($n = 131$); those with a briefer (20 sessions or less) time limit ($n = 449$); and those with a lengthier, but set, duration ($n = 64$). On average, 29% of clients dropped out of treatments that did not have a time limit, compared with a 17.8% dropout rate for treatments with a brief time limit and a 20.7% dropout rate for treatments with a somewhat lengthier time limit. Given that the length of the two time-limited treatments that were of a shorter or longer duration did not differ significantly from each other, we can assume that it is not just shorter treatments that result in lower rates of premature termination. Instead, it is possible that knowing from the start approximately how long the treatment is likely to last and how it will end leads to fewer treatment dropouts. Obviously, these are results that are being compared across studies with no direct manipulation of the duration expectation variable; however, the results do suggest that providing clients with duration estimates may reduce dropout rates by 9% to 11%.

One interesting study specifically examined whether providing clients with duration education, the first step in our recommendation to plan for appropriate termination, can lead to lower rates of premature discontinuation in psychotherapy. Swift and Callahan (2011) randomized 60 adult clients who were seeking services from a psychology department training clinic to one of two duration education groups. The clients randomized to the education group were told that research indicates that, on average, it takes approximately 13 to 18 sessions for 50% of clients to recover, whereas clients in the control group were not given this information. Clients were then asked to state their expectations with regard to how many sessions they thought they would attend. Those in the control group expected an average of $M = 6.43$, $SD = 4.86$, sessions, whereas those who received the education expected more than twice that amount, $M = 15.16$, $SD = 3.5$, representing a large effect, $d = 2.14$. Those are just expectations, however—the more important question lies in whether the education influenced actual duration and rates of premature termination. After expressing their expectations, the clients were assigned to a clinician via the regular clinic procedures. The clinicians worked with the clients as they routinely would, being blind to what study group they were in. At the end of therapy, treatment files were reviewed to find the actual number of sessions attended, and therapists were asked to classify each of their clients as having either dropped out or completed treatment. In terms of actual duration, those in the control group only attended an average of $M = 5.9$, $SD = 7.3$, sessions, whereas those in the education group attended an average of $M = 10.59$, $SD = 9.91$, sessions—almost twice as many. Last, in terms of dropout, 24 of the 31 control clients were classified as premature terminators, whereas only nine of the 29 clients who received the duration education were identified by their therapists as having dropped out. Thus, those clients who received the education were more than 3.5 times more likely to complete treatment compared with the control group clients. Although this was just one study, the results in favor of educating clients about typical treatment durations were dramatic.

Sheeran, Aubrey, and Kellett (2007) conducted another interesting study examining a different technique for addressing clients' thoughts about prematurely terminating. In their study, clients who were seeking treatment at a public sector mental health clinic were randomized to either an implementation intention or a control group. Those who were assigned to the former were told that clients can occasionally feel concerned about attending their appointments. They were then instructed to repeat the following statement four times: "As soon as I feel concerned about attending my appointment, I will ignore that feeling and tell myself this is perfectly understandable!" (p. 857). Eighty-three percent of the clients who repeated this information to themselves ended up attending their first appointment. In contrast, only 57% of those in the control group showed up for their initial appointment. Similar results have been found in other studies that asked clients to imagine attending sessions and state their reasons for why they are planning on completing therapy (Buckner et al., 2009; Sherman & Anderson, 1987).

PUTTING IT INTO PRACTICE

Similar to role induction, time should be taken early on in the therapy encounter to discuss and plan for appropriate termination. This information can be presented conversationally as a discussion between the patient and the therapist or through some type of educational media (i.e., video, pamphlet or handout, online). Rather than simply providing patients with facts, a rationale for the information should also be provided, thus increasing the patient's likelihood of accepting and buying into it. The rationale can be built from empirical research, the theoretical orientation of the therapist's particular approach, or information from the patient's own life. When providing this information, we always encourage patients to discuss their feelings about it with their therapists.

We have found that the dose–effect model of psychotherapy (Howard, Kopta, Krause, & Orlinsky, 1986) provides a good framework for discussing treatment length with patients. On the basis of data from thousands of patients, Howard and colleagues (1986) discovered the existence of a positive relationship between treatment length and the percentage of patients who recover—that is, with a greater number of sessions, a greater percentage of patients will have made a significant change. Over the past nearly 3 decades, their model has been widely replicated. For example, in 2001, with data from more than 10,000 patients, Lambert, Hansen, and Finch found that approximately 20% of patients recover after five sessions, 35% by 10 sessions, 50% by 20 sessions, and 70% by 45 sessions of therapy. The numbers we like to share with patients are based on a 2002 review by Hansen, Lambert, and Forman in which they concluded that it takes roughly 20 sessions for 50% of patients to show a clinically significant change. We believe that the exact number is of less importance; more essential is giving patients some type of expectation for how long treatment should last. We like couching this information in the dose–effect literature because the model is atheoretical, thus having broad application to many orientations. The dose–effect model also provides duration estimates in terms of chances of recovery, thus leaving it open for patients to recognize that the number of sessions is not a set standard, but that some patients will recover more quickly and other patients will take much longer. Clinicians may choose to adjust the information they share to be consistent with their own theoretical model.

As we mentioned earlier, there is adequate evidence indicating that different clients need different lengths of treatment (Baldwin, Berkeljon, Atkins, Olsen, & Nielsen, 2009; Barkham et al., 2006), and so some may question whether it is appropriate to provide education to clients based on the dose–effect model. Indeed, some clients will recover after a single session, and it would not make sense to tell those clients that they must attend 20 or more sessions. However, the majority of clients will not recover after a single session—for the majority it takes much longer. Although we may like to guess, as therapists we cannot always tell which clients are going to recover quickly and which clients will take more time. If we told all clients that there is a chance they would recover after two sessions (or even eight sessions), that information would not be applicable to most of them. Also, many might end up worrying that therapy was not working properly because they had not recovered in that short amount of time. To help clients set more realistic expectations, but also leave open the possibility for quicker or longer durations as necessary, we recommend providing them with information on the median number of sessions (about 20 sessions for 50% to recover) but then discussing how and why some individuals may need more or less than that median duration.

    Along these lines, in discussing how to recognize the appropriate timing for termination, collaboration in making decisions should always be emphasized. As therapists work to develop treatment goals with their patients, they should also help their patients learn to recognize when those goals are being met. Patients can be told by their therapists that together they will both look for the signs indicating that it may be time to end therapy, and they can both be open in sharing their opinions and feelings. Once feelings have been shared, a mutual decision to end or continue can be made and an appropriate plan for doing so can be set. Finally, therapists may want to tell patients that gradual endings to therapy are often best. This can be done by tapering sessions at the end and scheduling one or two follow-up appointments. In addition, patients might be assured that the door is open to their returning to therapy in the future should they feel the need.

    Therapists may also want to mention to patients that the goals and focus of therapy may change over time. As one problem gets addressed and resolved, another issue may come to the fore or be found to underlie what was previously assumed to be core problem. In other words, in psychotherapy you might not end up "dancing with the problem that brung you." Therefore, the therapy duration can become extended as new material and concerns are uncovered. Patients who are informed of this possibility will be less likely to worry if therapy continues longer than they originally expected.

    In this same discussion, therapists can also take time to normalize patients' potential thoughts about terminating therapy prematurely. They should encourage patients to share these types of thoughts if they arise, so that therapist and patient together can develop a different plan for therapy that might better fit the patient's needs and preferences. This would also be a good time for therapists to have patients state their reasons for wanting to complete therapy and have them complete some type of implementation induction for attending.

CLINICAL EXAMPLES

The following excerpt with Emily picks up where the role induction excerpt from Chapter 3 left off. Again, this is the end of her intake session. Here, the therapist is having a discussion with her about treatment length.

Therapist: Yes, it would be nice if there was just a quick, easy fix to the problems that you are going through right now. But sounds like you understand that that wouldn't really work. After all, based on what you shared with me today, it appears that you have been carrying around some pretty painful stuff for years. So it seems like it is not just the current difficulty in your relationship that you want to work on, but maybe some of those things from your past as well.

Emily: Right.

Therapist: When you set up an appointment with me, did you have any expectations about how many times you would need to come in?

Emily: No, I guess I was not really sure what to expect.

Therapist: Although it is different for everyone, there is some pretty good research on this topic. The research has generally found that it takes somewhere around 20 sessions for about half of all clients to recover. For some clients, it is more, and for some clients it is less, but based on my experience, those numbers are about right—about 20 sessions or so for many clients. What do you think about those numbers?

Emily: Wow—20 sessions—that is a lot more than I was expecting. Although I wasn't sure exactly how many would be needed, I was really thinking that it would only take about five or so.

Therapist: OK, so you were thinking maybe five or so sessions. Everyone is different, and each client has different needs, so it is possible that five sessions is all it will take. At the same time, I think it is important we both recognize that most clients do take longer than that. Some of these problems you have been facing most of your life, and so it often does take a good amount of time to work through them. I just don't want you to have unrealistic expectations; that way, if five sessions comes around and things are not completely better, you won't think that we are doing something wrong. In the end, it may not take longer than just a handful of sessions, but it may, so it is good to have that in mind too.

Emily: That makes sense to me.

Therapist:	How about we just plan on regularly checking in on it and see how things are progressing? As the fifth session comes around, we can talk and see if you think you are ready to be done, or we can see if there are more things that we would want to address in therapy.
Emily:	Sounds like a good plan.

The following excerpt with Robert focuses on normalizing thoughts of premature termination. It occurs at the end of the initial session.

Therapist:	Before we end today, I wanted to talk to you a little about ending treatment. You told me earlier that you have previously worked with many different therapists, and usually you have made the decision to end treatment on your own without discussing it with your therapist.
Robert:	Right, I just never felt like I was getting much from therapy, so I stopped showing up.
Therapist:	Well, I was wondering if you would be up for trying something different this time. At some point you are probably going to feel like dropping out here as well. I don't mean to be pessimistic, but it is common; many clients think about that at some point or another.
Robert:	OK—so when I think about dropping out you want me to just ignore those thoughts and keep coming anyway?
Therapist:	No, not necessarily. You will probably have some good reasons for feeling like you want to quit. Instead of immediately acting on them, though, what I want you to do is come in to the next appointment and we can talk about those reasons. Perhaps we will be able to change the way we do things in here to resolve your concerns, or perhaps we won't and I will be able to at least give you a good recommendation for a different therapist. All I am suggesting is that we take some time to talk about and try to problem-solve things together before you decide to stop. What do you think might be some of the benefits of doing it this way?
Robert:	I guess we may be able to address whatever concerns I have, and things will end up going really well. And . . . I may get a chance to actually feel like I have finished treatment. Even if we decide we can't address my concerns, at least I will get a referral, and I won't have to feel guilty about not showing up on you.
Therapist:	So, what do you think?
Robert:	OK, I'm on board.

In the first example, the therapist helped Emily plan for an appropriate termination by discussing treatment duration. The therapist first presented information based on the dose–effect model; however, the duration that the therapist shared was much greater than what Emily was expecting. The therapist tried to provide some validation for Emily's beliefs but also encouraged her to keep the possibility of a higher number of sessions in mind too. In the end, the therapist suggested a plan for collaboration in which they check in periodically to see how treatment is going and both share thoughts about continued sessions. This model serves as a good example of how to discuss treatment duration with clients who might have unrealistic duration beliefs. With Robert, the therapist focused less on the number of sessions that were required and instead discussed plans for making sure the termination is mutually agreed on. Again, in this case, the focus was on collaboration in making decisions about termination. Although these case examples demonstrate the two techniques separately, we would recommend that therapists include both when discussing termination with their clients.

CONCLUSION

Helping clients think about termination right from the start of treatment is another useful technique for reducing premature termination in practice. When clients know approximately how long treatment will last, they may be more likely to push through some of the ups and downs associated with engaging in therapy and less likely to mistake early improvements for recovery (both discussed in more detail in Chapter 6). Research has indicated that clients are less likely to drop out of treatments that have a set duration (Swift & Greenberg, 2012). Additionally, Swift and Callahan (2011) demonstrated that giving clients an idea of treatment duration based on the dose–effect model can lead to substantially lower rates of dropout. Two additional benefits of discussing termination with clients early on is that they are then able to recognize that desires to unilaterally terminate are normal and they know it is OK to talk to their therapists about their desires to end treatment. Although the results from Sheeran et al.'s (2007) study are promising, future research is needed to further test strategies for getting clients to commit to a full course of therapy.

6

PROVIDE EDUCATION ABOUT PATTERNS OF CHANGE IN PSYCHOTHERAPY

An investment in knowledge pays the best interest.
—Benjamin Franklin

Similar to providing clients with education about appropriate therapy roles (Chapter 3) and education about typical therapy durations (Chapter 5), therapists may be able to reduce premature termination in their practice by providing clients with education about patterns of therapeutic change. In William Shakespeare's play *Julius Caesar*, the title character is cautioned by a seer to "beware the Ides of March"—a warning that conspirators would soon attempt to take his life. Caesar did not heed this prediction, and he was assassinated on the very day that the soothsayer predicted. In contrast, had Caesar listened to the forewarning that had been given, his life might have been spared, and the Roman Republic might not have fallen the way it did.

Although clients may not be at risk of an assassination attempt, and the fate of nations may not be at stake, providing clients with a forewarning about patterns of change and potential setbacks can help them better navigate therapy and thus be better prepared for the struggles that they may face. When

http://dx.doi.org/10.1037/14469-006
Premature Termination in Psychotherapy: Strategies for Engaging Clients and Improving Outcomes,
by J. K. Swift and R. P. Greenberg

setbacks do come up, without forewarning clients may see these struggles as a sign that therapy is not working; thus they may perceive that their present therapy is having little benefit and anticipate that attending treatment will yield few benefits in the future. Just as a forewarning can assist in preparing clients for any setbacks that may come during the course of psychotherapy, discussions of early surface-level progress can also help clients remain in treatment when necessary. When immediate, surface-level improvements occur, and are associated with increased hope, clients may perceive that therapy has been of some benefit; however, they may also mistakenly think that the therapeutic work is done, thus anticipating little future benefit and deciding to drop out. However, further work is often needed to help clients make the deeper changes that are a sign of more long-lasting recovery. Thus, providing a forewarning to clients about both the good and bad is another strategy that can help them remain in psychotherapy for a full course of treatment.

DEFINITION AND DESCRIPTION

There are two distinct ways in which a lack of knowledge about patterns of change may lead to premature termination from therapy. First, clients may drop out because they expect therapy to be brief and they see initial improvements as a sign of recovery; second, clients may expect a linear pattern of progression but get discouraged when therapy becomes difficult or setbacks are encountered. In this chapter, we discuss our recommendation that therapists provide education about the possible courses of therapeutic change. This type of education, when provided early on, can help clients recognize and avoid certain assumptions that may lead them to drop out. Before discussing what type of education can be provided, let us first look at how premature termination might be related to mistaken expectations about change.

As mentioned in Chapter 5, clients generally expect therapy to work quickly. For some, the speed at which change occurs will not meet their expectations, and, as a result, they will experience disappointment and likely drop out. In contrast, others may mistake early gains as complete recovery and thus drop out thinking that they have finished the therapy endeavor. As discussed in the last chapter, according to the phase model of psychotherapy (Howard, Lueger, Maling, & Martinovich, 1993), most clients experience change in a predictable, steplike manner. First, they experience some early improvements in terms of their general sense of hope and well-being. These improvements, referred to as *remoralization*, generally occur within about four sessions. Clients who expect treatment to take only a few sessions may mistakenly view these early improvements as a resolution of their problems. However, according to data on the phase model, true recovery in terms of significant decreases in symptoms (remediation) or improved functioning (rehabilita-tion) takes much longer (Callahan, Swift, & Hynan, 2006; Haase et al., 2008; Howard et al., 1993; Stulz & Lutz, 2007). Thus, education about the phase model of psychotherapy may be useful in helping clients understand that last-ing change is likely to take some time.

In addition to expecting quick changes, many clients begin psycho-therapy believing it will result in a linear progression or change. However, therapy is not all a bed of roses; it can be difficult work. Instead of avoiding painful and threatening experiences and emotions, in therapy we ask clients to face them. For some, this may result in increased distress and symptoms. Although we do not endorse the adage that things have to get significantly worse before they get better, we expect that almost all clients will experience at least minor setbacks sometime during the course of therapy. In some cases the setbacks can be extreme. On the basis of results from one study, at least 10% of clients will experience sudden and significant deterioration during treatment (Lutz et al., 2013). For all clients, when a setback or increased distress is experienced, it can easily be seen as a sign that therapy is not working—that the benefits are not present. If therapy becomes too painful, clients may even see therapy as a burden. In both instances, clients may choose to drop out prematurely, believing the costs associated with attending outweigh any potential benefits that—in their mind—may not even come. Hence, educating clients about nonlinear patterns of change and the fact that potential setbacks are a routine occurrence in the process may also reduce the likelihood of premature termination in psychotherapy.

EMPIRICAL RESEARCH

To our knowledge, no research has directly examined whether providing clients with information from the phase model or warning them of potential setbacks in therapy by itself leads to lower dropout rates. However, general sup-port for this type of education can be seen in several related areas of research. For example, in Chapter 3, we discussed the literature demonstrating improved treatment outcomes and decreased therapy dropout associated with role induc-tion (Monks, 1996; Strassle, Borckardt, Handler, & Nash, 2011). Many of the studies testing role induction procedures have included some information about the course of therapeutic change with their description of client and therapist roles and behaviors. Accordingly, it is possible that education about therapeutic change may play some part in the positive findings for role induc-tion. However, this hypothesis needs to be empirically tested more thoroughly.

Preliminary support for educating clients about potential setbacks in treatment can also be seen in the literature on treatment feedback and patient-focused research (discussed in Chapter 10) and the research on many addiction interventions. Outcome feedback studies have clearly demonstrated that when therapists and clients detect negative trajectories early on, they are better able to discuss the deterioration and make the changes necessary before premature termination occurs (Lambert & Shimokawa, 2011). It may follow that even earlier warnings to clients about possible negative trajectories could set clients up to talk about deterioration as soon as it starts to occur, thus shifting the trajectory toward improvement rather than a premature ending. For example, most addiction treatments include a component of planning for lapses before they occur (Larimer, Palmer, & Marlatt, 1999). In the substance abuse field, when a lapse is viewed as a personal failure, individuals have more difficulty getting back to their abstinence goals. However, when they are able to recognize that a lapse is common, they often can view it as just a mistake and avoid slipping further into a full relapse. Similarly, if a psychotherapy client views a setback or minor deterioration as something that might be expected, he or she would be less likely to drop out because of a belief that treatment is failing completely.

PUTTING IT INTO PRACTICE

Education about patterns of therapeutic change can either be given simultaneously with role induction and duration education or presented separately. This type of information should also be presented early, perhaps even before the patient has met with the therapist but, at the latest, sometime during the initial appointments. Similar to the educational material discussed in the previous two chapters, information on patterns of change can be presented conversationally as a discussion between the patient and the therapist or through educational media. For example, Exhibit 6.1 is a patient handout that presents information on treatment duration as well as patterns of change. In addition to providing this information at the beginning of therapy, therapists may revisit these topics at key times when changes are observed.

We recommend providing patients with both basic education about the psychotherapy phase model and a warning that therapy progress may not occur linearly. The phase model of psychotherapy is an empirically derived model of change developed by Kenneth Howard and colleagues (1993). The model purports that successful patients go through three sequential phases of recovery: remoralization, remediation, and then rehabilitation. The phase of *remoralization* represents patients' improvements in their general sense of well-being (a lifting of their morale). These improvements are associated with building hope that psychotherapy will provide some aid to their suffering. The average patient likely sees some signs of remoralization early on, possibly even by session four. Subsequently, improved well-being leads to *remediation*, which represents a resolution of symptoms or the problems that

EXHIBIT 6.1
Example Handout of Education About the Course of Therapeutic Change

Patient Handout on the Course of Therapeutic Change

In starting to meet with a therapist, you probably have many questions, such as how long will treatment last, and how long before I start to feel better? The following handout offers some information on typical patterns of change for patients. The facts provided are based on empirical research and refer to averages for patients of all types. Your individual pattern of change may differ somewhat from what is described here. You are encouraged to discuss your own changed expectations with your therapist as well as any differences that you notice in your own pattern of change as therapy progresses.

How long should therapy last?

The exact length of therapy will depend on a number of factors, including what types of problems you are experiencing, how long the problems have been present, and what type of treatment approach you and your therapist are using. In all cases, however, it is good to keep in mind that therapy does not provide an overnight fix—change takes time! An extensive body of research looking at psychotherapy outcomes indicates that, on average, it takes approximately 4 to 5 months of weekly sessions for 50% of patients to experience substantial improvement and up to 50 sessions for 75% of patients to fully recover. Some patients may get better in a shorter amount of time and other patients may take much longer.

How soon will I start to notice things getting better?

Although it will probably take a little while for you to experience recovery from the problems that led you to seek out treatment, you will likely notice some improvements early on. Many patients will notice some gains in their general sense of well-being after just a few sessions. These early improvements may include increased hope and optimism or the relief that comes from sharing your problems with someone, knowing he or she understands, and that there is a way to overcome them. Although these early gains are a good sign, they do not always signify lasting change. There is more work to be done! It typically takes continued sessions and effort to notice a more enduring reduction in your symptoms and for things to get back to normal in your life (i.e., at work or school, with family and friends).

What if I feel worse?

Change doesn't always come easily! In therapy you may be asked to face some of your fears and pains. Although you should notice a general progression over time, there may be some ups and downs. Experiencing the downs or setbacks need not always be taken as a sign that therapy is failing. Instead, it may be a sign that you are doing some very difficult work. At the same time, the setbacks should not be all that you experience. When you do notice some setbacks, talk to your therapist and see if together a plan can be developed to get you through them as quickly as possible.

led the patient to seek out treatment. Remediation for patients is usually the result of learning and using more effective coping skills. For the average patient, improvements in this area usually occur sometime after 2 to 3 months of weekly sessions. Last, decreased symptoms typically result in the final stage, rehabilitation, which represents improved life functioning. This stage usually occurs once the patient and therapist are able to address the long-standing life patterns that have contributed to the patient's problems.

It is often the result of increased insight and ongoing practice of new coping skills. Improvements in this phase typically occur sometime after 4 or 5 months of continued work. Although patients may not need to know the details of the entire phase model, it would be useful for them to understand that they might start to feel better early on in therapy and that although these early improvements are a good sign, they typically do not indicate complete recovery. Longer lasting changes in symptoms and life functioning usually follow continued therapeutic work and may take several months to achieve.

In line with the idea that it may take practice to recognize and change old faulty assumptions and maladaptive patterns of behavior, the therapist may introduce the idea that homework or actions considered and tried out between sessions may prove useful. A review of the research evidence on homework shows a strong relationship between positive therapy outcomes and engaging in the out-of-session actions that have been discussed during the psychotherapy meetings (Scheel, Hanson, & Razzhavaikina, 2004). Compliance with homework is also a useful indicator of patient involvement and commitment to the therapy (and therefore a lower likelihood of dropout). Moreover, most therapists, independent of theoretical orientation, indicate that homework is a common treatment strategy (Kazantzis & Deane, 1999) and that it is generally regarded as a routine tool for facilitating healthy change (Scheel et al., 2004).

Additionally, we recommend that therapists alert their clients about the up-and-down nature of therapeutic progress. Clients should be informed that they are going to be helped to face their fears and pains, things they may usually try to avoid. They should be warned that this may be difficult and that as they work on solving their problems and making changes, they are going to continue to experience some good days and some bad days. It is important to recognize that bad days are normal and need not be taken as a sign that treatment is failing. Also, clients can be told that not every therapy session will be perfect, that there may be times of doubt or frustration in therapy. After the therapist normalizes these types of feelings and experiences, it is important to teach clients what to do with them—discuss them with the therapist and work together to adjust things so similar setbacks occur less often.

CLINICAL EXAMPLE

The following dialogue with Robert illustrates a discussion about patterns of change. This discussion took place in his intake session.

Therapist: Well, Robert, I am really excited to be able to work with you in tackling these anxiety problems.

Robert: I am looking forward to working with you, too.

Therapist: I know you have met with therapists before, but I still want to give you a heads up about some of the things you might expect as we work together.

Robert: OK.

Therapist: As we start working, you might notice some improvements in your general mood and life outlook pretty early on. This is usually a good sign that accompanies the initial steps of sharing your struggles with someone and developing a plan for working on those struggles.

Robert: Yeah, I know what you are talking about. I am already feeling a lot better just talking with you today. I have noticed that in the past too with the therapists that I have seen. It always starts off really good.

Therapist: You said you have noticed it in the past—what has ended up happening after that?

Robert: Oh . . . there have been times where I figured that things were better so I stopped going. And there have been other times where things just kind of fizzled out and didn't go anywhere beyond that.

Therapist: Hmm, sounds like it never quite turned out how you wanted it to. Well, I was going to say that although those early improvements are a good sign, they usually just signify the beginning—that things are just starting to move forward. That is just the first phase of therapy. From there we really get to start working on the problems, figuring out how to challenge some of your anxiety-provoking thoughts and face some of those feared situations. By continuing to work on these things, we will get to see some more lasting changes in your symptoms and functioning at work and in social situations.

Robert: That is what I need, more lasting change. In the past, things have never seemed to stick.

Therapist: Right, and so it's going to take some time and effort for things to stick better this time. It is not going to be easy, and there may be times, especially as you start facing some of your fears, that you may feel like the anxiety is too much or you want to give up. That's normal; there are going to be ups and downs. The important thing is to not give up when things are down. Instead, let's talk about it and see if we can adjust things some to help you get back on track.

In this vignette, the therapist was able to facilitate a conversation about patterns of change by first asking about the patterns that Robert has noticed in his previous treatment experiences. Notice how the therapist brought up both positive and negative patterns of change that could occur. This discussion was particularly important with Robert given that both of these patterns have led to his dropping out of treatment in the past. Although neither of these patterns may actually occur for Robert in this course of treatment, if they do happen, he is better prepared to recognize them for what they are. With this recognition, Robert and his therapist can then have a conversation about what is happening rather than Robert dropping out because he thinks therapy is done or because he thinks it is not working as it should.

CONCLUSION

In this chapter, we discussed the strategy of educating clients about potential patterns of change early in therapy. After receiving education about the phase model, clients will be able to recognize that early improvements in hope that occur in the first few sessions are a good thing (in fact, these are discussed as another dropout-reducing strategy in the next chapter) but not an indication that complete recovery has occurred. Additionally, when they have been educated about potential setbacks, clients will be able to recognize that a lack of a linear progression does not mean that therapy is failing. Instead, they will be prepared to talk with their therapist about the deterioration they notice early on so that changes can be made, rather than simply dropping out. Research from the role-induction, patient-focused research, and addiction fields all provide preliminary support for this dropout-reducing strategy; however, studies directly examining the efficacy of this strategy in psychotherapy are needed. We recommend that providers include this type of education early in treatment so it can serve as a forewarning, before the pattern has occurred. However, it may be useful to revisit these topic areas and more thoroughly discuss them if either pattern is noticed in clients. Discussing both strategies can help clients maintain their hope in psychotherapy, which is the focus of the next chapter. By recognizing early improvements, clients can hope that further improvements will follow, and by recognizing setbacks as temporary and normal, clients can maintain their hope that therapy will eventually bring about the change that they desire.

7

STRENGTHEN HOPE

We should not let our fears hold us back from pursuing our hopes.
—John F. Kennedy

Up to this point, we have discussed strategies for reducing premature termination in psychotherapy that are designed to prepare patients for treatment and ultimately to help them start off on the right foot. These strategies have focused largely on educating patients about therapy and helping them become more fully invested participants. Once therapy begins, hope is what motivates patients to continue on their journey.

In Jules Verne's classic science fiction novel, *A Journey to the Center of the Earth*, readers follow three travelers (the professor, his nephew, and their guide) as they descend miles and miles down into the depths of the unknown. After traveling underground for a little over a month, the professor's nephew somehow is separated from his traveling companions and finds that he is entirely alone. The book describes the young man's frenzied madness as he frantically searches for the others through the labyrinth of tunnels and the despair that follows as he loses his light and is left in utter darkness.

http://dx.doi.org/10.1037/14469-008
Premature Termination in Psychotherapy: Strategies for Engaging Clients and Improving Outcomes,
by J. K. Swift and R. P. Greenberg

Eventually, he is overcome with despair, and he falls down on the cold rock of the tunnel in a pool of his own tears. After 4 days in the darkness, however, a miracle happens. Somehow the fissures of the rock aligned just right so that he could faintly hear the voice of his uncle and their guide, even though they were miles away. Although exhausted, he was eventually able to make his way to a spot in the wall where he could communicate to them. Verne wrote of the young man's thoughts while he was talking to his uncle: "While he was speaking, my brain was at work reflecting. A certain undefined hope, vague and shapeless as yet, made my heart beat wildly." That vague and undefined hope initially resulted in frantic efforts to find a way out, but, with the help of his uncle, that hope led to strength and a strategy that brought the nephew back to his companions.

As therapists, we often play the role of the uncle. Our voice and the assistance that we offer can give patients' enough hope to continue on their journey until change has occurred. This strategy, perhaps most of all, speaks to the anticipated benefits associated with attending therapy. If clients have enough hope that the therapist and the treatment can bring about change, they will be willing to endure almost any perceived and anticipated cost associated with engaging in treatment.

DEFINITION AND DESCRIPTION

Hope, broadly defined, is the belief that one's goals are attainable through specific methods or routes and is paired with the willpower to make efforts to move toward those goals (Snyder, 1995). In an oft-cited paper that discusses the conceptualization of hope, Snyder (1995) indicated that it is similar to, but different from, the constructs of optimism and self-efficacy beliefs. Although optimism includes a belief that positive things will happen, it lacks direction or the accompanying willpower or motivation to make efforts to achieve one's goals. Self-efficacy theory (Bandura, 1977) acknowledges the importance of either a belief that a particular behavior will produce a given outcome or a belief that one can undertake that given behavior to achieve the outcome, but Snyder suggested that both conditions are necessary for hope to be present. Applied to psychotherapy, hope is sometimes referred to as positive-outcome expectations. It includes the belief that change or recovery is possible and that therapy is a promising route to bring about that change. Tying it back to Snyder's broader definition, hope in psychotherapy would also include the willpower or motivation to invest in treatment to bring about the desired change. Similar to the nephew's hope in *A Journey to the Center of the Earth*, when starting therapy, clients' hope can often be seen as vague and shapeless and may better be described as optimism. This vague and shapeless hope may be enough to motivate clients to start treatment, but it must be replaced with specific hopeful trust in the therapist and the prescribed treatment methods for it to remain.

Perhaps the best discussion of the role of hope and outcome expectations in treatment comes from Jerome Frank's conceptual framework for psychotherapy (Frank & Frank, 1991). According to Frank and Frank (1991), clients seek out treatment in a state of demoralization, feeling powerless to change their situation or problems on their own. Psychotherapy of any type then serves as a hope-inspiring mechanism by providing a plausible set of procedures that can be used to solve the problems. If clients believe in the set of procedures as a cure (outcome expectations), they will be more likely to fully engage in the procedures. Taking action in this manner and seeing that a potential cure is available helps restore the client's perception of power and control over the problems, which in turn results in an increased general sense of well-being. This increased well-being and engagement in therapy then translates into reduced symptoms and improved life functioning (Howard, Lueger, Maling, & Martinovich, 1993). Frank and Frank thus placed outcome expectations as the pivotal variable for change in psychotherapy. Although some would disagree with Frank and Frank's assertion that prognostic beliefs are the main mechanism of therapeutic progress, outcome expectations do seem to play an essential role in therapy. Regardless of theoretical orientation, if clients do not have some general hope or belief that psychotherapy (or the specific treatment techniques) will work, they will not fully engage in the therapy process (or those techniques) and will likely drop out prematurely.

Given the role that outcome expectations play in therapy engagement and premature discontinuation, it is critical for therapists to make an effort to bolster clients' positive prognostic beliefs as soon as possible. Frank and Frank (1991) suggested two main ways to use hope in therapy: first, to arouse it through early therapy cues; and second, to strengthen it through initial progress toward the therapeutic goals. With regard to hope-arousing cues, therapists should give consideration to how they present both themselves and their interventions. Strong (1968) originally proposed that therapists can be seen as more credible when they are perceived as being an expert, attractive, and trustworthy; decades of research support these three components (Hoyt, 1996). Research indicates that interventions can be seen as more credible when the treatment rationale is logical, when it fits with the client's beliefs, and when the therapist or other sources express faith in the specific treatment approach (Constantino et al., 2011; Greenberg, Constantino, & Bruce, 2006). Therapists can also present hope-arousing cues by strengthening their clients' self-efficacy beliefs early in therapy. As Frank and Frank suggested, not only is it essential for therapists to present hope-arousing cues at the start of therapy, but for hope to be maintained and strengthened, the benefits of therapy need to be experienced relatively quickly by the clients as well.

EMPIRICAL RESEARCH

A large body of research has found evidence linking client hope and outcome expectations to actual treatment outcomes. Perhaps the clearest link between outcome expectations and treatment success can be seen in studies demonstrating positive effects for placebo treatments. Placebos are interventions thought to be inert or to lack the specific ingredients proposed as necessary to treat a given ailment (Shapiro & Shapiro, 1997). Given that they lack the specific ingredients, any improvements observed while a client is on a placebo treatment is thought to be due to the positive effects of hope and outcome expectations. Interestingly, study after study has consistently found that many clients recover from their psychological problems and impairment while only receiving these "inert" treatments (Fisher & Greenberg, 1997).

In the psychotherapy literature, placebo treatments are similar to bona fide treatments in variables such as contact with the therapist and a supportive environment but lack the specific techniques that are unique to the given intervention (e.g., cognitive restructuring for cognitive therapy). In one review, Baskin, Tierney, Minami, and Wampold (2003) attempted to calculate the difference in effectiveness between structurally equivalent active and placebo psychotherapies. They found only a negligible difference ($d = 0.15$) in favor of the actual treatments. This finding illustrates the power of placebo conditions in psychotherapy (Wampold, Minami, Tierney, Baskin, & Bhati, 2005). However, psychotherapy placebo conditions contain many ingredients that could be contributing to their effectiveness (e.g., presence of a therapeutic relationship), and so it is difficult to tease out which effects are due to outcome expectations and hope alone.

The picture is a little clearer, however, when looking at the use of pill placebos. Making a comparison with antidepressants, one review of 182 studies (36,385 clients) found an average response rate for pill placebos to be 37.3%, whereas the average response rate for the bona fide antidepressants was 53.8% (Walsh, Seidman, Sysko, & Gould, 2002)—only a 16.5% difference. Others have found even smaller differences in outcome between antidepressants and placebos (Greenberg & Fisher, 1997). In fact, Kirsch, Moore, Scoboria, and Nicholls (2002) analyzed all the data reviewed by the U.S. Food and Drug Administration in the process of initially sanctioning the six most widely used antidepressants approved between 1987 and 1999 and found that antidepressants were not even 10% more effective than placebos. They concluded that the difference was not clinically meaningful.

If the active ingredients are not present in these placebo conditions, the client's beliefs and hopes for the treatments must be responsible for the changes observed (Bandura, 1977; Frank & Frank, 1991).

As it has turned out, the use of a double-blind research design (the gold standard), in which neither the patients nor the investigators are supposed to be aware of who is receiving the active medication and who is receiving the placebo, has given a false sense of security. The design was supposed to prevent the natural prodrug expectations and desires of the investigators and patients from biasing outcome ratings. However, studies have shown that participants in these antidepressant studies can predict with a high degree of accuracy who is receiving the drug and who is getting the placebo, and this likely translates into enhanced ratings for medication (Greenberg & Fisher, 1994, 1997). One of the tipoffs is the side effects produced by active drugs. When active placebos (those including ingredients that mimic drug side effects such as dry mouth, thus producing the strongest expectations for success) are used as comparisons, the already small antidepressant–placebo differences fade even more. It is of interest that despite the articles and books documenting the lack of blindness in double-blind studies, it was not until 2010 that *The American Journal of Psychiatry* finally acknowledged in a commentary that the double-blind is not really blind (Perlis et al., 2010).

Another interesting observation emerged from a meta-analysis of the placebo response in antidepressant trials (Rief et al., 2009). The investigators recognized that the improvements in placebo groups accounted for a large part of the expected drug effects. They wanted to determine just how large the placebo effects actually were. They examined the placebo effects produced in studies conducted between 1980 and 2005. To their surprise, they discovered that not only did placebos produce almost 70% of the effects reported for antidepressants, but that the placebo effects were growing stronger over time. The rate of response to placebos had increased dramatically. According to observer ratings, effect sizes in placebo-treated groups more than doubled between 1980 and 2005, demonstrating the powerful belief in medication use for psychological problems that is now present in our society. The authors concluded that whereas the placebo effect needed to be controlled in clinical research trials, clinical practice should attempt to use its full power by helping instill positive outcome expectations in clients.

In addition to the implications of results from placebo studies, research directly comparing patients' outcome expectations to treatment success similarly show the value of hope in psychotherapy. In 2011, Constantino and colleagues conducted a meta-analysis directly examining the relationship between patient expectations and outcomes. Their meta-analysis included data from 46 studies and over 8,000 patients. In aggregating data for each study they found an effect size of $r = .12$, indicating a statistically significant positive relationship between high expectations and good treatment outcomes. Although this effect size may be considered small, it is significant when considering the number of process variables that play a role in determining treatment outcomes. One broader, but non-statistical review of the psychotherapy research literature estimated an even larger effect for patient expectations—explaining approximately 15% of the variance in patient change (Norcross & Lambert, 2011).

But what about the relationship between hope and dropout? While not as many studies have been conducted directly examining the relationship between outcome expectations and premature discontinuation, several do exist. In the well-known National Institute of Mental Health Treatment of Depression Collaborative Research Program (TDCRP) study, Elkin and colleagues (Elkin, 1994) compared outcomes for patients who were randomly assigned to either cognitive behavior therapy (CBT), interpersonal psychotherapy (IPT), imipramine plus clinical management, or placebo plus clinical management for the treatment of depression (Elkin, 1994). Prior to assignment however, participants were asked to state how effective several different techniques would be for treating their depressive symptoms. Participants were then identified as belonging to either a CBT, IPT, or medication profile based on which intervention they believed would be most effective. In analyzing the data, Elkin et al. (1999) found that while only 5% of those patients who received the treatment they felt would be most effective dropped out, 21% of patients who received a treatment they felt would be less effective prematurely terminated. Similar to the results from this study, a number of reviews have indicated that patients' belief in their treatments play an important role in determining whether or not they will prematurely terminate (Devilly & Borkovec, 2000; Greenberg et al., 2006; Horvath, 1990; Ilardi & Craighead, 1994; Kazdin & Krouse, 1983).

Although research has clearly demonstrated that treatment outcome expectations and premature termination are linked, the relationship between these two variables may not be a straight linear one. Nock and Kazdin (2001) conducted another interesting study examining the exact pattern of the relationship between these two variables with child patients. In this study they asked the parents of the patients to rate how likely it was that the treatment their child was about to receive would help their child improve, and they actually found a curvilinear relationship between outcome expectations and premature termination. Specifically, when expectations were too optimistic (e.g., expecting to recover in just one or two sessions) or when expectations were very low (not expecting treatment to help at all), the patients were more likely to drop out. Similarly, Swift and Callahan (2008, 2011) demonstrated in two studies the importance of considering both duration and outcomes when assessing expectations. Although we want to strengthen patients' early

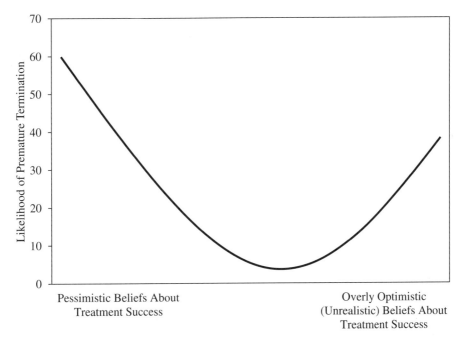

Figure 7.1. Hypothetical likelihood of premature termination based on type of outcome expectations. The hypothetical curve in this figure represents the likelihood of
premature termination (*x*-axis) based on beliefs about treatment success (*y*-axis). At
the left end of the scale, clients who do not believe that treatment will be of any help
are likely to drop out prematurely. As beliefs about treatment success become more
positive, the likelihood of dropout also decreases. However, it is hypothesized that
as beliefs become overly optimistic, clients again become more likely to dropout.
For example, a client who believes that she is going to be 100% cured after two
sessions will likely dropout after just a few sessions if recovery has not occurred.

hopes and beliefs in the efficacy of therapy, overly optimistic expectations
are also likely to result in premature discontinuation of services. Figure 7.1
represents a hypothetical curvilinear relationship between outcome expectations and treatment dropout.

The literature discussed above illustrates the importance of clients'
general expectations that the treatment or therapy will help them recover
from their distress and impairment. However, earlier in this chapter, we mentioned that expectations for the therapist also play an important role. In
other words, not only is it important for clients to believe that the treatment
will help, they should also believe in the effectiveness of their therapists.
Hoyt (1996) conducted a meta-analysis that included 13 studies examining
the influence of perceived therapist credibility on therapy outcomes. Overall,
a large significant effect ($d = 0.83$) was found, indicating that more positive
therapy outcomes are obtained when clients perceive their therapists to be

credible. The therapist credibility effect was the largest for client satisfaction with therapy ($d = 1.33$); however, moderate effects were still observed for the influence of perceived therapist credibility on therapeutic attitude ($d = 0.69$) and behavior ($d = 0.41$) changes.

PUTTING IT INTO PRACTICE

Strategies for strengthening and maintaining clients' early hope generally fall into three broad categories: (a) techniques for making therapy and the specific treatment seem more credible, (b) methods for increasing clients' faith in their therapists, and (c) efforts to raise clients' self-efficacy beliefs.

First, therapists can strengthen clients' initial levels of hope by building their confidence in therapy and the specific treatment that will be used. Building clients' general confidence for therapy can be done by sharing with them some general research findings. For example, a therapist might share that decades of research representing thousands of studies have consistently found psychotherapy to be an effective treatment for most psychological disorders and clients. More specifically, a therapist might share that comprehensive reviews of the research indicate that about 65% of those who stick with therapy will have a positive outcome compared with only about 35% of those who do not receive a treatment (Lambert, 2013). Clients can also be informed that those who receive psychotherapy typically show comparable if not superior outcomes compared with those who receive other treatments such as medication (Fisher & Greenberg, 1997; Lambert, 2013).

Efforts to strengthen clients' beliefs in psychotherapy can also be more localized. For example, one primary care mental health service clinic in the United Kingdom (Primary Care Mental Health Service, Leeds Community Healthcare National Health Service Trust) is conducting a pilot project examining the effectiveness of sharing some of their clinic-level outcome data with their clients. For this pilot study, clients who seek mental health services from their site will be told that a recent report (Royal College of Psychiatrists, 2011) "found that 90% of their clients reported high levels of satisfaction with the treatment that they received" and that "one out of two people fully recover from their difficulties within a fairly brief period of treatment (less than 6 months)" (J. Delgadillo, personal communication, April 25, 2013). This type of clinic- or system-level information can help strengthen clients' initial levels of hope before they even meet with a therapist.

Not only is it important to build up patients' general beliefs in the effectiveness of therapy, therapists should also work to help patients develop confidence in the specific treatment they will receive. In Chapter 3, we discussed the importance of providing patients with a treatment rationale so they know what to expect from treatment. We include it here as well because it is important not only for patients to know what to expect but also for them to believe that the specific treatment will be a means to bring about change. Thus, here we emphasize that the treatment rationale should be credible and presented in a way that inspires hope. Treatment rationales will be more effective in building patients' hope when they are specific and tailored to the patient's presenting problems and when the causal explanation incorporates the patient's beliefs about why they are facing the problems that they are experiencing. Treatment rationales are also more likely to inspire hope when the therapist expresses his or her confidence in the treatment approach.

Second, in addition to believing in the treatment, patients must believe in their therapist's ability to be a helping agent. As mentioned earlier in this chapter, Strong (1968) originally proposed that therapists can be seen as more credible when they are perceived as being an expert, attractive, and trustworthy. The expertise of a therapist is most easily conveyed by the use of reputational cues (e.g., a title, displaying degrees in the office) and demonstrations of psychological knowledge (e.g., using psychological jargon, referring to research when discussing the case conceptualization or treatment rationale). Therapists are seen as more attractive when they are seen as similar to the patients with whom they work. Some of the similarity may be based on demographics (e.g., age, ethnicity, gender), something over which the therapist has little control. However, therapists can also seek to demonstrate similarity by dressing in a manner that is appropriate to the patients with whom they work. For example, in Alaska, it might be appropriate for a therapist to wear jeans and a polo shirt when working with patients, whereas in New York it may be more fitting for the therapist to wear slacks and a blazer. Underneath patients' desires to have a therapist who is similar to them is a desire to have a therapist who will understand their background and situation (Swift & Callahan, 2013; Zane, Hall, Sue, Young, & Nunez, 2004). Thus, even when dissimilarities are present in terms of demographic characteristics, therapists can focus on emphasizing the similarities they do share with their patients and seek to gain an understanding of the ways in which similarities do not exist. As the last piece to Strong's theory, therapists can be seen by their patients as more trustworthy when they seek to display genuineness, warmth, and empathy.

A related body of work indicates that positive expectations and hope can be engendered even before the patient and therapist meet. Greenberg (1972) presented a brief review showing that the referral process can alter the way the therapist and the initial therapy interactions will subsequently be perceived and evaluated. Building on classic research from the social psychology literature, a case is made that individual perceptions and attitudes toward the therapist and therapy are often predetermined by information given before patients meet their therapists. Objective evaluations of encounters may be distorted to agree with previous expectations of what patients are led to believe they should see. Thus, a series of studies showed that giving information about a therapist's experience and personality traits, as in a referral, could enhance the perception of the initial therapy encounters and render individuals more open to the therapist's influence (Greenberg, 1969; Greenberg, Goldstein, & Perry, 1970; Greenberg & Land, 1971). It is also the case that these early efforts can provide other benefits because therapists are likely to respond in more therapeutic ways to those they see as cooperative, invested, "good" patients. In sum, this research suggests that those making referrals can help therapy get off to a good start by providing positive information about the experience, warmth, and usual helpfulness of the therapist being recommended.

Another way therapists can increase their patients' faith in them is to express their confidence in their ability to help the patient. Therapists should not, of course, make promises that cannot be met (remember that overly optimistic expectations can also lead to premature termination), or express so much confidence that they appear boastful and not genuine. However, modest expressions of confidence can go a long way to help increase patients' initial levels of hope. These expressions of confidence could include simple statements indicating that one has previously helped patients successfully get through similar difficulties or statements indicating that the patient's type of problems fits in to one's specialty or focus area. In situations in which the therapist has little expertise (i.e., trainees), the therapist can still appeal to the expertise of others, such as emphasizing supervision from a seasoned psychologist or having attended trainings from experts in the field. One novel way to demonstrate one's credibility is to actually report outcomes to patients (e.g., see http://www.jasonseidel.com/effective2.html). For example, on a practice website, therapists may choose to report the average amount of change that their patients experience, the percentage of their patients that drop out prematurely, or the percentage that show a clinically significant change by the end of treatment.

Last, therapists can work to strengthen patients' early levels of hope by expressing faith in the patient. Not only is it important for patients to believe in a given treatment or a particular therapist, patients also need to believe that the therapist and treatment can work for them (Constantino et al., 2011; Frank & Frank, 1991). Therapists may choose to point out to the patient how well suited he or she is for the particular treatment or mention the patient's strengths that increase the likelihood of success in therapy.

In one of our clinics, we have asked clinicians to add a strength-recognizing statement to the initial preintake registration paperwork. After completing the required demographic and contact information, patients are shown a script that says:

> Thank you for calling the clinic to set up an initial appointment. We recognize that a lot of times individuals will call in to our clinic when things are really tough or at their worst. We also recognize that it can be very difficult to call in and seek out help. Although difficult, calling in to schedule an appointment is a good sign. It actually shows two important things about you: (1) that you are able to recognize when you are having problems and (2) that you are willing to take the necessary steps to address those problems. Those two things will serve you well in your future treatment. Based on those two things, we are optimistic that you will be able to get the help you need to overcome your problems.

Clients often seek out help when they are at their lowest—when they have given up almost all other hope. When they call a therapist, they are often focused almost entirely on their weaknesses. In this initial conversation, clinicians too often only focus on the clients' problems, wanting to make sure they have an adequate understanding of whether and how they might be able to help. Although the initial phone call may spark hope in clients by helping them gain a belief that a solution to their problems may be available, they often end the call not feeling any better about their self-perceived incompetence. In contrast, this script is designed to help clients begin to recognize some of their strengths. Thus, clients can base their hope not just in a potential therapist and treatment but in themselves and their own abilities as well. In addition, this script encourages clients to continue to draw on those strengths and abilities throughout therapy, thus inspiring active client engagement right from the start of treatment.

Although it is perhaps most important during the early phases of treatment, therapists should make efforts to strengthen clients' hope throughout the therapeutic endeavor. In the early phases, hope can help with clients' willingness to begin treatment. Later on, clients may need hope-instilling efforts to help keep them going, particularly if the therapeutic work has been difficult or if they have experienced a setback. At the end of treatment, encouragers of hope should focus on the client's ability to successfully navigate life and problems without the regular help of the therapist or a structured weekly treatment.

Strengthening client hope along with the strategies discussed in the next two chapters (enhancing motivation and fostering the therapeutic alliance) are three techniques that are particularly important for clients who do not enter therapy on their own accord (e.g., court-ordered clients, clients who seek therapy at a significant other's request). These clients may see little need to change and thus perceive and anticipate little benefit associated with attending psychotherapy. By providing these clients with some early improvements in an area that is of value to them (even if it is not the area of focus for the court or the significant other), they may be more willing to engage in therapy and perhaps even work on some of the things that have been requested by others.

CLINICAL EXAMPLES

This excerpt with Emily occurred at the end of her fifth therapy session. It demonstrates the therapist's attempts to strengthen Emily's hope by expressing faith in the therapy process and in Emily.

Therapist: Today it seemed like you brought up some more difficult topics. You talked some about some of the continued difficulties you are having with your boyfriend, but then we were able to start processing some of the trauma that you experienced as a child and the helpless feelings that you had, feeling like you were left to face this horrible thing all alone, but feeling like you were powerless to do anything about it. You had mentioned some of the events to me before, but today was the first day that I felt like we really got to explore and process it. How did it feel to share more about the trauma with me today?

Emily: It was really difficult.

Therapist: Uh huh . . .

Emily: I am not quite sure why I brought it all up. I mean, things still aren't going well in my relationship and I feel like I have plenty there to focus on. I guess I just feel like it was time.

Therapist: Felt like it was time?

Emily: Yeah, I guess I am starting to feel a little more comfortable in here and I know that some of these issues from my childhood are contributing to the conflicts I am having now with my boyfriend.

Therapist: Like it would be easier to talk about your current relationship, but maybe more valuable to start to work on your traumatic experiences as a child.

Emily: Exactly, today's session definitely wasn't easy.

Therapist: I think it took a lot of courage to start talking about the things that you did today. It wasn't easy, but you did it anyway because you felt like that was what you needed to do in order to start feeling better. I think that's a definite strength you have, one that will serve you well as we continue to work together. As we talk about your experiences and feelings there will be times when it's difficult and painful, but the courage to approach those feelings and keep going is what is going to help you move past them. I am confident that as we keep moving in this direction, we will see the change that you were looking for when you started therapy.

The following dialogue with Robert occurred in the treatment planning phase right after a treatment rationale was presented but before Robert and his therapist decided on individual sessions. This excerpt demonstrates the therapist's attempts to convey his expertise.

Robert: Sounds like you know what you're talking about in terms of this treatment. So I am guessing there must be others out there who have problems similar to mine?

Therapist: I know that sometimes when you experience something like social anxiety, it feels like you are the only one who feels that way. Almost like everyone else is completely confident in social situations. I am glad you asked, though. Social anxiety is actually quite common and normal. Almost everyone at one point or another experiences some anxiety in social situations. That anxiety actually serves as a motivator to help us perform well. For example, it might motivate someone to practice before giving a public speech or dress up when going to a job interview. However, for some people, that anxiety can be debilitating at times. That is actually quite common too, and it is estimated that about 7% of the population experience it at the level that causes marked impairment.

Robert: So does anyone ever get better? It seems like I have had this anxiety problem my entire life.

Therapist: I can't see into the future, so I don't know exactly how things will work out for you, but I am pretty confident that by working together, we can get over this anxiety problem. I have actually been working with people with similar anxiety problems my entire career. This is the area that I focus on most in my clinical work, and I have seen a lot of success over the years, particularly with the cognitive–behavioral approach that we will be using. I have even worked with some patients who started off having a really hard time just stepping out of their front door and then, by the end of

therapy, they were initiating conversations and relationships with others. So I am optimistic that if we work hard,
we can help you reach your goals, too.

Robert: Sounds like there is some definite hope then.

Although both of these vignettes provide examples of a therapist's
attempts to instill hope, the therapists went about it in two different ways.
For Emily, the hope-instilling statements focused on her strengths. This was
particularly important given that Emily had a somewhat taxing session. These
hope-encouraging statements helped her realize that even though the work
was hard, she was doing the right thing. For Robert, the hope-instilling statements focused on building Robert's beliefs in the therapist. These types of
statements are usually most appropriate in the initial sessions of treatment.
In this case, the therapist believed they would be particularly useful given
that Robert had discontinued treatment prematurely with other therapists
in the past.

CONCLUSION

Throughout the course of psychotherapy, therapists can work to
reduce premature termination by strengthening their clients' levels of hope.
Hope-instilling efforts can focus on building clients' beliefs in the treatment
(outcome expectations), in their therapists, and in themselves. When a high
level of hope is present, clients will not only anticipate the benefits associated
with therapy but also will be more willing to endure many of the costs. A large
body of research has found a significant association between outcome expectations (Constantino et al., 2011; Greenberg et al., 2006) and therapist credibility beliefs (Hoyt, 1996) and treatment outcomes and dropout. However,
to our knowledge, research has yet to empirically examine whether recognizing clients' strengths can also improve hope and have positive treatment
effects. Given its potential benefits and theoretical justification, we believe
that there is a tremendous need for research in this area. Additionally, further
research investigating whether an optimal level of hope exists is needed (as
illustrated in Figure 7.1). Although a curvilinear relationship can be surmised
given that clients who hold overly optimistic expectations for how quickly
recovery will occur end up attending fewer sessions and are more likely to be
classified as treatment dropouts (Swift & Callahan, 2011), further empirical
evidence of the relationship is needed. On the basis of the existing evidence,
however, we feel confident that therapists' efforts to optimize their clients'
hope will lead to fewer treatment dropouts in their practice. When hope is
present, clients will be truly motivated to engage in psychotherapy.

8

ENHANCE MOTIVATION FOR TREATMENT

If you're going through hell, keep going.

—Winston Churchill

In Chapter 7 we discussed how increasing clients' levels of hope can result in enough motivation to help them initially engage in treatment despite the many costs that are often associated with attending therapy—scheduling difficulties, weekly fees, potential embarrassment. However, hope alone may not be enough of a motivator to sustain attendance. In this chapter, we discuss further strategies for enhancing patients' motivation so that they can face the inconveniences, embarrassments, and difficulties associated with treatment and carry on until the benefits are more fully realized.

We started Chapter 3 by telling of Samwise Gamgee, J. R. R. Tolkien's character from *The Lord of the Rings* and the slight hesitation he had when he first began his journey with Frodo Baggins. As their mission to destroy the evil ring was nearing its end, the weight of the journey had taken its toll on both Sam and Frodo. They had faced numerous struggles and trials along the way, and then just a few hundred yards from their goal, Frodo, the ring

http://dx.doi.org/10.1037/14469-009
Premature Termination in Psychotherapy: Strategies for Engaging Clients and Improving Outcomes,
by J. K. Swift and R. P. Greenberg

bearer, felt like he could go no further. Seeing that Frodo was about to give up, Sam turned to him and cried, "I can't carry it for you, but I can carry you." Although the journey had been challenging for him too, somehow Sam found the strength and motivation to pick his friend up and carry him so they could finish their mission.

Likewise, therapists can work with patients to make sure they have the drive to continue in psychotherapy even when the journey becomes difficult. Motivation for treatment can come in a number of ways. In Chapter 4, we discussed how patients will be more motivated for treatments in which they personally choose to engage. When clients are able to plan for an appropriate treatment ending (Chapter 5), they will be motivated to see therapy through to that end. In the previous chapter (Chapter 7), we also talked about how motivation can be the result of hope based on a belief that a therapist and a treatment might be able to help. In Chapter 9, we talk about how motivation for treatment can be strengthened by building a strong therapeutic relationship with clients. In this chapter, we focus directly on working with a client's level of motivation as a method for reducing premature termination from psychotherapy.

DEFINITION AND DESCRIPTION

Motivation in psychotherapy refers to a patient's willingness to engage in the therapeutic efforts that are necessary to bring about improvement and recovery (Ogrodniczuk, Joyce, & Piper, 2005). It can include both motivation to enter psychotherapy and motivation to change (Bohart & Wade, 2013). Perhaps the best-known theory of motivation in psychotherapy is Prochaska and DiClemente's (1983) stages of change model. According to this trans-theoretical model, patients progress through a series of five successive stages: precontemplation, contemplation, preparation, action, and maintenance. Norcross, Krebs, and Prochaska (2011) described individuals who are in the *precontemplation* stage as individuals who, despite problems, have no intention to seek help or make changes to their behavior. Individuals at this stage may not even recognize that they have a problem and usually only enter therapy at the behest or request of someone else. Individuals in the *contemplation* stage recognize that problems exist, but they are still not quite ready to commit to efforts to overcoming those problems. The *preparation* stage includes those individuals who are committed to change and are just starting to take the initial steps to do so. Finally, individuals in the *action* stage are actively working on addressing their problems, and those in the maintenance stage are continuing with their initial actions and working to prevent a relapse of the problem behavior or emotion from occurring. The stages of change model was originally proposed as a process that applies to smoking behavior, but the model has been applied to many other problem areas that might lead one to seek treatment, including alcohol and substance abuse, anxiety, borderline personality disorder, depression, eating disorders, gambling, posttraumatic stress disorder, and relationship problems (see Norcross et al., 2011, for review).

Although initially one might expect only precontemplators as being at a high risk of premature termination from psychotherapy, patients at any stage could drop out if the intervention does not match their current motivation level and needs. As mentioned previously, at precontemplation, patients are frequently forced into therapy by someone else and thus have difficulty seeing a need to remain in treatment. Patients at this stage may actually work to find excuses to drop out of treatment, but if they are unable to (e.g., therapy has been court ordered), they may continue without fully engaging. Individuals in the contemplation stage may have some motivation for therapy, but if the therapist moves too quickly to push them into action, they too may drop out prematurely. Even though motivation may be much higher for patients in the preparation, action, and maintenance stages, patients in these stages may find little benefit to therapy if their therapists seek to address their ambivalence and commitment rather than working on specific concrete strategies to encourage and sustain change. Additionally, patients at this stage are at risk of losing their motivation if they become bored with treatment and the strategies that are discussed or if the strategies do not result in continued gains.

EMPIRICAL RESEARCH

A number of studies have found a strong link between motivation and premature termination from psychotherapy. For example, Frayn (1992) compared 20 patients who terminated prematurely with 20 therapy completers on a set of 16 psychological variables, one of which was motivation for treatment. Although the two groups differed significantly on 10 of the 16 variables that were studied, the largest differences were found for motivation ($p < .001$). Not only do treatment completers and dropouts differ in their levels of overall motivation, they also differ in the stage of change to which they belong. This finding was illustrated by Brogan, Prochaska, and Prochaska (1999), who tracked the course of therapy for 60 patients who had been seeking services from a university counseling center, a community mental health clinic, or a doctoral training clinic. Using a discriminate function analysis, they found that the patient's stage of change could correctly predict termination status (premature or not) for 91.67% of the patients. By and large, those who prematurely terminated in their study had been classified as precontemplators. The findings from these two studies have been replicated in a number of different trials. In a review of the literature that included data from 24 studies, Norcross et al. (2011) found a significant effect size ($d = 0.42$), demonstrating the moderately strong relationship between the stages of change and premature termination from psychotherapy.

Although a number of studies have demonstrated a relationship between motivation and premature termination status, fewer studies have tested whether interventions to increase patient motivation actually result in fewer treatment dropouts. In one review of strategies for reducing premature termination from psychotherapy, Oldham, Kellett, Miles, and Sheeran (2012) only identified three studies that tested motivation as an intervention. In the first, Milton, Crino, Hunt, and Prosser (2002) randomly assigned 40 participants who were seeking treatment for gambling problems to cognitive behavior therapy (CBT) or CBT plus strategies to address motivation. Although only 35% of those who received CBT alone completed treatment, 65% of those who received the added motivational intervention did. In the second study, Westra and Dozois (2006) randomly assigned 55 patients who were seeking treatment for anxiety problems to either CBT alone or CBT plus three sessions of pretreatment motivational interviewing. Whereas 84% of those who got the pretreatment motivational interviewing went on to complete the CBT treatment, only 63% of those who did not receive the pretreatment completed their course of CBT. In the final study Oldham et al. identified, Zanjani, Bush, and Oslin (2010) randomized 113 primary care patients to motivational or control conditions. Those who were assigned to the motivational group received one or two pretherapy telephone calls that addressed motivation for treatment, whereas those in the control group received no such phone call. Zanjani et al. found that only 32% of the control group showed up for their initial appointment, but 70% of the motivational enhancement group did. In addition, the motivational enhancement group attended almost twice the number of sessions of therapy as those patients who were placed in the control group. In one other motivation enhancement study that was not included in Oldham et al.'s review, Taft, Murphy, Elliott, and Morrel (2001) examined the efficacy of integrating motivational interviewing techniques into their standard group procedures for 189 male perpetrators of domestic violence. Taft et al. found a 30% dropout rate for those who received the treatment as usual but only 15% for those who received the treatment with the integration of motivational interviewing.

PUTTING IT INTO PRACTICE

Several strategies can be used to increase a client's motivation for therapy. In general, on the basis of our conceptualization of premature termination presented at the start of this book, it can be assumed that as clients experience and anticipate more benefits and experience and anticipate fewer costs they will be more motivated to continue to attend. Thus, all of the strategies that we have recommended and will recommend can be considered methods that also have the potential to indirectly increase clients' motivation for treatment. However, techniques for directly focusing on client motivation can also be recommended. In many research studies, motivational enhancement is included by adding a session or two of treatment specifically addressing these issues before the start of therapy; in practice, however, clinicians may also want to include these types of strategies whenever needed throughout the course of therapy.

Motivational interviewing (Miller & Rollnick, 2013) provides one useful and well-supported framework for addressing client motivation in treatment. The goal of motivational interviewing, as proposed by Miller and Rose (2009), is to work with clients' ambivalence by evoking and strengthening their verbalizations of desires to change and decreasing their resistance or verbalizations of desires not to change. In essence, instead of trying to convince clients that they need to change their behaviors, therapists allow them to argue for their own change desires. In so doing, these change desires become solidified, and clients are more strongly motivated to follow through with the therapeutic recommendations.

Levensky (2003) and Fischer and Moyers (2012) presented a number of specific strategies for working with clients on their motivation, and we believe that their suggestions could also prove useful for reducing premature termination with clients. In general, the strategy that is used needs to match the stage of change. Broadly speaking, Norcross et al. (2011) described the different roles the therapist takes on with each of these stages as: a nurturing parent for precontemplation, a Socratic teacher for contemplation, an experienced coach for preparation, and a consultant for action and maintenance.

More specifically, at the precontemplation and contemplation stages of change, therapists can focus on eliciting self-motivational statements from their clients, expressing understanding of desires to change and not to change, and rolling with resistance. First, therapists can seek to elicit self-motivational statements in their clients. Rather than specifically stating all of the reasons why the client should be in therapy or work on his or her problematic behaviors, therapists ask clients open-ended questions that allow them to state why they want to be in therapy, how their behaviors have been causing problems, and why they want to work on them. For example, a therapist might ask, "In what ways do you think regularly attending our sessions might be of a benefit to you in your life?" Therapists may also choose to provide the clients with feedback or information about the negative consequences that could result if they do not work on their problems; however, if therapists choose to provide this type of feedback, they should be careful not to sound like they are lecturing or confronting the client about the problematic behavior.

Second, as clients express desires to change and not to change, therapists work hard to express empathy and understanding of their opinions on both sides. When working with a client who has expressed some desire to discontinue treatment early due to a busy schedule, instead of stating all of the reasons why continued attendance in therapy is needed, the therapist could say,

> You sound conflicted: On the one hand, you believe therapy is important and you are just starting to make some gains, on the other hand, things have gotten busy in your life now, and you are finding it difficult to find enough time to take care of yourself.

This example leads directly to the next set of therapist behaviors: rolling with resistance. Rather than confronting or arguing with clients when they express resistance, therapists can simply use restatements, reflections, and reframes to help clients confront their resistance themselves. When a client believes that his or her therapist understands how difficult change can be, the client no longer needs to convince the therapist of that point. Additionally, when a client knows that the therapist will support whatever change decision he or she wants to make, there will be a growing recognition that the decision to change is his or her own.

These three strategies apply largely to clients who are in the precontemplation and contemplation stages of change. These early stages are perhaps the times when clients are at the highest risk of dropping out. However, clients in one of the later stages of change are also at risk of premature termination if their motivation falters. As mentioned earlier, motivation in the preparation, action, and maintenance stages may become a problem if therapists seek to address client ambivalence and commitment, if the change strategies used are static and become boring or mundane to clients, when the therapeutic work becomes difficult, and when a setback or even plateau of change is experienced.

For clients in these later stages, it is important for therapists to recognize when their clients are ready for action. For some clients, this may be in the initial appointment; for others, it may only come after months of work. Whatever the timing, when clients are ready for action, therapists can best help their clients maintain their motivation by helping them develop an individually tailored change plan and carry out dynamic activities that will lead to positive treatment outcomes. In thinking about the steps and activities that should be taken, therapists can help clients maintain their motivation by planning strategies that are not only challenging but also have a high likelihood of success. While working on these activities, therapists can provide encouragement and affirmations. If a setback does occur and the client's motivation wanes, the therapist can revert back to the earlier strategies of eliciting self-motivational statements, expressing understanding of desires for and against change, and rolling with resistance to help their clients get back on track.

Given the importance of matching the strategy to the stage of change, therapists should also develop skills in assessing motivation. First, they can often assess their clients' level of motivation by listening to change talk. Clients who are ready for action will make more statements affirming their individual desire to change for themselves and fewer statements indicating their desires to hold on to their problem behaviors. Therapists can also assess motivation by looking at their clients' behaviors inside and outside of therapy. Clients who lack motivation often cite others as the reason for their problems, have sought out treatment only at the request of others, and have taken few if any steps to change on their own. Additionally, clinicians may choose to use the University of Rhode Island Change Assessment Scale (DiClemente & Hughes, 1990) as a self-report measure that assesses the four stages of change that we have discussed throughout the chapter or the Stages of Change Readiness and Treatment Eagerness Scale (Miller & Tonigan, 1996) as a self-report measure that assesses problem recognition, ambivalence, and taking steps as two well-supported measures of motivation.

CLINICAL EXAMPLE

In the following excerpt, we pick up with Emily a few sessions from where we left off in Chapter 7. She had begun to process her childhood traumas, but the work continued to be difficult. At the start of this session, she expressed some desire to give up and discontinue treatment.

> *Emily:* To be honest with you, as I was getting ready to get in my car and head over here for our appointment today, I thought about just calling in and canceling. I decided to come in, but on the drive over, I just got to thinking that maybe we should make this our last session.

> *Therapist:* I am glad that you did come in and really appreciate that you have shared these feelings with me rather than just stopping without ever talking about it. What do you think has brought on these feelings of wanting to discontinue?

> *Emily:* I am just not sure I am ready for the work we have been doing.

> *Therapist:* Uh huh . . .

> *Emily:* At first, therapy seemed pretty easy as we were talking about some of the conflicts that I am having with my boyfriend, but now recently we have started talking about my childhood experiences, and it has been really difficult. I sometimes just dread coming in and facing all of that again.

Therapist: I can tell how difficult and painful it has been for you. Approaching topics like this is never easy, and I can completely understand how it would be easier to avoid them.

Emily: Yeah, and I just don't know if it is worth it.

Therapist: Emily, I want you to know that I respect your opinion on wanting to stop. After all, therapy is for you, and we should be doing the things in here that are going to be of the most benefit for you. Although these topics are difficult, a few sessions back something motivated you to start talking with me about your childhood traumas. What was that?

Emily: Well, I have been carrying around these secrets for a long time now and keeping them bottled up was just wearing me out. I could tell that it was affecting things with my boyfriend, and so I figured it was time to address them and see what happens.

Therapist: So even though you thought it would be difficult, you felt like it was time. But maybe now you are finding that it is a little more difficult than you thought, and you are ready to maybe bottle them back up again?

Emily: No, I guess I don't want to do that either. I know it is time to work on them, it's just so hard.

Therapist: You said you know it is time to work on them, it is just so hard. Sounds like you know what you want to do, it is just a matter of working up the strength to do it. What do you think would happen if you didn't want to work up the strength—if we did just stop here?

Emily: I am sure it would start getting in the way of my relationship again and then I would probably lose my boyfriend even though I really love him. I can't let that happen, I think I am ready to go on.

Therapist: Despite how painful it can be, you're ready to push through because you recognize the benefits that can come if you do.

Emily: Yeah, I am.

Therapist: I am glad to hear you say that; I think you have a lot of courage and strength. I think we have made some real progress so far in therapy and I believe that if we keep going, we will get to the place where things aren't as painful and you won't have to work so hard at keeping your previous abuse and your feelings a secret and bottled up.

Hearing clients express concerns about attending therapy just when things seem to be progressing can be concerning for therapists. As a result, therapists may be tempted to try to convince their clients of why it is important to continue to meet with them. Rather than trying to tell Emily all of the reasons why stopping now would be a bad idea, Emily's therapist first tried to understand where her concerns were coming from. Emily quickly shared how difficult the past few sessions had been. In the dialogue that followed, notice how the therapist tried to validate and empathize with Emily's concerns. The therapist also emphasized that the decision to attend or not attend was completely up to Emily; however, the therapist also had Emily think about what had motivated her to open up in the past and what the outcomes would be if she were to choose to stop or continue to attend now. These techniques allowed Emily to start to engage in more change talk and realize on her own that she was still motivated to work on her problems.

CONCLUSION

The strategy of directly enhancing motivation for the patient's willingness to engage in the therapeutic effort to bring about change builds on all of the previous strategies that we have discussed so far in this book. All these strategies may indirectly increase motivation by helping clients perceive and anticipate more benefits and fewer costs associated with treatment. A significant amount of research has demonstrated the value of directly addressing motivation in treatment and tailoring interventions based on clients' readiness to change (Norcross et al., 2011). However, most of this research has been conducted in the addictions domain, and further research is needed examining the efficacy of motivational enhancement strategies for decreasing treatment dropout with clients who experience other psychological problems.

In this chapter specifically, we have focused on ways to work with clients according to their current level of motivation. For clients in the precontemplation or contemplation stages, efforts should focus on eliciting self-motivational statements, expressing understanding of desires to change and not to change, and rolling with resistance. For clients in the action and maintenance stages, efforts should focus on developing and carrying out plans and providing encouragement and affirmations. For these clients, therapists should work to make sure the plans are ones that are interesting and challenging to their clients and ones for which there is a high likelihood of success. It is also important for therapists to recognize that motivation is not a stable characteristic and that client motivation may falter if the client experiences a significant setback. In these situations, therapists can seek to normalize that setback and revert back to some of the earlier motivational strategies to get the client back on track. In the end, a more motivated client is more likely to establish a stronger relationship with his or her therapist, another important factor for reducing premature termination that is discussed in Chapter 9.

9

FOSTER THE THERAPEUTIC ALLIANCE

I think people are isolated because of the nature of human consciousness and they like it when they feel connection between themselves and someone else.

—James Taylor

Once clients have been properly prepared for treatment, and once they have at least enough hope and motivation to initially engage, therapists can work to establish and foster a strong therapeutic relationship—our next strategy for reducing premature termination in psychotherapy. Although the concept of the therapeutic alliance originally grew out of the psychodynamic tradition, this construct is currently acknowledged almost universally across theoretical orientations as an important variable in determining treatment outcomes for patients. However, when Freud originally discussed the role of this variable, he did so in terms of premature termination. As stated by Horvath, Del Re, Fluckiger, and Symonds (2011):

> In some of his writings (Freud, 1912/1958; 1913), he noted the apparent paradoxical situation clients find themselves in the beginning of treatment; the therapy process itself activates the client's defenses which should make the client flee the therapeutic situation, yet, in successful

http://dx.doi.org/10.1037/14469-010
Premature Termination in Psychotherapy: Strategies for Engaging Clients and Improving Outcomes, by J. K. Swift and R. P. Greenberg

treatments, clients persist to collaborate with the therapist in unearthing disturbing material. As a solution to this contradiction, he proposed the presence of a positive or "unobjectionable" transference which binds the client to the person of the therapist and assists the client to remain in treatment despite the increased level of anxieties. (p. 10)

Freud's writings speak directly to the costs–benefits conceptualization of premature termination we proposed in Chapter 1. When the therapeutic alliance is strong, the perceived benefits of working collaboratively with an understanding and empathic therapist can help outweigh almost any other costs associated with attending therapy. In contrast, if the therapeutic alliance is weak, the lack of a relationship itself may lead a client to prematurely terminate from psychotherapy.

DEFINITION AND DESCRIPTION

Even though Freud wrote about the therapeutic alliance in the early 1900s, according to Horvath et al. (2011), the term itself was not coined until the 1950s, first by Zetzel (1956) and then further elaborated by Greenson (1967). Over the past half-century, many variations in this construct have been put forward; however, perhaps the most commonly recognized definition of the therapeutic alliance today was first proposed by Bordin (1979), who suggested a pantheoretical definition of the therapeutic alliance that includes three central components: (a) agreement on the therapeutic goals, (b) agreement on the assignment of tasks for therapy, and (c) the development of a bond between the client and the therapist. The first two components of this definition are related and relatively straightforward. Although each theoretical approach proposes its own set of objectives and methods for reaching those purposes, for a client and therapist to work together, they must have at least some level of agreement as to what those objectives and methods are to be. These two aspects of the therapeutic alliance are closely linked to the domains of role expectations (Chapter 3) and preferences (Chapter 6). If clients and therapists are not on the same page about the purposes of therapy or the most appropriate ways to achieve those purposes, clients are not likely to remain in treatment.

The therapeutic bond, the third component of Bordin's (1979) definition, includes the feelings that the client and the therapist share for one another. The bond is often considered to be strengthened by the therapist's ability to display Carl Rogers's *necessary* and *sufficient* conditions for therapeutic change such as unconditional positive regard, accurate empathy, and genuineness (Rogers, 1957) as well as nonpossessive warmth and respect for the client. A therapist's display of these characteristics in turn leads to the client's feelings of safety, trust, liking, and respect for the therapist. In addition to making it possible for a client to feel safe to be open with the therapist and trust the goals and techniques the therapist proposes, the bond is what keeps the client coming back even when the therapeutic work might be difficult. Without a positive relationship with the therapist to keep them in therapy, clients are likely to follow any number of competing reasons to discontinue.

In addition to developing the therapeutic alliance early on in therapy, therapists should seek to maintain the alliance throughout the therapeutic process. Safran, Muran, and Eubanks-Carter (2011) pointed out that in therapy there can occasionally be a tension or breakdown of the relationship between the client and the therapist—something they referred to as an *alliance rupture*. They indicated that an alliance rupture is similar to the concepts of an empathic failure (Kohut, 1984), therapeutic impasse, and misunderstanding event (Rhodes, Hill, Thompson, & Elliot, 1994). Although the therapeutic alliance may be one of the best ways to keep a client in therapy despite other costs that might be present, a client's perceptions of being hurt by his or her therapist will almost surely lead to premature termination unless it is recognized and ameliorated quickly. In contrast, when the therapist is successful in perceiving and repairing an alliance rupture, the bond between the client and therapist will likely be strengthened, making it all the less likely that the client will discontinue prematurely.

EMPIRICAL RESEARCH

A large body of research has found a strong relationship between the therapeutic alliance and patient outcomes across settings, patients, disorders, and even treatment models (Lambert, 2013). This relationship is demonstrated in the results of a meta-analysis that included 190 studies and more than 14,000 patients (Horvath et al., 2011). Across studies an aggregate effect size of $r = .28$ was found, indicating that approximately 7.5% of the variance in treatment outcomes is accounted for by the strength of the therapeutic alliance alone. Although this effect size was only moderate, it was highly reliable, 95% confidence interval [0.25, 0.30], and large compared with the size of the relationship that is seen between many other variables and treatment outcomes (Wampold, 2001).

The relationship between the therapeutic alliance and treatment outcomes was further demonstrated by another meta-analysis examining therapists' efforts to repair alliance ruptures (Safran et al., 2011). Safran and colleagues (2011) actually conducted two meta-analyses, the first examining the effectiveness of repairing efforts and the second examining the effects of repairing training for therapists. In the first, a significant relationship ($r = .24$) between rupture repairing episodes and treatment outcome was found, indicating that if therapists were able to heal the alliance when it was broken, then patients were more likely to show positive therapy outcomes. A significant and large effect ($r = .65$) was also found for repairing training, indicating that therapists had better treatment outcomes with their patients after they were trained in methods for fixing the alliance compared with their pretraining patient outcomes.

More pertinent to premature termination from psychotherapy, a meta-analysis conducted by Sharf, Primavera, and Diener (2010) directly examined the relationship between the therapeutic alliance and dropout. It included 11 studies, all of which were adult focused and all of which were for individual therapy. They found a significant overall effect of $d = 0.55$, which translates to an r effect size of about .30. The direction of this effect size indicates that patients with weaker therapeutic alliances were more likely to drop out of psychotherapy. In their additional analyses, Sharf et al. further discovered that weaker alliance scores were more strongly associated with dropping out for patients who had a lower level of education, who were in inpatient settings, and for treatments that were of a longer duration.

One additional study conducted by Muran et al. (2009) directly compared efforts to repair ruptures in the alliance and patient continuation in psychotherapy. In this study, 128 patients and their therapists were asked to complete rupture intensity and resolution ratings after each of their first six sessions of psychotherapy. Muran et al. found that rupture resolutions, as rated by either the therapist or the patient, were significantly correlated with dropout, such that when a resolution occurred, regardless of the intensity of the initial rupture, patients were less likely to prematurely terminate. Interestingly, this result was consistent across three different types of treatments: brief relational therapy, cognitive behavior therapy, and short-term dynamic psychotherapy. Although the results from this study are promising, additional research is needed to replicate their findings.

PUTTING IT INTO PRACTICE

Given the relationship that exists between the therapeutic alliance and premature termination from psychotherapy, a number of suggestions can be made for therapists to apply in fostering the therapeutic alliance. The first would be to make sure that there is some agreement on the goals and tasks of therapy before jumping into treatment. Therapists may sometimes take this step as a given, assuming that they understand what their patients want from therapy and assuming their patients agree with them about the best ways to proceed. However, in one study we actually found that agreement was the exception to the rule (Swift & Callahan, 2009). Swift and Callahan (2009) asked 151 patient and therapist dyads to separately identify the goals and tasks of their work together after the third session of treatment. In only 31.1% of the cases were the patient and the therapist in agreement about the focus of the treatment, and in only 46.4% of the cases were they in agreement about the activities that should predominately be used in therapy. It is easy to see how a significant number of patients would want to prematurely terminate if about two thirds of the time they felt like their therapist was working toward a goal that did not match what they wanted out of treatment.

To achieve a greater consensus on the goals and tasks for therapy, therapists can make sure, particularly in the beginning, to work collaboratively with their clients. This recommendation matches the recommendations made in Chapters 3 and 4. To increase collaboration, therapists can follow the strategies mentioned in those chapters to educate clients about appropriate therapeutic roles and about the different treatment options that might be available and to provide a rationale for why one might choose one treatment approach over another. They should also allow clients to express their preferences about the options and seek to accommodate those preferences whenever possible. It is important for clients to feel like therapy is a joint effort, not just another instance when someone is telling them what they are doing wrong and how they should change.

The second recommendation to therapists for fostering the therapeutic alliance is to focus on developing a relational bond with their clients. Therapists can work on developing a bond by listening to their clients, displaying characteristics of warmth and acceptance, seeking to really understand clients' individual problems rather than just deciding on a diagnosis, and seeking to respond empathically to what the client shares. Research indicates that clients value these types of therapist characteristics most when they seek out treatment. Using a delay-discounting method, Swift and Callahan (2010) asked clients how much they would be willing to sacrifice in terms of treatment effectiveness to have an empathic and accepting therapist or one with whom they could develop a therapeutic relationship. These participants ($n = 57$) indicated that they would rather receive a treatment that research indicates has a lower client recovery rate by 38.14% to ensure that they could receive a therapist with whom they could develop a positive working relationship, and a lower recovery rate by 48.54% to ensure that they would receive a therapist who could be described as warm, empathic, and accepting. A similar result was noted by Greenberg (1969), who found that individuals were more drawn to therapists described as possessing the positive personality characteristic of "warmth" than therapists described as having more years of experience. It appears that for clients, the therapist's possession of relationship-enhancing personality characteristics trumps years of experience in a desirable clinician. In summary, it is essential for therapists to remember the value of the bond, not to sacrifice that bond to deliver an intervention, and to use all of the basic therapy skills (e.g., listening, being present, responding empathically) to relate on an affective level with their clients.

Third, therapists can work on fostering the therapeutic alliance by routinely monitoring their clients' perspectives of it throughout therapy. Just as therapists sometimes have difficulty recognizing their clients' goals and tasks, therapists often have trouble identifying clients' feelings about the therapeutic relationship. In a meta-analysis that included 53 studies, Tryon, Blackwell, and Hammel (2007) found a correlation of $r = .36$ between therapists' and clients' ratings of the alliance. Additionally, clients' feelings about the alliance frequently fluctuate from session to session as well as within a single session. To monitor these fluctuations and to receive more objective data, therapists may ask their clients to complete a standardized measure of the therapeutic alliance on a regular basis. The most commonly used measure in the literature of the therapeutic alliance is the Working Alliance Inventory (WAI; Horvath & Greenberg, 1989). The WAI is a 36-item self-report questionnaire with three subscales measuring the three components of Bordin's (1979) pantheoretical definition of the therapeutic alliance: goals, tasks, and bond. Although it does not have the same level of empirical support, a short version of the measure with only nine items (three for each domain) also exists (Hatcher & Gillaspy, 2006). Another measure of the therapeutic alliance that is not as commonly used by researchers but that is popular among practitioners is the Session Rating Scale (SRS; Duncan et al., 2003). The SRS includes four self-report items that also fit Bordin's definition of the alliance. Additionally, this measure is easy to use and was designed for use on a session-by-session basis.

Our final suggestion for fostering the therapeutic alliance is for therapists to seek to repair alliance ruptures as soon as they occur. Based on their own research and review of the literature, Safran et al. (2011) suggested six specific interventions that can be used to repair alliance ruptures. The first three strategies are surface-level techniques to help get the working relationship back on track. First, they suggested that therapists repeat the therapeutic rationale. Because collaborative work on goals with agreed-on methods (tasks) is essential to the therapeutic alliance, therapists may choose to get the alliance back on track by reminding their clients what the previously agreed-on goals and tasks were. However, sometimes a conflict in the relationship occurs because clients' opinions and needs have shifted over the course of treatment. This shift can occur because clients have gained actual experience with the various techniques, which may inform their new opinions and desires. Likewise, they may have made some initial changes, and the old goals and tasks are no longer relevant. In such situations, Safran et al. suggested that the therapist modify his or her behaviors so they better fit what the client currently wants. Third, Safran et al. suggested that therapists can seek to repair alliance ruptures by clarifying misunderstandings at a surface level. For example, if the client seems upset by something the therapist has said, the therapist seeks to understand and recognize the client's feelings and then seeks to validate them as being legitimate within the context of the relationship.

Safran et al.'s (2011) next three suggestions for repairing alliance ruptures attempt to help clients learn and grow from the rupture. First, therapists can help clients explore relational themes associated with the rupture. The themes that come up may then become the focus of future work. However, we would suggest that this strategy not take place until after the therapist sought to repair the alliance at the surface level. Similarly, therapists can also attempt to help the client link the alliance rupture to common patterns in the client's life. Last, Safran et al. recommended that therapists can seek to repair alliance ruptures by creating new relational experiences for their clients. Even if they do not specifically talk about the relational themes or common patterns that were showing up in the rupture, creating new experiences can help clients break the maladaptive themes and patterns in which they have been caught. According to the situation and the client's need, a therapist can choose to use any one or multiple strategies when alliance ruptures have occurred. Whatever strategy is chosen, we suggest that therapists take a nondefensive stance when a rupture has occurred, validate their clients' feelings and concerns, and tread lightly with clients until the relationship can get back on track.

CLINICAL EXAMPLES

This dialogue with Emily was taken from a later session after she had shown significant reductions in her symptoms and distress level. In it, Emily described to the therapist how the therapeutic alliance had helped her progress in therapy.

> *Therapist:* Emily, we have been meeting for a few months now, and I feel like you have made a lot of changes. Coming in today, you are smiling, and you look happy. I wonder, is there something in particular that has brought about this happiness?

> *Emily:* No, nothing in particular. Things just seem to be getting better. Maybe things aren't 100% with my boyfriend yet, but I am just feeling better now and I think therapy has really helped.

Therapist: Well, that's great! What was it about therapy that you think helped bring about these changes?

Emily: Hmm. . . . When I first came in to meet you I was really worried. I was really worried about what you would think of me and worried that you would just tell me that everything was my fault. But it wasn't that way at all. In the beginning you really listened to me, and I started to feel like you understood me and what I was going through. It also felt like you didn't necessarily have your own agenda, but you were willing to follow my lead. That made me feel like you really trusted me, and because of that, I think I trusted you a lot more. Eventually, as I started to share more and express a side of me that I don't really let others see, I still felt like you accepted me. This actually helped me start to open up a lot more with my boyfriend, and I think that has helped our relationship.

Therapist: I am grateful that you felt that trust in me and were willing to open up and share. I know that opening up is often difficult, but I am glad that I got to be a part of it.

In this example with Robert, the therapist attempted to repair an alliance rupture after one had occurred.

Therapist: For your exposure homework this week, you were going to initiate a conversation with someone in a checkout line at least four separate times. How did it go?

Robert: Not so hot.

Therapist: No?

Robert: Well I had it all planned out. After we met last week I was going to go straight to the grocery store to get a few things for dinner on my way home. I was really excited to give it a shot. I got my stuff and then made my way to the checkout area. I picked a line that had a couple of people in it already. There was another guy there at the back of the line who I thought I might be able to talk to. But then, as I was thinking what to say, he started texting on his phone. I didn't want to interrupt him, so I was just going to wait until someone came up behind me. But then no one did. After that I figured I would just say something to the lady ringing me up, but then I couldn't think of the right thing to say, so I paid, said thank you, took my groceries, and went home. I kind of gave up after that and didn't even try to say anything to anyone when I went to the store later in the week.

Therapist:	Sounds like you got really anxious that first time you were there in line and you just couldn't work up the courage to say something like you had wanted to.
Robert:	*Silent, with an expression of surprise and some anger.*
Therapist:	It seems like something I said maybe upset you?
Robert:	How could you say that I didn't have any courage? I don't know why I am even doing this anyway. You wanted me to go to the grocery store and initiate conversations with people I hadn't even met before and you act like that's easy. Not too long ago when I would go to the grocery store, I would use the self-checkout lines and avoid people all together. I felt like it took a lot of courage to use the line that other people were in. Things just didn't work out so I could talk to them like you wanted me to.
Therapist:	You're right, I do think I misspoke. You have made a lot of progress over the past couple of weeks and the fact that you got in a line with other people and where you would have to interact with the person at the cash register was a big step. You even said "thank you" as you paid, and that took a lot of courage. I am sorry that I missed that.
Robert:	I guess it really was such a small thing. I should have done more!
Therapist:	What do you think about that? Although I do think exposures can be beneficial, I don't want you to feel like you have to do them just for me. Maybe these exposures aren't what we should be working on right now?
Robert:	No, I agree. I know I need to do them, and I know that this is what is going to help me get better. Maybe we are just going a little too fast.
Therapist:	OK, what do you think would be a better exercise for this week—one that will push you to face your fears some, but not so much that it seems impossible?
Therapist:	(*later on, toward the end of the session*) Before we end today, I want to say that I think it took a lot of courage for you to share your feelings with me the way you did when we were talking about your homework. When you felt like I had said something wrong and was pushing you too hard, you let me know. As a result, we were able to work through those concerns and come up with a better plan.
Robert:	Oh, it wasn't anything important.

Therapist: It may feel like a small thing, but I also remember that a little while back, you told me that people tend to walk all over you—that the social anxiety always gets in the way of you standing up for yourself. But here was an example where you did share your concerns with me, and I am glad that you did.

Both of these examples demonstrate in somewhat different ways how the therapeutic alliance can be used to provide new experiences for clients. In the first case, Emily simply shared how working with a male therapist whom she grew to trust allowed her to realize that she can be more open and trusting with other men in her life—namely, her boyfriend. Although this was a realization that Emily came to on her own, she may not have ever fully arrived there if the therapist had not given her a chance to express what she felt had been helpful in therapy.

In the second case, Robert also had a new experience, but it came only after an alliance rupture. In response to Robert's not completing his homework, his therapist suggested that perhaps he did not have quite enough "courage" to follow his goal through. Although the therapist was well meaning in this comment, Robert felt judged by it. At that point, Robert was at a high risk of dropping out and probably would have if not for two things. First, the therapist noticed Robert's reaction and asked about it. Second, up until this point, the therapist had built a strong enough relationship with Robert that he was willing to break his normal pattern of interacting with others and share his anger with the therapist. The therapist quickly took a non-defensive stance, apologized for the judgment that was perceived in his words, empathized with Robert's feelings, and then, at the end of the session, used the rupture to point out some of Robert's strengths. Notice how the therapist recognized the "courage" that it took for Robert to share his feelings with the therapist, the very thing that Robert felt judged on earlier in the session. Through these efforts, the therapist was actually able to turn the rupture into a learning and alliance-building experience for Robert.

CONCLUSION

Among the therapeutic variables, the therapeutic alliance has consistently been found to be one of the strongest predictors of treatment outcomes (Horvath et al., 2011), so it makes sense that it would likewise also play a role in premature termination from psychotherapy. A strong therapeutic alliance, in and of itself, can be a strong perceived benefit that can motivate clients to stay in treatment despite the costs that also may be present. Indeed, although the body of research examining the therapeutic alliance and premature termination is much smaller, a significant relationship between these two variables has been found (Sharf et al., 2010). Continued studies examining the relationship between the alliance and dropout are needed to add to the preliminary evidence that has already been found. In particular, studies examining whether clients choose to drop out shortly after alliance ruptures would be helpful, as well as studies more fully investigating whether alliance-repairing strategies can result in fewer prematurely terminating clients.

Given the solid preliminary evidence, we strongly recommend that therapists seek to foster the therapeutic relationship as a strategy for reducing treatment dropout. Efforts to foster the therapeutic relationship should occur throughout treatment, starting as early as the first session. Therapists should work to display the Rogerian common factors of unconditional positive regard, warmth, and empathy. It is also important for therapists to be aware that alliance ruptures can frequently occur in psychotherapy, even when a strong and long-standing positive relationship currently exists. Using a standard measure of the alliance such as the WAI or the SRS may be one way to routinely check on the relationship. In addition, therapists should watch for ruptures in the moment-by-moment interactions of each session and work on repairing them as soon as they occur. Alliance ruptures can often lead to more global deterioration, which is discussed in more detail in the Chapter 10. By tying alliance ruptures to existing relationship themes or recurring patterns in the client's life, and by providing a new experience through the rupture repair, therapists can often help clients gain insight into some of their problems and make the rupture a growth and learning experience rather than one that leads to dissatisfaction and premature termination.

10

ASSESS AND DISCUSS TREATMENT PROGRESS WITH CLIENTS

Feedback is the breakfast of champions.

—Ken Blanchard

In Chapter 9, we suggested that one step to foster the therapeutic relationship is to periodically check in with clients about the relationship, whether through objective self-report measures or an in-session discussion. The present chapter builds on that strategy: By periodically asking clients for feedback on how therapy is going (whether through objective self-report measures or an in-session conversation), premature termination from psychotherapy can also be reduced. Through feedback, an individual can recognize and fix shortcomings and mistakes early on, before there are major negative consequences. Similarly, assessing client progress is one way for therapists to recognize early on those clients who are heading toward premature termination. With this early feedback, therapists can implement changes to make sure therapy gets back on track, thus decreasing the probability of client dropout. In addition, discussing progress with clients and possible changes that could take place helps to build strong collaborative relationships between clients

http://dx.doi.org/10.1037/14469-011
Premature Termination in Psychotherapy: Strategies for Engaging Clients and Improving Outcomes,
by J. K. Swift and R. P. Greenberg

and therapists. As discussed in Chapter 9, a collaborative relationship makes it difficult for a client to discontinue treatment prematurely.

DEFINITION AND DESCRIPTION

Although many have discussed the importance of tracking client progress (e.g., Carl Rogers, 1957, discussed outcome tracking methods in his article on the *necessary* and *sufficient* conditions for therapeutic change), the idea of routine outcome monitoring for individual clients was first fully conceptualized by Ken Howard and colleagues in the 1990s. In a seminal article on the topic, Howard, Moras, Brill, Martinovich, and Lutz (1996) indicated that there are three fundamental questions that can be asked about psychotherapy or any particular intervention: (a) Does it work under experimental conditions (efficacy)? (b) Does it work in practice (effectiveness)? and (c) Is it working for a particular client? Although Questions 1 and 2 are important for establishing the research base for a given treatment, Howard and colleagues (1996) pointed out that Question 3 is the "crucial, immediate question posed by the practitioner" (p. 1059). For practitioners, information about which treatment outperforms which other treatment might be useful in our treatment planning and decision-making process. However, when we sit down with an individual client, we are less concerned about outcomes on a group level. Instead, we want to know whether the client sitting across from us is getting better, and if not, what we can do to better help him or her change. Howard et al. (1996) originally referred to the idea of assessing treatment progress of individual clients as *patient profiling*, but it later became known as *patient-focused research* (Lambert, 2001). Specifically, patient-focused research includes three main components: (a) routine tracking of a client's progress, (b) comparing that progress with trajectories of change that would be expected if the client is likely to recover while in therapy, and (c) providing feedback to the therapist on the comparison between the client's progress and the expected trajectory.

First, progress and outcomes need to be routinely tracked for individual patients. Rather than simply relying on clinician judgment regarding patient change, it is important for the therapist to gather objective data from the patient. But why? Why can't clinicians just rely on their own judgment regarding patient progress and change? Unfortunately, research dating back to the 1950s has found that clinical judgment is not always accurate (Garb, 2005; Grove, Zald, Lebow, Snitz, & Nelson, 2000). Two studies demonstrate this observation for judgments about patient outcomes. In the first, Hannan et al. (2005) asked 48 clinicians from a university counseling center to make a prediction about eventual treatment outcome for 550 of their patients.

These therapists predicted deterioration for only three of the 550 patients, when in actuality 40 patients had deteriorated by the end of therapy (only one of whom was predicted to do so). In contrast, therapists predicted just over 500 of their patients to have a positive outcome, but only slightly more than 200 did. So not only did the therapists miss identifying the patients who got worse in therapy, they also missed the patients who failed to change by the end of treatment.

In the second study, Swift, Callahan, and Levine (2009) compared therapists' judgments regarding premature termination for their patients against actual patient change. At the end of therapy for 135 patients who were seen for treatment in a psychology department clinic, therapists were asked to label each of their patients as having either dropped out or completed treatment. Additionally, outcome scores were calculated for each patient to determine the level of progress that was actually made. As can be seen in Figure 10.1, the treating therapists classified 100 of the 135 patients as having dropped out (i.e., failed to make adequate progress by the end of treatment) and the remaining 35 as completers. In reality, as indicated by an outcome monitoring

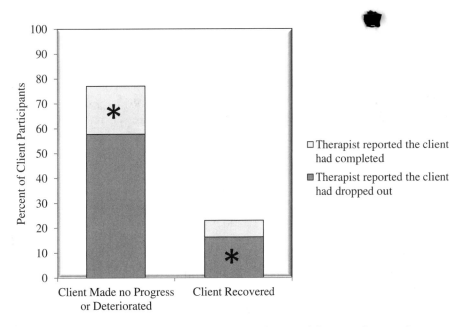

Figure 10.1. Comparison between therapists' judgment of dropout after termination and actual patient progress made during treatment. Marked portions indicate an error in therapist judgment. In the left bar, the marked portion indicates the percentage of clients who had made no progress or deteriorated but their therapists indicated that they had completed treatment. In the right bar, the marked portion indicates the percentage of clients who had made a clinically significant change but their therapists indicated that they had dropped out.

system, 104 patients failed to make adequate progress in therapy, and only 31 actually improved. Based on those numbers, therapist judgment does not sound too bad—the numbers seem to be pretty close. Even though the overall numbers are close, however, ratings of the individual patients were actually off. A closer inspection of the data reveals that 26 of the patients that the therapists said had completed therapy had either made no progress or had gotten worse. Additionally, 22 of the patients that the therapists said had dropped out of treatment had actually recovered from their previous levels of distress. The results from this study and the study conducted by Hannan and colleagues (2005) illustrate that therapists sometimes miss when some of their patients are improving, but, more important, they are not able to recognize when their patients are failing or getting worse.

Given that therapists are not always good predictors of patient progress and change, it is vital for clinicians to have some type of objective method for assessing when patients might be getting worse or at risk of dropping out of therapy. Of course, therapists can ask patients directly about their progress and their satisfaction with therapy. Although we are in favor of such an action, directly asking a patient this question may be limited in that he or she may be hesitant to report negative experiences or dissatisfaction to the therapist. Additionally, a global question of progress or satisfaction may not capture all of the nuances that accompany change or the many domains in which change can occur (e.g., well-being, symptoms, functioning). An alternative method for more objectively measuring patient progress and change is for patients to frequently complete self-report measures of symptoms, distress, and/or impairment. By having patients complete self-report measures normed on clinical and nonclinical populations, therapists can see how their patients' endorsement of symptoms, distress, and impairment matches up to others who do not have the same clinical complaints. Additionally, by having patients routinely complete these measures, we can see whether their symptoms, distress, and impairment improve over the course of therapy.

These two concepts (pre–post and norm comparisons) make up what is referred to in the treatment-outcome literature as *clinically significant change*. Clinically significant change is a concept introduced by Jacobson and Truax in 1991 as a statistical method for determining meaningful change for patients. For a patient to demonstrate clinically significant change, his or her end score on a norm-referenced measure should be closer to the average score of a nonclinical population than to the average score of a clinical population. Additionally, the amount of change a patient demonstrates on the measure should be large enough to represent a reliable change, as opposed to fluctuations due to error in the measurement instrument. This concept is illustrated in Figure 10.2. Take, for example, a hypothetical instrument that measures patient distress. As can be seen in Figure 10.2, the average score for

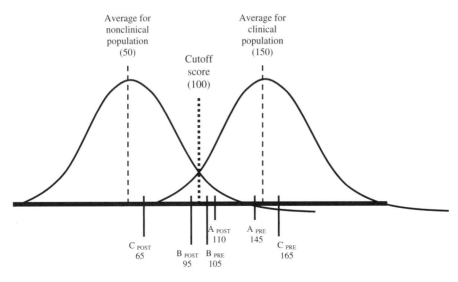

Figure 10.2. A hypothetical example of the construct of clinically significant change. For a client to demonstrate a clinically significant change, he or she would have to exhibit an improvement on a measure that is reliable (≥ 20 points on this hypothetical measure) and have a score that crosses over into the nonclinical range (< 100 on this hypothetical measure). Although Client A has made a reliable change, this client's score is still in the clinical range. Client B's posttherapy score is no longer in the clinical range, but the amount of change that was made was not reliable. In contrast, Client C's pre-to-post progress demonstrates a clinically significant change.

clinical populations on this instrument is 150, whereas the average score for nonclinical populations is 50. The midway point between these two averages is 100: If a patient scores less than 100, he or she resembles more closely an individual from a nonclinical population than an individual from a clinical population; if the patient scores more than 100, he or she should be associated more closely to with individuals from a clinical population rather than from a nonclinical population. Now, take three hypothetical patients (A, B, and C), all of whom start therapy with scores in the clinical range (145, 105, and 165, respectively). By the end of therapy, Patient A obtains a score of 110 on our hypothetical measure. Although this patient has improved, she has failed to make a clinically significant change because her score is still more similar to the clinical population than it is to the nonclinical one. By the end of therapy, Patient B obtains a score of 95. This score represents a move into the nonclinical population, but the amount of change is small (10 points) and may not be reliable compared with the error of measurement in the instrument. Patient C, in contrast, obtains an end score that falls in the nonclinical range (65), and the amount of change from the start to the end of therapy is reliable (100 points). Patient C would be determined to have made a clinically significant change. If Patient C had only decreased to an end score of 115, even though this is a reliable improvement (50 points), it is not clinically significant because it has not crossed into the nonclinical range (≤ 100).

Using routine measures of client progress as well as the construct of clinically significant change, therapists are able to tell more accurately when a client has recovered in therapy and when further treatment might be necessary. However, this information alone does not really help us reduce the number of our clients who drop out. Some type of early warning system is needed for when a client might be at risk for premature discontinuation or ending treatment with a negative therapy outcome. This brings us back to the second component of patient-focused research: a comparison between the client's progress and a trajectory of progress expected if the client is going to recover by the end of therapy. On the basis of either theory or empirical data from thousands of clients, various researchers have charted typical client session-by-session change for good prognosis—clients who start therapy at varying levels of disturbance on a given outcome measure. Although each client might be expected to change in his or her own way in his or her own given time, one might predict that if an individual client deviates too far in a negative direction from the trajectory than is typical, he or she might be more likely to drop out as a result of experiencing dissatisfaction with the lack of progress.

Figure 10.3 shows an example with two clients. Both clients started with a score of 150 on the hypothetical measure just discussed. On the basis of data from many other clients who have begun therapy with a similar start score, a trajectory of change over time can be plotted. In general, clients whose change follows this approximate trajectory end therapy having recovered and having made a clinically significant change. However, data from previous clients indicate that those whose patterns of change do not follow the trajectory are at an increased risk for dropping out and ending therapy without having recovered. In this example, both clients (A and B) have attended 12 sessions of therapy. Whereas Client A is right on track for eventually showing a clinically significant change, Client B is not and is probably experiencing some dissatisfaction with therapy. Clients who are dissatisfied and making little to no change are at high risk for dropping out of therapy prematurely. Given that little to no change has occurred, it may be difficult for such clients to see any benefits for continued attendance that would outweigh the associated costs.

In a study mentioned earlier in this chapter, Hannan and colleagues (2005) demonstrated that these types of trajectories can be very accurate. In making a prediction of treatment outcomes for 492 clients at a university counseling center, they found that one such empirical method accurately

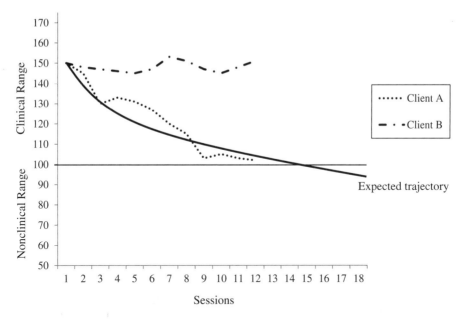

Figure 10.3. Plot comparing progress for two hypothetical clients to an expected trajectory. An example of patient profiling for a hypothetical measure where scores below 100 represent the nonclinical range and scores above 100 represent the clinical range. Based on data from successful clients who started treatment at a score of 150, an expected trajectory of progress over sessions has been plotted (solid black line). Client A's pattern of change closely follows the expected trajectory, and this client is likely to complete treatment successfully. In contrast, Client B's pattern of change deviates from the expected trajectory, and as a result, this client is likely to drop out of treatment with a high level of dissatisfaction.

guessed the treatment outcome for 83.1% of the clients. Remember, that outcome is compared with the much more modest accurate-prediction rate of approximately 50% via therapist judgment. Additionally, whereas therapists were only able to accurately predict 2.5% of those who had a negative treatment outcome, the particular empirical method that was tested predicted 100% of the clients who had gotten worse during therapy.

The third and final step of patient-focused research is to provide the therapist with feedback regarding his or her client's progress and how that progress compares with the expected trajectory that eventually leads to client recovery. Once given feedback, therapists have many options available to them. If the client is on track, the therapist can continue with the approach he or she has been taking. He or she can also talk to the client about what has been working in therapy and can make sure to do more of it. If the client is not on track, the therapist can also discuss this variance with the client and together develop a plan for what needs to be done in therapy to get the client to where he or she needs to be. For clients who are not on track to recover, not only will these types of discussions help solve problems that might be getting in the way of therapy, they will also show the client that the therapist cares and desires to work collaboratively to make sure change occurs. Clients will be less likely to prematurely discontinue treatment when they feel that the therapist cares and that changes are going to take place to better direct the treatment to address their needs.

EMPIRICAL RESEARCH

Although patient-focused research and the idea of providing therapists with client feedback are relatively new concepts for psychotherapy, they already have a large body of empirical support. In 2011, Lambert and Shimokawa conducted a meta-analysis examining the effects of collecting client feedback in therapy. In their meta-analysis, they examined results separately for two feedback systems: the Partners for Change Outcome Management System (PCOMS; Miller, Duncan, Sorrell, & Brown, 2005), which included data from three empirical studies comparing feedback and no feedback conditions; and the OQ outcomes questionnaires system (based on the Outcome Questionnaire—45; Lambert et al., 2004), which included data from six empirical studies comparing feedback and no feedback conditions. They had decided to examine the results separately because studies of the PCOMS included all clients (those who were making adequate progress and those who were not) in one group to determine the relationship between client feedback and treatment outcomes. In contrast, studies with the OQ system separated clients into groups based on whether their progress was on track, with the belief that feedback is of the most value for clients who are not making adequate progress and are thus at risk for prematurely terminating or ending therapy with a negative treatment outcome.

Overall, both sets of analyses found positive results in favor of the feedback groups. The aggregated effect size for the PCOMS ($k = 3$, $n = 558$) was $r = .23$. In addition to the general relationship between feedback and outcome, they found that those in the feedback group had 3.5 times higher odds of experiencing reliable change while in therapy and were half as likely to drop out of therapy in a deteriorated state. For the OQ system, data were reported for conditions in which the therapist was provided feedback, both the therapist and client were given feedback, and the therapist was given feedback on general outcome as well as feedback on the therapeutic alliance, social support, stressful life events, and motivation to change (together referred to as the Clinical Support Tools). When the therapist alone was provided feedback ($k = 4$, $n = 454$), the aggregated effect size was $r = .25$. Additionally, those in the feedback condition were 2.6 times as likely to experience reliable change and half as likely to deteriorate. The effects for feedback to the client and therapist ($k = 3$, $n = 495$) were almost identical: aggregated effect size was $r = .25$, approximately three times more likely to experience reliable change and about a third less likely to deteriorate. However, feedback on overall outcomes and using the Clinical Support Tools outperformed the other two groups in almost all areas. This higher level of feedback ($k = 3$, $n = 535$) resulted in an aggregate effect size of $r = .33$, and clients who were in the feedback condition were almost four times more likely to display a reliable change but only about one fourth as likely to drop out of therapy having deteriorated.

PUTTING IT INTO PRACTICE

Although many feedback systems exist, the three most commonly used are the Clinical Outcomes in Routine Evaluation (CORE; Mellor-Clark, Barkham, Connell, & Evans, 1999) system based on the CORE outcome measure (CORE–OM; Evans et al., 2000), the OQ system, and the PCOMS system. Each system uses a general outcome measure that is administered to patients on a session-by-session basis. Each system is also set up to provide therapists with visual feedback of patient progress toward clinically significant change. All three of the systems and the outcome measures that they include have also been well validated with adequate to excellent psychometric properties.

CORE System

The CORE system is the most widely used feedback system in the United Kingdom. The original outcome measure for the system, the CORE–OM, was developed by Michael Barkham and colleagues in the 1990s. The CORE–OM is a patient self-report questionnaire designed to be administered before and after an entire course of therapy. It includes 34 items that cover the three phase model domains (subjective well-being, symptoms, and life functioning) as well as an assessment of risk and harm. Each item on the measure is scored on a 5-point Likert-type scale ranging from 0 to 4, and a total score is calculated by averaging scores across all items. Thus, total scores also range from 0 to 4 with higher scores representing greater impairment. The clinical cutoff score for men on the measure is 1.19 and for women is 1.29. Barkham and colleagues (2001) reported that reliable change is indicated by a change of 0.48 points with one sample; however, they also indicate that calculations of reliable change are population-specific, and so reliable change calculated with one sample may not apply to another.

Given that the CORE–OM was designed to be administered before and after an entire course of therapy, this measure alone can only be used to determine a patient's outcome and the level of progress that has been made. However, two shorter versions of the main measure (one with 10 items and one with five items) have been developed for session-by-session monitoring of patient progress by therapists. Although these versions provide therapists with session-by-session feedback on how current patient impairment compares to pretherapy patient impairment and progress toward the nonclinical range, the CORE system is limited in that it does not include expected trajectories for patient progress, and so clinicians must guess whether their patients are on or off track to achieve clinically significant change in therapy.

In addition to the full CORE–OM and the two short versions, the CORE system comes with a number of tools to aid clinicians in their gathering of patient feedback. Some of these additional tools include the CORE progress tracking chart (provides clinicians with visual feedback of session-by-session patient progress), the Young Persons CORE (YP–CORE; for youth ages 11–16 years), CORE—Learning Disabilities (CORE–LD; tailored to adults with learning disabilities), and the Agnew Relationship Measure—5 (ARM–5; five-item measure of the therapeutic alliance). All of the CORE system measures and tools are available for download and use free of charge from http://www.coreims.co.uk. Paper versions can also be purchased in packs of 100 for a modest fee. A web-based CORE system has also been developed allowing patients to complete measures and therapists to view progress forms electronically.

OQ System

The OQ system is the most developed and well researched of the existing patient feedback systems. The main questionnaire for the system, the OQ–45.2, was originally developed by Michael J. Lambert and colleagues in the 1990s. The OQ–45.2 is a patient self-report questionnaire designed to be administered on a session-by-session basis. It includes 45 items that cover three domains: symptom distress, interpersonal functioning, and social role performance. Each item on the measure is scored on a 5-point Likert-type scale ranging from 0 to 4, and a total score is calculated by summing responses to all items. Total scores range from 0 to 180, with higher scores representing greater distress and impairment. The clinical cutoff score for the measure is 64, and a reliable change is signified by a change of 14 or more points. Patients are typically asked to complete the measure before the start of each therapy session.

One major advantage of the OQ system over the CORE system is the inclusion of patient trajectories and visual progress reports based on those trajectories. A line of expected progress can be plotted across sessions based on a patient's intake score on the measure. This line represents an average course of change from previous patients who started therapy at a similar level of distress but recovered from their impairment by the end of treatment. Thus, for each session, a therapist can compare his or her patient's observed OQ score with where it should be based on the average successful patient. At any given session, if a patient's observed score is worse than 68% of patients who started at a similar level of disturbance, then a yellow warning signal is provided; if the patient's observed score is worse than 95% of patients who started at a similar level of disturbance, then a red warning signal is provided. These warnings signal to the therapist that his or her patient is currently not on track to achieve clinically significant change by the end of therapy and is at risk of ending with a negative therapy outcome. Therapists can then use the feedback to make changes as appropriate to get their patients back on track.

The OQ system comes with a number of feedback tools. In addition to the full 45-item measure, briefer 10- and 30-item versions have been developed. Versions for children and adolescents, severely mentally ill populations, groups, and for postdeployment military personnel have also been developed. Additionally, within the OQ system the Clinical Support Tools have been developed for clients who signal as being off track. The Clinical Support Tools include questions assessing the therapeutic alliance, the client's motivation to change, the client's social support network, and the client's experience of recent stressful events. These additional items can provide therapists with more information about why a client may have signaled on the OQ-45.2 and ideas about which area might be most appropriate to address. Paper versions of the OQ are available for a minimal charge at http://www.oqmeasures.com. However, given the number of items, therapists may find it difficult to score the measure before a session and thus would not likely be able to calculate their clients' progress until after a session is over. This limits the utility of the paper measure given that changes would have to wait until the following session; however, off-track clients may have already dropped out of treatment by that point. In contrast, the web-based system for the OQ automatically calculates a client's score, charts the client's session-by-session progress, and identifies whether the client is on or off track to achieve clinically significant change in therapy.

PCOMS system

Compared with other feedback systems, the PCOMS system is relatively new but is quickly gaining popularity among practicing clinicians. The two main measures for the PCOMS system, the Session Rating Scale (SRS; Duncan et al., 2003) and the Outcome Rating Scale (ORS; Miller, Duncan,

Brown, Sparks, & Claud, 2003), were developed by Barry Duncan and Scott Miller at the turn of the century. Both measures were designed to be ultra-brief alternatives to existing measures of client change and the therapeutic alliance. The ORS includes just four self-report items in which clients are asked to rate their general well-being, personal well-being, interpersonal functioning, and social functioning. The measure is generally completed before the start of a session. Clients respond to each item by placing a hash mark on a line that measures 10 centimeters in length with marks to the left representing more impairment and marks to right representing higher levels of functioning. A total score for the measure (0–40) is obtained by totaling the number centimeters from the left to the client's hash mark for each item. The clinical cutoff score for the ORS is 25, and a reliable change is indicated by a change of 5 or more points. The SRS also includes just four client self-report items. The measure is completed at the end of each therapy session to assess how the preceding session went. Items include an assessment of the relationship, consensus on goals and topics of the session, consensus on the approach or method that was used, and an overall rating of the session. Similar to the ORS, clients respond to each item by placing a hash mark on a line that measures 10 centimeters in length with marks to the right representing a more positive session. The clinical cutoff score for the SRS is 35.

Similar to the OQ system, the OCS provides predictive trajectories and confidence intervals based on data from almost 100,000 clients. With the comparisons that are available, therapists are able to see how their clients' session-by-session scores match up with both previous successful and unsuccessful clients. If an individual client's scores look more similar to the average unsuccessful client, then his or her therapist can work with him or her to make necessary changes to the treatment.

In addition to the regular versions of the ORS and the SRS, a number of additional versions and formats are available. Both measures are available as child and young child scales. Additionally, a group version and a supervision version of the SRS have been developed. Paper versions are available for free download and use at http://www.scottdmiller.com/performance-metrics. Given the brevity of the measure and the ease with which a therapist could plot her or his clients' session-by-session change, the paper version seems to be a viable option. However, the paper version of the measure does not allow a comparison with the predictive trajectories. Fortunately, a web-based PCOMS system that plots clients' scores with trajectories is available.

Other Practice Recommendations

Although we highly recommend the use of one of the preceding feedback systems for reducing premature termination in psychotherapy, a few alternative or adjunctive recommendations can be made for assessing and discussing treatment progress with clients. First, therapists may choose to assess client outcomes with measures not included in the existing feedback systems. For example, a therapist who works primarily with clients who suffer from depression may want to use an instrument that focuses on depressive symptoms. Or a therapist who works in an agency that already has a routine measurement battery in place for clients may want to use the existing measures. Fortunately, therapists can calculate clinically significant change on any measure as long as they can find normative and reliability statistics for the measure, both of which are typically found in a measure's administration manual. Remember, clinically significant change is signified when a client's score is associated more closely with a nonclinical population than a clinical population and when there is an improvement that is reliable. A cutoff score for any measure can be calculated by finding the middle score between the average for clinical and nonclinical samples. The amount of change needed to be considered reliable can be found using Jacobson, Follette, and Revenstorf's (1984) and Jacobson and Truax's (1991) formula for the reliable change index:

$$RC = 1.96 \times \left(\sqrt{2\left[SD\sqrt{1 - r_{xx}} \right]^2} \right),$$

where SD is the population standard deviation for the measure and r_{xx} is the test–retest reliability of the instrument. By calculating the clinically significant change criteria for the measure that will be used, therapists will better be able to tell how their clients' session-by-session progress compares with a standard objective measurement of recovery. An online calculator for reliable change can be found at http://www.clintools.com/products/rcg/reliable_change_generator.html.

Whether or not a therapist decides to use an objective measurement of client change, we recommend that all therapists seek to discuss client feedback frequently with their clients. If outcome measures are used, therapists can refer to scores on the measure to start the discussion. If not, we would suggest that therapists simply start by asking clients how they think therapy is going. They can then further probe for specifics about what has been working well in treatment, recommendations from the client about changes that could be made, areas in the client's life that have improved, and areas that need further work. In general, clients may be hesitant to share feedback that they think might be critical. Thus, therapists should work hard to develop an atmosphere of trust and show that they value the client's honest and frank opinion.

CLINICAL EXAMPLES

This portion of a session with Emily came a little over midway through therapy. The therapist had been using an outcome tracking system, and for a while Emily's scores had been steadily improving. Still, the therapist was interested in getting Emily's opinion on how therapy had been going.

    Therapist: Before we end today I want to take a few minutes to talk about how therapy has been going. Your scores on the measure that you complete every week have been showing steady progress, but I wanted to ask how you feel you have been doing.

    Emily: You know, that measure is a funny thing. Most of the time as I go about my week, I don't really think that things are changing. But then, as I sit down to take that measure right before our session and I reflect on it a little bit, I do notice that I am answering the questions differently and that I really am getting better.

    Therapist: Funny how that works—taking the time to stop and think about it helps you realize how far you have come since when you first came in. Of the things that we have been doing in therapy, what do you think has been helpful in bringing about those changes?

    Emily: Well, just coming in and talking about things has helped me see things a little clearer. I think I understand a little more how the conflicts in my relationship with my boyfriend might be linked to some of those abuses that I experienced as a child and the thoughts about men that I have held on to ever since.

    Therapist: Uh huh . . .

    Emily: But it's not perfect yet . . . I still feel like I have a long way to go.

    Therapist: What do you think we can do in here to help you continue to progress and get to where you want to go?

    Emily: Well, I guess we should just keep on doing what we have been doing. It's been working so far, right?

    Therapist: Right, we can definitely keep going in this direction. If you could change anything about our work, though, is there anything that comes to mind?

    Emily: Maybe you can just keep me focused a little more. I know sometimes I don't talk about my past when I really should because I think it will just be painful. I know that I have complained about how difficult it is to talk about those things before, but now I think I am ready to be more focused. Maybe if you recognize that I am not talking about something, you can call me out on it.

Therapist: OK, so if I get the sense that you are avoiding something, I can bring that up. Anything else?

Emily: No, that's it. I really do think therapy has been going great. I appreciate all the help you've given me.

Five sessions into treatment with Robert, his therapist had noticed that his scores had gotten slightly worse over the course of therapy. Although Robert hadn't significantly deteriorated from where he started, the feedback system indicated a potential for treatment failure. Robert's therapist started the session by discussing his scores.

Therapist: I was hoping we could start our session today by discussing your scores on the measure that you have been completing every week. Is that OK with you?

Robert: Sure.

Therapist: When you first came in, your score on the measure was pretty high, indicating that you were experiencing a significant amount of distress. At the time, we talked some about what that score meant.

Robert: Right.

Therapist: (*showing Robert a graph of his scores over the past five sessions of therapy*) If we look here at this figure, it shows that your scores have actually gotten slightly worse as we have worked together, that you are experiencing a little more distress compared with when you first came in.

Robert: Oh, really? I guess that's probably right.

Therapist: As I look at these scores, I wonder if maybe therapy isn't on the right track. I know you have been working really hard at recognizing the errors in your thinking about social situations and trying to challenge your maladaptive thoughts, but I wonder if maybe we should be working on something else? Or if something that I am doing isn't quite right?

Robert: No, I think we are doing things right in here, and I think you are really helping me. I do like this cognitive restructuring stuff that we have been doing, and I think I am just getting the hang of it. You know, I think maybe my scores haven't been changing because of things that have been going on with my family. Not too long ago, I found out that my dad has cancer, and it is not looking good for him.

Therapist: I'm sorry to hear that. I can understand how that could be contributing to the distress that you have been experiencing. Maybe we want to spend some time talking about that a little bit today.

Robert: Thanks for offering. Actually, I would like to talk about it a little. But I am also hoping we can continue with the thought challenging that we have been working on today too. Like I said, I think that is going well, and I want to make sure I am getting it right and I keep up what I've been learning.

Therapist: Sounds good.

Although these examples differ in that Emily was making good progress and Robert was not, both therapists approached discussing treatment progress with their clients with the same goals in mind: (a) gaining an understanding of the client's view of how treatment has been going, (b) determining with the client the reasons for the progress or lack thereof, and (c) seeing whether there is anything different that could be done in therapy to further facilitate change. Having routinely administered an outcome questionnaire, both therapists had an idea of the amount of progress that their clients had made. With Emily, the conversation took place as a routine check in, and the timing of the discussion was less important given the improvements that she had made. Still, the therapist came away from the conversation with some ideas of how to better continue their work together. With Robert, the timing of the conversation was more critical. Robert had not been getting better and was at a high risk of dropping out because of the lack of progress. If the therapist had not been using a routine outcome measure, he might not have known that this type of conversation needed to take place with Robert. However, because they did talk about progress, the therapist was able to learn about an additional stressor that Robert had been facing, one that could have resulted in a shift of therapy goals and tasks.

CONCLUSION

Tracking client progress is an important strategy that can help therapists better recognize when their clients are not progressing as expected and thus are at an increased risk of dropping out. With the advance warning that can be had through outcome tracking systems, therapists can make the necessary changes to help their clients before it is too late. Although the idea is relatively new, outcome tracking already has a strong and established research base of support (Lambert & Shimokawa, 2011). In addition to just tracking outcomes, discussing treatment progress with clients allows therapists to gain an understanding of clients' opinions about why improvements have or have not been made and how to further facilitate change. Building on the recommendations presented in Chapter 9, these types of discussions are an additional way to demonstrate a collaborative working relationship with clients. By adequately preparing clients for treatment, continually enhancing their hope and motivation for change, and fostering a collaborative working relationship, therapists will be able to better reduce the occurrence of premature termination in their practice.

III

CONCLUSION

11

CONCLUSIONS AND FUTURE DIRECTIONS

If all economists were laid end to end, they'd never reach a conclusion.
—George Bernard Shaw

Patient dropout and premature termination is a significant problem in psychotherapy that all practitioners, whether trainees or experienced providers, face at some time or another during their career. Additionally, psychotherapy researchers, whether they study the effectiveness of psychotherapy in naturalistic settings or the efficacy of specific treatment approaches in controlled settings, also must concern themselves with methods for assisting their patients in completing a full course of treatment. As evidence shows, those who remain in therapy achieve better outcomes than those who drop out. The aim of this book has been to provide readers (practitioners, students, clinical supervisors, and researchers) with an in-depth understanding of why some patients choose to drop out, situations when dropout is more likely, and methods that have been empirically shown to work in reducing dropout. With this understanding, readers are better able to take steps to reduce the occurrence of premature discontinuation by their patients. In this chapter,

http://dx.doi.org/10.1037/14469-012
Premature Termination in Psychotherapy: Strategies for Engaging Clients and Improving Outcomes,
by J. K. Swift and R. P. Greenberg

we provide a brief review of some of the main concepts and findings presented in the previous sections of the book, discuss some potential strategies for reducing premature termination that have less empirical support than those already reviewed, and indicate some directions for future research on psychotherapy dropout.

DEFINING AND CONCEPTUALIZING
PREMATURE DISCONTINUATION

In Chapter 1, we defined *premature termination* as occurring when patients unilaterally (without approval or agreement from their therapists) decide to discontinue treatment before meeting their therapeutic goals. These goals could include gaining insight into a problem or showing a significant amount of improvement from the symptoms, functional impairment, and distress that led them to seek out treatment. Many methods for measuring premature termination exist (e.g., duration-based, missed appointment, failure to complete, therapist judgment), and although each has its strengths and weaknesses, we recommend an operationalization based on clinically significant change. According to this method, a patient has dropped out when he or she stops treatment and has failed to make a reliable and clinically significant improvement (reliable improvement alone could be used as a more lenient criteria) on an objective outcome (e.g., OQ–45.2) or symptom measure (e.g., Beck Depression Inventory—II). Practitioners and researchers may want to integrate this method of measurement with therapist judgment to fully capture the construct; however, we would not recommend that therapists use their judgment alone given the many errors and biases that are often involved in clinical judgments (Garb, 2005; Grove, Zald, Lebow, Snitz, & Nelson, 2000; Hannan et al., 2005; Hatchett & Park, 2003; Swift, Callahan, & Levine, 2009).

Although each premature terminator has her or his personalized reasons for dropping out of therapy, premature termination can be broadly conceptualized as being more likely to occur when the patient's perceived or anticipated costs associated with attendance in therapy outweigh the perceived or anticipated benefits. The potential benefits associated with attending therapy include things such as having someone who will listen in a nonjudgmental way, improvements in one's general sense of well-being, decreased symptoms, improvements in work or school performance, better social relationships, increased understanding of oneself, and so on. In contrast, the potential costs associated with engaging in therapy include having to face and talk about problems, the stigma associated with attending therapy, scheduling conflicts, therapy fees, and more. Strategies that will be most successful in reducing premature termination in therapy are those that decrease patients' perception and experience of therapy costs and increase their perception, experience, and anticipation of therapy benefits.

WHEN IS PREMATURE TERMINATION MOST LIKELY TO OCCUR?

In Chapter 2, we reported the results of a meta-analysis that sought to identify an average rate of premature termination of adult psychotherapy and identify the treatment, client, setting, and therapist variables associated with higher rates of treatment dropout. This meta-analysis included data from 669 studies and almost 84,000 clients. The average dropout rate across all studies was only 19.7%, with a 95% confidence interval of 18.7% to 20.7%. Although this rate is much lower than estimates made more than 2 decades ago (Wierzbicki & Pekarik, 1993), this average still indicates that one of every five clients is dropping out of psychotherapy prematurely. In further examining the dropout rates reported by individual studies, we noticed a significant amount of variance among them. Although many studies reported that less than 5% of their clients dropped out of therapy prematurely, other studies reported dropout rates higher than 70%. Statistical calculations did find a significant degree of heterogeneity in the rates that were reported, $Q(668) = 7694.74, p < .001, I^2 = 93.32$. This high degree of heterogeneity supports the need to more closely examine potential client, provider, treatment, and setting variables that may be able to predict when clients are more likely to discontinue treatment prematurely.

We found, from moderator and meta-regression analyses, that dropout rates did not differ based on client race or ethnicity, marital status, employment, or education level; therapist race or ethnicity, age, or gender; the type of orientation or approach used (cognitive–behavioral, integrative, psychodynamic, solution-focused, and supportive/client-centered), or whether an individual or group treatment was provided. In contrast, dropout rates did differ by a number of other client, provider, treatment, and setting variables. First, clients who had a personality disorder or eating disorder diagnosis were more likely to drop out of treatment than were clients who were seeking services for an anxiety, mood, or psychotic disorder. Younger clients were also found to be more likely than older clients to discontinue treatment prematurely. Second, although younger therapists did not have higher dropout rates compared with older therapists, trainee therapists experienced more premature termination by clients than did therapists who had already completed their training. Third, dropout rates were lower for manualized than nonmanualized treatments and for treatments that were time limited (regardless of what that time limit was) than for treatments without a prespecified time limit.

Last, efficacy studies (highly controlled settings) had lower dropout rates than effectiveness studies (naturalistic settings), and university-affiliated clinics (psychology department training clinics and university counseling centers) reported higher rates of premature termination than outpatient clinics affiliated with a hospital or medical school, private and public outpatient clinics, research/specialty clinics, and inpatient settings. A number of reasons for the higher dropout rates in these settings and situations could be hypothesized; however, perhaps it is more important simply to recognize that these are situations and settings in which there is an increased risk of premature termination by clients. By recognizing that the risk is elevated, providers will be able to more strategically use the dropout-reducing strategies that we have presented in this book.

EIGHT STRATEGIES FOR REDUCING PREMATURE TERMINATION IN PRACTICE

Although a number of possible strategies exist for reducing premature termination in practice, in this book we have reviewed eight strategies that have strong empirical and theoretical support. Given the high level of support for these strategies, we recommend that clinicians focus their dropout-reducing efforts on them first. To begin with, four of these strategies aim to reduce perceived and anticipated costs and increase perceived and anticipated benefits by adequately preparing clients for the psychotherapy endeavor: provide role induction, incorporate client preferences, plan for an appropriate termination, and provide education about patterns of change. Although many of these strategies would be appropriate at multiple times during therapy as the treatment process unfolds, these strategies are particularly recommended for the first couple of sessions. The remaining strategies (strengthen hope, enhance motivation, foster the therapeutic alliance, seek client feedback, with the addition of client preferences in the group as well) focus on reducing perceived and anticipated costs and increasing perceived and anticipated benefits by helping clients feel like a collaborative investor throughout the therapy process. Although some overlap in the strategies does exist, specific techniques for therapist action can be recommended for each. We now provide a brief summary of each technique.

Provide Role Induction

Patients are often unfamiliar with the therapy process and what is expected of them when they go in to meet with a therapist. Even patients who have had previous experience with therapy may not know exactly what to expect from a new provider or setting. Fear of the unknown and uncertainty about the proper process of therapy can translate into a significant cost that leads a patient to discontinue treatment prematurely. *Role induction*—the process of providing patients with some education about appropriate therapy behaviors—is one technique for addressing this type of cost. We believe that providing role induction to patients should include a discussion of three main domains: (a) the general behaviors of an ideal patient; (b) the general behaviors the patient can expect from the therapist; and (c) the specific nature, purpose, and behaviors associated with the particular treatment approach.

Incorporate Preferences Into the Treatment Decision-Making Process

With adequate role expectations in mind, clients are better prepared to express their preferences for treatment. Preferences include clients' hopes and desires for therapy and can include favoring particular modes of treatment to be used, the characteristics of the ideal therapist, and the roles and behaviors most appropriate for therapy. Preferences typically represent clients' beliefs about what conditions will most likely lead to treatment success for them. When therapists integrate their clients' preferences into the treatment decision-making process, clients can experience a benefit by perceiving that their therapist values their opinion and recognizes their wisdom and authority in making decisions about their own life. In contrast, when preferences are ignored, clients may view this as a cost and may choose to abandon treatment rather than stick with a therapy approach or therapist they do not believe in (little anticipated benefits). Therapists can seek to incorporate preferences by (a) sharing relevant information about treatment options with clients, (b) eliciting the preferences, and (c) collaboratively coming to a decision about the appropriate course of action. Even when preferences cannot, or should not, be accommodated, discussing them will at least help clients recognize the collaborative nature of the therapeutic relationship.

Assist in Planning for Appropriate Termination

Just as many patients experience uncertainty about appropriate therapy roles, many start therapy without an adequate understanding of the timing of and process for ending treatment. The majority of patients who come in for treatment have mistaken beliefs about how long treatment should last, with the majority believing five sessions or less will be more than adequate (Mueller & Pekarik, 2000; Pekarik, 1991; Pekarik & Wierzbicki, 1986; Swift & Callahan, 2008, 2011). Unfortunately, patients rarely attend more sessions than they originally state they expect to attend. Unrealistic duration expectations can often be addressed by simply providing clients with research-based information about more appropriate treatment durations (approximately 20 sessions are needed for 50% of clients to recover). Of course, the exact duration that is presented to clients can be based on a number of factors, such as client symptom severity, the goals of treatment, and the therapist's theoretical orientation. Even with appropriate duration expectations in mind, some patients may worry about how to bring up the topic of ending treatment without hurting their therapist's feelings. By simply talking about and planning for the end of therapy early on, patients are better able to commit to a full course of treatment and will better know how to end therapy when it is time. Additionally, therapists can help patients plan for thoughts of premature termination by informing them that these thoughts may arise and that it is best to meet with the therapist for at least one more session so that the thoughts can be discussed and an appropriate plan of action can be made.

Provide Education About Patterns of Change in Psychotherapy

Another area of uncertainty for many patients is the process of change that can be expected. Patients may be at an increased risk of prematurely terminating if they expect immediate and global changes and they mistake initial improvements as a complete recovery from all of their symptoms and problems, or if they expect linear progress but periods of setback or deterioration occur. As such, we recommend that patients be provided education on the phase model of psychotherapeutic change (Howard, Lueger, Maling, & Martinovich, 1993). According to the phase model, patients progress through three successive stages in therapy, beginning with remoralization (increased hope), followed by remediation (decreased symptoms), then rehabilitation (improved life functioning). In addition, when clients are provided with a warning about ups and downs early in therapy, they will be able to better recognize these minor setbacks for what they actually are—signs that they are doing difficult but meaningful work with their therapist. This type of information can also be incorporated into the presentation of role induction.

Strengthen Early Hope

Once clients are able to start psychotherapy off on the right foot, with appropriate expectations and with treatment decisions based on their preferences in place, therapists can work to strengthen their hopes for change. *Hope* in this context refers to clients' outcome expectations—the belief that the treatment and the therapist can help produce change. While some level of hope must be present for the client to call and schedule an initial meeting with a therapist, this initial hope must be nurtured for positive prognostic beliefs to remain. Therapists can work to build their clients' early hope in a number of ways. First, they can work to strengthen clients' broad beliefs in therapy and their more specific beliefs in the exact treatment approach to be used. To strengthen these beliefs, not only should therapists present a convincing treatment rationale, they may also choose to inform clients about the research demonstrating psychotherapy's effectiveness or recent findings from an empirical trial that established the efficacy of a certain approach (perhaps even information about what percentage of clients improved and recovered while receiving the treatment). Second, therapists should work to increase their clients' faith in them as therapists. This can be done by discussing one's training and experience in successfully working with a given population, displaying degrees and awards in the office, judiciously using psychological jargon, dressing in a professional and culturally appropriate way, and focusing on the similarities they have with their clients, to name a few. Third, therapists should work to raise their clients' self-efficacy beliefs. As mentioned earlier, integrating client preferences into the treatment decision-making process is one way to recognize and validate clients' authority and opinions. Therapists may also choose to point out how a client is well suited for a particular treatment or mention the client's strengths that increase his or her likelihood of success in therapy.

Enhance Motivation for Treatment

With a high level of hope in place, clients will be more motivated to engage in a full course of therapy. In addition to instilling hope, therapists can take a number of steps to increase their clients' motivation, which will in turn reduce the occurrence of premature termination of treatment. Therapists can best use motivation as a strategy to prevent premature termination by first assessing the stage of change that their clients are in, and then by using the techniques that are best suited to a client's readiness. In general, precontemplators and contemplators are usually at the highest risk of dropping out; however, clients in the preparation, action, and maintenance stages may still drop out if the therapist works a step behind them. Based on the suggestions of Norcross, Krebs, and Prochaska (2011), motivational interviewing techniques may be most appropriate for clients in the precontemplation and contemplation stages. In contrast, clients in the preparation stage need to be allowed to make choices regarding how their treatment and intervention plan should proceed. Finally, when working with clients who are in the action and maintenance stages, therapists should reinforce and provide encouragement for the progress that has been made.

Foster the Therapeutic Alliance

Fostering the therapeutic alliance is another important way therapists can work to increase client motivation and reduce premature termination in their practice. The *therapeutic alliance* is conceptualized as including agreement between the client and therapist on the therapeutic goals and tasks and the development of a bond. Many clients will view a strong therapeutic relationship in and of itself as a benefit of therapy that outweighs many costs associated with session attendance. In contrast, clients are not likely to stay in treatment long if they do not get along with their therapist or if their therapist says or does something—even unintentionally—that hurts them. To develop the therapeutic alliance, agreement on the therapeutic goals and tasks comes initially from working collaboratively with the client to make treatment decisions and, later, by checking in with the client to make sure the techniques being used still fit with her or his hopes and desires. Although clients differ in their specific expectations of the therapist, the therapeutic bond is often thought to be generally strengthened by the therapist's ability to show unconditional positive regard, accurate empathy, and genuineness. Given the importance of the therapeutic relationship in therapy, therapists may want to objectively measure clients' feelings about the relationship on a regular basis throughout therapy. In many cases, at some point in treatment, the client will indicate a rupture in the therapeutic alliance. In such situations, it is important for therapists to quickly and nondefensively work to repair the rupture by clarifying misunderstandings, validating clients' feelings and concerns, exploring why the rupture has occurred, and seeking to change behaviors to get the alliance back on track (Safran, Muran, & Eubanks-Carter, 2011).

Assess and Discuss Treatment Progress With Clients

Patients who are progressing in therapy are more likely to continue to attend due to the high level of perceived benefits. On the other hand, patients who make little progress (low perceived benefits) or who experience deterioration (patients may see this as perceived cost) are not likely to continue with treatment for long. Luckily, therapists can now use outcome and feedback systems to help identify patients who are likely to have a negative therapy outcome before they have dropped out of treatment. Some of the more popular outcome monitoring packages include the CORE, OQ, and PCOMS systems. Therapists can pair the use of one of these systems with informally checking in with patients about their perceptions of treatment progress on a regular basis. When patient progress is not on track or there is dissatisfaction with the amount of progress made, therapists can seek to change the emphasis in the techniques being used so they better fit the needs of the patient.

ADDITIONAL STRATEGIES

Each of the eight strategies for reducing premature termination that we discussed in Part II of this book has strong empirical or theoretical support for its use. However, there are also a number of other strategies that may be lacking empirical support at this time or that are simple enough that they can be presented in just a paragraph or two.

Appealing and Culturally Sensitive Office Space

As basic as it may be, the therapist's office space can play a role in patients' decisions to terminate therapy prematurely. Being located in a busy or traffic-laden part of town, having limited or expensive parking, being located on an upper floor without an elevator, and/or being located in an unsafe neighborhood may all be considered insignificant details but can still represent extra costs that may contribute to a patient's decision to drop out of therapy. Additionally, therapists' office décor can play a role in their patients' decisions to drop out. Patients may be less willing to return to an office with broken or dirty furniture, one that seems cluttered, or if they worry their privacy will not be maintained because of inadequate soundproofing between the rooms. Additionally, some office décor may be considered offensive by certain cultural groups. Although therapists should have the freedom to decorate their office in a way that is pleasing and meaningful to them, they should recognize that certain decoration choices may drive some patients away. Given that an office space can provide patients with an initial impression of a therapist, clinicians may want to make sure their office is decorated and set up in an appealing way.

Time From the Initial Call to the First Appointment

To increase the likelihood of attendance, it is also important for therapists to meet with their patients as soon as possible after they call to schedule an appointment. One study tracked the course of treatment for 57 individuals who had called in for an initial appointment in a training clinic setting (Swift, Whipple, & Sandberg, 2012)—specific interest was in identifying which variables could predict attendance at the initial appointment. This study found that both previous therapy experience and amount of time that patients had to wait from the initial phone call to the initial appointment significantly predicted who would show up for that appointment. Those with previous therapy experience were much more likely to attend, and for each day of wait from the initial phone call to the initial appointment, patients were 1.5 times less likely to show up. This result may have been observed because patients, especially those who are novices to therapy, frequently do not seek out help until their distress has become severe, they cannot identify other possible means for solving their problems on their own, and they are highly motivated to find a solution. Therapists who can meet with patients quickly after they call in capitalize on their patients' motivation for change and demonstrate to their patients that providing them with help is a priority.

Regular Appointment Times

Once clients have attended an initial appointment, therapists can reduce the likelihood of premature termination by helping them get into an attendance habit. Scheduling regular appointment times is a common practice for most therapists and clients, and in our experience, the clients who are the most hesitant about scheduling a recurring weekly appointment are the ones who are most likely to prematurely terminate. When clients are hesitant about scheduling a recurring appointment, therapists may want to further explore their resistances and make sure there are appointment options that can easily fit within their schedules.

Reminder and Missed-Appointment Calls

Amid the chaos that many clients experience in their lives, some will have difficulty keeping track of all of their appointments. Many professions (e.g., dentists, doctors, hairstylists) use reminder calls to confirm appointments a day in advance. Likewise, at the end of the day, therapists may choose to call their next day's appointments not only to remind clients of the session time but also to allow clients the opportunity to reschedule if needed and to discuss any attendance-related concerns over the phone. In their meta-analysis, Oldham, Kellett, Miles, and Sheeran (2012) found that clients who received such calls were significantly less likely to prematurely terminate from therapy compared with clients who did not receive a reminder ($d = 0.42$). In addition to serving as a reminder, the simple act of calling can also demonstrate to the client that the appointment is important to the therapist. Making reminder calls can be particularly useful for initial appointments or when a change in the routine scheduling has occurred. However, reminder calls may not be needed (and could potentially be found annoying by some clients) once a pattern of attendance has been demonstrated. Although some clinicians choose to make reminder calls on their own, these types of calls could also be made by an office secretary. In one review of the efficacy of reminder calls, Clough and Casey (2011) found that they were most effective when they were made by the therapist and when they were close to the appointment date.

Even with reminder calls and regular attendance among clients, appointments can be missed. After a missed appointment, a client may worry about having disappointed or angered the therapist and then drop out of treatment altogether to avoid the confrontation (seen by some clients as a significant cost that keeps them from coming back). Therapists can seek to ease their worries by initiating a call shortly after the missed appointment. This action gives the therapist the opportunity to show the client that he or she is not angry and to schedule another session.

Imagining Attendance

A few studies have found that rates of premature termination can be reduced by having clients imagine they will attend their sessions. In Oldham et al.'s (2012) meta-analysis they found a small but significant effect for this type of intervention ($d = 0.20$–0.26 depending on the type of imagination). Using this strategy involves simply asking clients to spend some time imagining that they are going to attend their therapy sessions. This can be done at the start of treatment during an intake appointment or at a later point if thoughts of premature termination should arise. We should caution that some clients may think it is silly to sit and actually imagine arriving at the clinic. Instead, this imagination can take the form of mentally stating to oneself, "Rather than dropping out, I will attend my next session to talk about my concerns with my therapist."

Appropriately Pacing Treatment

In Chapter 7, we discussed how helping patients make early improvements can strengthen their hope that therapy can bring about change. Indeed, the pacing of treatment can play an important role in patients' decisions to drop out of therapy. Therapists are sometimes eager to help free their patients from the symptoms they are experiencing; they may know a specific technique that is well suited for a set of symptoms and think the faster they can implement those techniques, the faster those symptoms will go away. We have noticed this pattern with trainees (who experience the highest rates of premature termination) in particular, who sometimes have trouble understanding why their patients will not fully engage in the manualized intervention they are trying to administer. From the phase model of psychotherapeutic change, we know that improvements in patients' general sense of well-being generally precede improvements in other areas such as decreased symptoms and increased life functioning. This conclusion would suggest that patients want to feel heard, understood, and safe before the therapist tries to jump in and fix things. Additionally, patients' initial motivation for change may not be at a stage that is ready for active strategies. Focusing on the common factors of listening in a nonjudgmental way, showing unconditional positive regard and empathy, being genuine, and showing warmth in the first few sessions can set the stage for symptom-specific techniques that may follow. Additionally, when therapists do start to focus on symptom-specific techniques, they may want to focus on areas that seem most amenable to change. For example, a therapist who always tries to start at the top of the exposure hierarchy when working on anxiety will probably notice more of his or her patients dropping out than those who start with easy exposures and work their way up. Early improvements in the amenable areas will help raise patients' hopes that further change is possible, and they will then have more strength to address the more difficult topics and problems. Moving too fast may be a particular concern for patients who have experienced a previous trauma. Patients who are forced to discuss their trauma too early may feel exposed, which could deter them from coming back in for another session. In general, to decrease rates of premature termination, we recommend therapists first focus on helping the patient feel safe and understood, then focus on the more amenable symptom and problem areas, and then follow the patients' cues before jumping in to the more difficult and painful topics.

LESSENING THE NEGATIVE IMPACT OF PREMATURE TERMINATION WHEN IT DOES OCCUR

Although the strategies that we have discussed in this book should reduce the occurrence of premature termination in psychotherapy practice, despite the therapist's best efforts, some clients may still choose to drop out. Even though this negative therapy event is still likely to occur on occasion, therapists can take steps to lessen its deleterious effects. First, many of the strategies that we have already presented in the book will help even those who choose to prematurely terminate (e.g., many of the strategies focused on building the client's sense of collaboration in the therapeutic process, such as preferences, the therapeutic alliance, discussions of treatment progress). Not only can these strategies help clients be more invested in treatment, their use also helps clients see themselves as capable of solving their own problems. Along these same lines, in Chapter 7, we suggested that therapists express their faith in their clients. Even if they do prematurely terminate, if clients have even a little more hope and faith in their own abilities, they will be better able to face their problems on their own.

Second, therapists can work to include some of the strategies that are typically saved for the termination sessions much earlier on in treatment. For example, during a termination session, many therapists ask clients what they found particularly useful (and not so useful) in leading to change. By doing this, therapists can then suggest ways that clients can include more of the useful techniques into their daily life outside of therapy. Therapists can do this much earlier as they get feedback from clients (Chapter 10), so that clients will have some tailored daily strategies in place should they end treatment early. Additionally, some therapists will help clients develop a specific plan for steps that can be taken to promote continued progress. Instead of waiting until the last session to develop such a plan, although it may not be as detailed or tailored, therapists can provide clients with suggestions of things they can regularly do on their own outside of treatment to promote change. Also, in the termination phase, many therapists process the therapeutic relationship and what it means to end that relationship. In Chapter 9, we suggested that therapists seek to process their relationships with clients often; even in these early discussions, therapists may want to ask clients how they will feel when treatment ends.

Third, therapists can seek to lessen the negative impacts of premature termination by ending on a good note. Premature terminators may often feel guilty for ending treatment early and may even wonder if they hurt their therapists' feelings. These client fears may be justified given that many therapists do feel frustrated when their clients prematurely terminate. Although it is important to help clients recognize the value of psychotherapy and the importance of following through with commitments, expressing frustrations to clients after they have ended treatment rarely results in positive outcomes. Sometimes these frustrations may come out in a phone conversation that occurs after a missed appointment or through a brief letter that simply states that the client's file will soon be closed. Instead, therapists may seek to make the last contact with a premature terminator a positive one. In a follow-up phone conversation or letter, therapists can mention how much they enjoyed working with the client and some of the clients strengths that were apparent in the time that they had together. Additionally, therapists can seek to recognize clients' needs to discontinue treatment but express that they would welcome the client back if he or she ever felt a desire for further work together. Obviously, some clients choose to drop out because of a lack of fit with the therapist. Therapists can help these clients by recognizing the lack of fit in a collegial way and then recommending other providers who might be a better fit for the clients' current needs.

Last, after a client prematurely terminates, therapists can seek to lessen the deleterious impacts they experience by spending time in self-reflection. When clients choose to drop out of therapy, therapists often blame themselves. They may ruminate over what they may have done wrong and may even start to question their efficacy as a therapist in general. Although self-reflection can be a good thing if it is focused on strategies for growth, if it is only focused on shortcomings, it can lead to demoralization, which in turn can lead to burn-out. It is important for therapists to remember that even the most seasoned professional is going to have some clients who end treatment prematurely. Additionally, while not ignoring possible ways to improve their skills and competencies, therapists can recognize that it is clients who choose to ter-minate prematurely. It may be of value to remember that a decision to do so does not always mean dissatisfaction; instead, clients may make this choice because of their own personality characteristics, their relationship patterns, outside stressors and demands that they are currently facing, or a lack of fit. Just because one, or even a few, clients choose to end treatment prematurely does not mean that the therapists will not be effective in helping other clients progress.

LIMITATIONS AND FUTURE DIRECTIONS IN RESEARCH ON PREMATURE TERMINATION

The research on premature termination in adult psychotherapy has made significant progress in identifying how many patients drop out of therapy; identifying which patients, therapists, settings, and treatments are associated with higher rates of dropout; and identifying specific techniques to help reduce the number of patients who choose to drop out of psychotherapy. However, a number of areas need further research attention.

First, it is essential that researchers of premature termination in psycho-therapy adopt a universal operationalization for the construct. Studies and reviews have repeatedly found that the numerous existing methods for assess-ing dropout do not converge in what they measure; a patient labeled as a premature terminator in one study using therapist judgment might be labeled as a completer in another study using a duration-based method. Duration-based methods, which identify patients as dropouts if they have failed to attend a certain number of sessions, are particularly prone to error, and we recommend discontinuation of their use. Although slightly less egregious, similar errors are made when operationalizations based on missed appoint-ments and failures to complete a protocol are used. Classifications of dropout based on therapist judgment have long been considered the gold standard method; however, therapist judgments are frequently biased. It is for these reasons that we strongly recommend the collective use of the operationaliza-tion we presented in Chapter 1 of this book: to base judgments of dropout and completion on reliable improvement or clinically significant change. This type of operationalization best matches how the construct is conceptualized and defined in the field. Clinicians may want to integrate their own judgment when making these classifications, but it is important that clinical judgment not be used alone given the numerous studies showing that mistakes are made with this method (Swift et al., 2009). Use of a common operationalization for premature termination across the field is essential to compare results from one study to the next.

Numerous studies examining patient variables associated with higher rates of premature termination from psychotherapy have recently been conducted. However, these studies have focused primarily on identifying the demographic variables that predict whether a patient will drop out. Although the findings from these studies are important, little research has sought to identify the patient attitudinal and personality characteristics (e.g., motivation, psychological insight) that are linked to premature termination as well as the therapeutic process variables (e.g., alliance ruptures, lack of treatment compliance) that predict its occurrence. It is important for future studies to focus more heavily on studying these variables given that the results will have more direct implications for the development of strategies to reduce premature termination in therapy.

Additionally, the research in the field has also largely been correlational with the focus on identifying the variables that are associated with therapy dropout, or case-control studies in which dropouts are compared with completers by analyzing a number of variables. Although this type of research does increase our understanding of the phenomena and its occurrence, the lack of experimental control does limit some of the conclusions that can be made. For example, a researcher could never randomly assign clients to either dropout or completer conditions. Thus, even though research has indicated that dropouts express more dissatisfaction and are less well-adjusted then those who complete treatment, we cannot be certain that additional sessions would have an impact. It is possible that those clients who drop out would be just as dissatisfied or less well-adjusted no matter how many sessions they attended. However, this issue would be difficult to test. One way to study this issue would be to examine the outcome results associated with the dropout-reducing strategies that have been discussed in this book. If a strategy (e.g., role induction) results in fewer dropouts than a control group and those who received that strategy also show more improvements in psychotherapy, one might infer that those clients who would have dropped out, but didn't because they received the strategy, made gains that were not seen in the control group. However, in this hypothetical situation, it is also possible that the strategy simply had a direct impact on treatment outcome for all clients, not just those who would have dropped out. Another possible way to examine this issue might be to randomly contact a group of dropouts and somehow entice them to resume their treatment. This would be a difficult task, but if it could be done, one could test whether those who were randomly assigned to return to treatment showed additional gains that were not present in those who were randomly assigned to remain a dropout.

Similarly, researchers can focus more attention on developing and testing strategies for reducing the number of clients who drop out of psychotherapy, and they may want to start with the eight strategies discussed in this book. Although each does have some theoretical or empirical support for its use, further research is needed to refine the procedures used to maximize their effectiveness. Recommendations for specific future research steps for each strategy can be found in the individual chapters. As researchers seek to develop new strategies for reducing premature termination, they may want to consider the conceptual model for the construct—that is, what strategies can practitioners use to decrease the perceived and anticipated costs associated with engaging in treatment and increase the perceived and anticipated benefits.

CONCLUSION

Premature termination is a negative therapy event that occurs frequently in psychotherapy. It occurs when clients perceive and anticipate more costs than benefits associated with attending therapy. Although it is the client who chooses to prematurely terminate, providers and clinical researchers do not have to simply stand by and watch them do so. On the basis of the literature that we have presented in this book, providers and researchers can better recognize the situations and settings (client, therapist, treatment, and setting variables) when premature termination is most likely to occur. Additionally, based on the practical, research-informed strategies herein, providers and researchers can actively take steps to reduce its occurrence. More than 50 years of research has clearly demonstrated that psychotherapy is a wonderfully effective treatment. Now, by using the strategies that we have recommended to reduce premature terminations, providers will be able to help more of their clients take full advantage of psychotherapy and thus maximize the effectiveness of their efforts.

REFERENCES

Acosta, F. X. (1980). Self-described reasons for premature termination of psycho-therapy by Mexican American, Black American, and Anglo-American clients. *Psychological Reports, 47,* 435–443. doi:10.2466/pr0.1980.47.2.435

Acosta, F. X., Evans, L. A., Yamamoto, J., & Wilcox, S. A. (1980). Helping minority and low-income psychotherapy clients "Tell It Like It Is." *The Journal of Bio-communication, 7,* 13–19.

Acosta, F. X., Yamamoto, J., Evans, L. A., & Skilbeck, W. M. (1983). Preparing low-income Hispanic, Black, and White clients for psychotherapy: Evalua-tion of a new orientation program. *Journal of Clinical Psychology, 39,* 872–877. doi:10.1002/1097-4679(198311)39:6<872::AID-JCLP2270390610>3.0.CO;2-X

Ahmed, M., & Westra, H. A. (2009). Impact of a treatment rationale on expectancy and engagement in cognitive behavioral therapy for social anxiety. *Cognitive Therapy and Research, 33,* 314–322. doi:10.1007/s10608-008-9182-1

American Psychological Association. (2002). Ethical principles of psychologists and code of conduct. *American Psychologist, 57,* 1060–1073. doi:10.1037/0003-066X.57.12.1060

American Psychological Association. (2006). Evidence-based practice in psychology. *American Psychologist, 61,* 271–285. doi:10.1037/0003-066X.61.4.271

American Psychological Association Publications and Communications Board Work-ing Group on Journal Article Reporting Standards. (2008). Reporting standards for research in psychology: Why do we need them? What might they be? *American Psychologist, 63,* 839–851. doi:10.1037/0003-066X.63.9.839

Arnkoff, D. B., Glass, C. R., & Shapiro, S. J. (2002). Expectations and preferences. In J. C. Norcross (Ed.), *Psychotherapy relationships that work* (pp. 335–356). New York, NY: Oxford University Press.

Aubuchon-Endsley, N. L., & Callahan, J. L. (2009). The hour of departure: Predicting attrition in the training clinic from role expectancies. *Training and Education in Professional Psychology, 3,* 120–126. doi:10.1037/a0014455

Bados, A., Balaguer, G., & Saldana, C. (2007). The efficacy of cognitive-behavioral therapy and the problem of drop-out. *Journal of Clinical Psychology, 63,* 585–592. doi:10.1002/jclp.20368

Baekeland, F., & Lundwall, L. (1975). Dropping out of treatment: A critical review. *Psychological Bulletin, 82,* 738–783. doi:10.1037/h0077132

Bakker, A., Spinhoven, P., Van Balkom, A. J. L. M., Vleugel, L., & Van Dyck, R. (2000). Cognitive therapy by allocation versus cognitive therapy by preference in the treatment of panic disorder. *Psychotherapy and Psychosomatics, 69,* 240–243. doi:10.1159/000012402

Baldwin, S. A., Berkeljon, A., Atkins, D. C., Olsen, J. A., & Nielsen, S. L. (2009). Rates of change in naturalistic psychotherapy: Contrasting dose–effect and good-enough level models of change. *Journal of Consulting and Clinical Psychology*, 77, 203–211. doi:10.1037/a0015235

Bandura, A. (1977). Self-efficacy: Toward a unifying theory of behavioral change. *Psychological Review*, 84, 191–215. doi:10.1037/0033-295X.84.2.191

Barkham, M., Connell, J., Stiles, W. B., Miles, J. N. V., Margison, F., Evans, C., & Mellor-Clark, J. (2006). Dose–effect relations and responsive regulation of treatment duration: The good enough level. *Journal of Consulting and Clinical Psychology*, 74, 160–167. doi:10.1037/0022-006X.74.1.160

Barkham, M., Margison, F., Leach, C., Lucock, M., Mellor-Clark, J., Evans, C., . . . McGrath, G. (2001). Service profiling and outcomes benchmarking using the CORE–OM: Toward practice-based evidence in psychological therapies. *Journal of Consulting and Clinical Psychology*, 69, 184–196. doi:10.1037/0022-006X.69.2.184

Barrett, M. S., Chua, W. J., Crits-Christoph, P., Gibbons, M. B., & Thompson, D. (2008). Early withdrawal from mental health treatment: Implications for psychotherapy practice. *Psychotherapy: Theory, Research, Practice, Training*, 45, 247–267. doi:10.1037/0033-3204.45.2.247

Baskin, T. W., Tierney, S. C., Minami, T., & Wampold, B. E. (2003). Establishing specificity in psychotherapy: A meta-analysis of structural equivalence of placebo controls. *Journal of Consulting and Clinical Psychology*, 71, 973–979. doi:10.1037/0022-006X.71.6.973

Beck, A. T., Steer, R. A., & Brown, G. K. (1996). *Manual for the Beck Depression Inventory—II*. San Antonio, TX: Psychological Corporation.

Bedi, N., Chilvers, C., Churchill, R., Dewey, M., Duggan, C., Fielding, K., . . . Williams, I. (2000). Assessing effectiveness of treatment of depression in primary care: Partially randomized preference trial. *The British Journal of Psychiatry*, 177, 312–318. doi:10.1192/bjp.177.4.312

Berg, A. L., Sandahl, C., & Clinton, D. (2008). The relationship of treatment preferences and experiences to outcome in generalized anxiety disorder. *Psychology and Psychotherapy: Theory, Research, and Practice*, 81, 247–259. doi:10.1348/147608308X297113

Bergin, A. E., & Garfield, S. L. (1994). *Handbook of psychotherapy and behavior change* (4th ed.). New York, NY: Wiley.

Berzins, J. I., Herron, E. W., & Seidman, E. (1971). Patients' role behaviors as seen by therapists: A factor-analytic study. *Psychotherapy: Theory, Research and Practice*, 8, 127–130. doi:10.1037/h0086638

Björk, T., Bjorck, C., Clinton, D., Sohlberg, S., & Norring, C. (2009). What happened to the ones who dropped out? Outcome in eating disorder clients who complete or prematurely terminate treatment. *European Eating Disorders Review*, 17, 109–119. doi:10.1002/erv.911

Bohart, A. C., & Wade, A. G. (2013). The client in psychotherapy. In M. J. Lambert (Ed.), *Bergin and Garfield's handbook of psychotherapy and behavior change* (6th ed., pp. 219–257). New York, NY: Wiley.

Bordin, E. S. (1979). The generalizability of the psychoanalytic concept of the working alliance. *Psychotherapy: Theory, Research and Practice, 16*, 252–260. doi:10.1037/h0085885

Borenstein, M., Hedges, L. V., Higgins, J. P. T., & Rothstein, H. R. (2005). *Comprehensive Meta-Analysis, Version 2*. Englewood, NJ: Biostat.

Borenstein, M., Hedges, L. V., Higgins, J. P. T., & Rothstein, H. R. (2009). *Introduction to meta-analysis*. Chichester, England: Wiley. doi:10.1002/9780470743386

Brehm, J. W. (1966). *A theory of psychological reactance*. Oxford, England: Academic Press.

Brogan, M. M., Prochaska, J. O., & Prochaska, J. M. (1999). Predicting termination and continuation status in psychotherapy using the transtheoretical model. *Psychotherapy: Theory, Research, Practice, Training, 36*, 105–113. doi:10.1037/h0087773

Buckner, J. D., Cromer, K. R., Merrill, K. A., Mallott, M. A., Schmidt, N. B., Lopez, C., . . . Joiner, T. E., Jr. (2009). Pretreatment intervention increases treatment outcomes for clients with anxiety disorders. *Cognitive Therapy and Research, 33*, 126–137. doi:10.1007/s10608-007-9154-x

Cahill, J., Barkham, M., Hardy, G., Rees, A., Shapiro, D. A., Stiles, W. B., & Macaskill, N. (2003). Outcomes of clients completing and not completing cognitive therapy for depression. *British Journal of Clinical Psychology, 42*, 133–143. doi:10.1348/014466503321903553

Callahan, J. L., Aubuchon-Endsley, N., Borja, S. E., & Swift, J. K. (2009). Pretreatment expectancies and premature termination in a training clinic environment. *Training and Education in Professional Psychology, 3*, 111–119. doi:10.1037/a0012901

Callahan, J. L., Swift, J. K., & Hynan, M. T. (2006). Test of the phase model of psychotherapy in a training clinic. *Psychological Services, 3*, 129–136. doi:10.1037/1541-1559.3.2.129

Carpenter, P. J., Del Gaudio, A. C., & Morrow, G. R. (1979). Dropouts and terminators from a community mental health center: Their use of other psychiatric services. *Psychiatric Quarterly, 51*, 271–279. doi:10.1007/BF01082830

Clough, B. A., & Casey, L. M. (2011). Technological adjuncts to increase adherence to therapy: A review. *Clinical Psychology Review, 31*, 697–710. doi:10.1016/j.cpr.2011.03.006

Constantino, M. J., Glass, C. R., Arnkoff, D. B., Ametrano, R. M., & Smith, J. Z. (2011). Expectations. In J. C. Norcross (Ed.), *Psychotherapy relationships that work* (2nd ed., pp. 354–376). New York, NY: Oxford University Press. doi:10.1093/acprof:oso/9780199737208.003.0018

Cooper, J. (2012). Cognitive dissonance theory. In P. A. M. Van Lange, A. W. Kruglanski, & E. T. Higgins (Eds.), *Handbook of theories of social psychology* (Vol. 1, pp. 377–397). Thousand Oaks, CA: Sage.

Cuijpers, P., van Straten, A., Schuurmans, J., van Oppen, P., Hollon, S. D., & Andersson, G. (2010). Psychotherapy for chronic major depression and dysthymia: A meta-analysis. *Clinical Psychology Review, 30,* 51–62. doi:10.1016/j.cpr.2009.09.003

Cuijpers, P., van Straten, A., Warmerdam, L., & Smits, N. (2008). Characteristics of effective psychological treatments of depression: A meta-regression analysis. *Psychotherapy Research, 18,* 225–236. doi:10.1080/10503300701442027

DeGeorge, J., Constantino, M. J., Greenberg, R. P., Swift, J. K., & Smith Hansen, L. (2013). Sex differences in college students' preferences for an ideal psychotherapist. *Professional Psychology: Research and Practice, 44,* 29–36. doi:10.1037/a0029299

DeLeon, P. H., Kenkel, M. B., Garcia-Shelton, L., & VandenBos, G. R. (2011). Psychotherapy, 1960 to the present. In J. C. Norcross, G. R. VandenBos, & D. K. Freedheim (Eds.), *History of psychotherapy: Continuity and change* (2nd ed., pp. 39–62). Washington, DC: American Psychological Association. doi:10.1037/12353-002

Devilly, G. J., & Borkovec, T. D. (2000). Psychometric properties of the credibility/expectancy questionnaire. *Journal of Behavior Therapy and Experimental Psychiatry, 31,* 73–86. doi:10.1016/S0005-7916(00)00012-4

Dewan, M. J., Steenbarger, B. N., & Greenberg, R. P. (Eds.). (2012). *The art and science of brief psychotherapies: An illustrated guide* (2nd ed.). Washington, DC: American Psychiatric Publishing.

DiClemente, C. C., & Hughes, S. O. (1990). Stages of change profiles in alcoholism treatment. *Journal of Substance Abuse, 2,* 217–235. doi:10.1016/S0899-3289(05)80057-4

Draycott, S., & Dabbs, A. (1998). Cognitive dissonance 1: An overview of the literature and its integration into theory and practice of clinical psychology. *British Journal of Clinical Psychology, 37,* 341–353. doi:10.1111/j.2044-8260.1998.tb01390.x

Duncan, B. L., Miller, S. D., Sparks, J. A., Claud, D. A., Reynolds, L. R., Brown, J., & Johnson, L. D. (2003). The Session Rating Scale: Preliminary psychometric properties of a "working" alliance measure. *Journal of Brief Therapy, 3,* 3–12. Retrieved from http://www.myoutcomes.com/documents/The_Session_Rating_Scale_Psychometric_Properties_of_a_Working_Alliance_Scale.pdf

Elkin, I. (1994). The NIMH Treatment of Depression Collaborative Research Program: Where we began and where we are. In A. E. Bergin & S. L. Garfield (Eds.), *Handbook of psychotherapy and behavior change* (4th ed., pp. 114–139). Oxford, England: Wiley.

Elkin, I., Yamaguchi, J. L., Arnkoff, D. B., Glass, C. R., Sotsky, S. M., & Krupnick, J. L. (1999). "Client–treatment fit" and early engagement in therapy. *Psychotherapy Research, 9,* 437–451. doi:10.1093/ptr/9.4.437

Ersner-Hershfield, S., Abramowitz, S. I., & Baren, J. (1979). Incentive effects of choosing a therapist. *Journal of Clinical Psychology, 35,* 404–406. doi: 10.1002/1097-4679(197904)35:2<404::AID-JCLP2270350235>3.0.CO;2-0

Evans, C., Mellor-Clark, J., Margison, F., Barkham, M., Audin, K., Connell, J., & McGrath, G. (2000). CORE: Clinical Outcomes in Routine Evaluation. *Journal of Mental Health, 9*, 247–255. doi:10.1080/713680250

Fadden, G., Bebbington, P., & Kuipers, L. (1987). The burden of care: The impact of functional psychiatric illness on the client's family. *The British Journal of Psychiatry, 150*, 285–292. doi:10.1192/bjp.150.3.285

Farber, B. A. (1983). Psychotherapists' perceptions of stressful client behavior. *Professional Psychology: Research and Practice, 14*, 697–705. doi:10.1037/0735-7028.14.5.697

Festinger, L. (1957). *A theory of cognitive dissonance.* Stanford, CA: Stanford University Press.

Fiedler, F. E. (1950a). A comparison of therapeutic relationships in psychoanalytic, nondirective and Adlerian therapy. *Journal of Consulting Psychology, 14*, 436–445. doi:10.1037/h0054624

Fiedler, F. E. (1950b). The concept of an ideal therapeutic relationship. *Journal of Consulting Psychology, 14*, 239–245. doi:10.1037/h0058122

Fischer, D. J., & Moyers, T. B. (2012). Motivational interviewing as a brief psychotherapy. In M. J. Dewan, B. N. Steenbarger, & R. P. Greenberg (Eds.), *The art and science of brief psychotherapy: An illustrated guide* (2nd ed., pp. 27–41). Washington, DC: American Psychiatric Publishing.

Fisher, S., & Greenberg, R. P. (Eds.). (1997). *From placebo to panacea: Putting psychiatric drugs to the test.* New York, NY: Wiley.

Foa, E. B., Hembree, E. A., Cahill, S. P., Rauch, S. A. M., Riggs, D. S., Feeny, N. C., & Yadin, E. (2005). Randomized trial of prolonged exposure for posttraumatic stress disorder with and without cognitive restructuring: Outcome at academic and community clinics. *Journal of Consulting and Clinical Psychology, 73*, 953–964. doi:10.1037/0022-006X.73.5.953

Frank, J. D., & Frank, J. B. (1991). *Persuasion and healing: A comparative study of psychotherapy* (3rd ed.). Baltimore, MD: Johns Hopkins University Press.

Frayn, D. H. (1992). Assessment factors associated with premature psychotherapy termination. *American Journal of Psychotherapy, 46*, 250–261.

Freud, S. (1912/1958). The dynamics of transference. In J. Strachey (Ed. & Trans.), *The standard edition of the complete psychological works of Sigmund Freud* (Vol. 12, pp. 99–108). London, England: Hogarth Press.

Freud, S. (1913). On the beginning of treatment: Further recommendations on the technique of psychoanalysis. In J. Strachey (Ed. & Trans.), *The standard edition of the complete psychological works of Sigmund Freud* (Vol. 12, pp. 122–144). London, England: Hogarth Press.

Fuller, T. C. (1988). The role of patient preference for treatment type in the modification of weight loss behavior. *Dissertation Abstracts International, 49*, 2932.

Garb, H. N. (2005). Clinical judgment and decision making. *Annual Review of Clinical Psychology, 1*, 67–89. doi:10.1146/annurev.clinpsy.1.102803.143810

Garfield, S. L. (1963). A note on clients' reasons for terminating therapy. *Psychological Reports, 13*, 38. doi:10.2466/pr0.1963.13.1.38

Garfield, S. L. (1994). Research on client variables in psychotherapy. In A. E. Bergin & S. L. Garfield (Eds.), *Bergin and Garfield's handbook of psychotherapy and behavior change* (4th ed., pp. 190–228). New York, NY: Wiley.

Greenberg, R. P. (1969). Effects of presession information on perception of the therapist and receptivity to influence in a psychotherapy analogue. *Journal of Consulting and Clinical Psychology, 33*, 425–429. doi:10.1037/h0027816

Greenberg, R. P. (1972). The influence of referral information upon the psychotherapeutic relationship. *Psychotherapy: Theory, Research and Practice, 2*, 213–215. doi:10.1037/h0086730

Greenberg, R. P. (2012). Essential ingredients for successful psychotherapy: Effect of common factors. In M. J. Dewan, B. N. Steenbarger, & R. P. Greenberg (Eds.), *The art and science of brief psychotherapies: An illustrated guide* (2nd ed., pp. 15–26). Washington, DC: American Psychiatric Publishing.

Greenberg, R. P., Constantino, M. J., & Bruce, N. (2006). Are client expectations still relevant for psychotherapy process and outcome? *Clinical Psychology Review, 26*, 657–678. doi:10.1016/j.cpr.2005.03.002

Greenberg, R. P., & Fisher, S. (1994). Suspended judgment. Seeing through the double-masked design: A commentary. *Controlled Clinical Trials, 15*, 244–246. doi:10.1016/0197-2456(94)90041-8

Greenberg, R. P., & Fisher, S. (1997). Mood-mending medicines: Probing drug, psychotherapy and placebo solutions. In S. Fisher & R. P. Greenberg (Eds.), *From placebo to panacea: Putting psychiatric drugs to the test* (pp. 115–172). New York, NY: Wiley.

Greenberg, R. P., & Goldman, E. D. (2009). Antidepressants, psychotherapy, or their combination: Weighing options for depression treatments. *Journal of Contemporary Psychotherapy, 39*, 83–91. doi:10.1007/s10879-008-9092-2

Greenberg, R. P., Goldstein, A. P., & Perry, M. A. (1970). The influence of referral information upon client perception in a psychotherapy analogue. *Journal of Nervous and Mental Disease, 150*, 31–36. doi:10.1097/00005053-197001000-00005

Greenberg, R. P., & Land, J. M. (1971). The influence of some hypnotist and subject variables on hypnotic susceptibility. *Journal of Consulting and Clinical Psychology, 37*, 111–115. doi:10.1037/h0031249

Greenberg, R. P., & Zeldow, P. B. (1980). Sex differences in preferences for an ideal therapist. *Journal of Personality Assessment, 44*, 474–478. doi:10.1207/s15327752jpa4405_5

Greenson, R. R. (1967). *The technique and practice of psychoanalysis* (Vol. 1). New York, NY: International Universities Press.

Grove, W. M., Zald, D. H., Lebow, B. S., Snitz, B. E., & Nelson, C. (2000). Clinical versus mechanical prediction: A meta-analysis. *Psychological Assessment, 12*, 19–30. doi:10.1037/1040-3590.12.1.19

Haase, M., Frommer, J., Franke, G., Hoffmann, T., Schulze-Muetzel, J., Jager, S., . . . Schmitz, N. (2008). From symptom relief to interpersonal change: Treatment outcome and effectiveness in inpatient psychotherapy. *Psychotherapy Research, 18*, 615–624. doi:10.1080/10503300802192158

Hannan, C., Lambert, M. J., Harmon, C., Nielsen, S. L., Smart, D. W., Shimokawa, K., & Sutton, S. W. (2005). A lab test and algorithms for identifying clients at risk for treatment failure. *Journal of Clinical Psychology, 61*, 155–163. doi:10.1002/jclp.20108

Hansen, N. B., Lambert, M. J., & Forman, E. M. (2002). The psychotherapy dose–response effect and its implications for treatment delivery services. *Clinical Psychology: Science and Practice, 9*, 329–343. doi:10.1093/clipsy.9.3.329

Hardy, G. E., Stiles, W. B., Barkham, M., & Startup, M. (1998). Therapist responsiveness to client interpersonal styles during time-limited treatments for depression. *Journal of Consulting and Clinical Psychology, 66*, 304–312. doi:10.1037/0022-006X.66.2.304

Hatcher, R. L., & Gillaspy, J. A. (2006). Development and validation of a revised short version of the Working Alliance Inventory. *Psychotherapy Research, 16*, 12–25. doi:10.1080/10503300500352500

Hatchett, G. T., & Park, H. L. (2003). Comparison of four operational definitions of premature termination. *Psychotherapy: Theory, Research, Practice, Training, 40*, 226–231. doi:10.1037/0033-3204.40.3.226

Hoehn-Saric, R., Frank, J. D., Imber, S. D., Nash, E. H., Stone, A. R., & Battle, C. C. (1964). Systematic preparation of patients for psychotherapy: I. Effects on therapy behavior and outcome. *Journal of Psychiatric Research, 2*, 267–281. doi:10.1016/0022-3956(64)90013-5

Horvath, A. O., Del Re, A. C., Fluckiger, C., & Symonds, D. (2011). Alliance in individual psychotherapy. In J. C. Norcross (Ed.), *Psychotherapy relationships that work* (2nd ed., pp. 25–69). New York, NY: Oxford University Press. doi:10.1093/acprof:oso/9780199737208.003.0002

Horvath, A. O., & Greenberg, L. S. (1989). Development and validation of the Working Alliance Inventory. *Journal of Counseling Psychology, 36*, 223–233. doi:10.1037/0022-0167.36.2.223

Horvath, P. (1990). Treatment expectancy as a function of the amount of information presented in therapeutic rationales. *Journal of Clinical Psychology, 46*, 636–642. doi:10.1002/1097-4679(199009)46:5<636::AID-JCLP2270460516>3.0.CO;2-U

Howard, K. I., Kopta, S. M., Krause, M. S., & Orlinsky, D. E. (1986). The dose–effect relationship in psychotherapy. *American Psychologist, 41*, 159–164. doi: 10.1037/0003-066X.41.2.159

Howard, K. I., Lueger, R. J., Maling, M. S., & Martinovich, Z. (1993). A phase model of psychotherapy outcome: Causal mediation of change. *Journal of Consulting and Clinical Psychology, 61*, 678–685. doi:10.1037/0022-006X.61.4.678

Howard, K. I., Moras, K., Brill, P. L., Martinovich, Z., & Lutz, W. (1996). Evaluation of psychotherapy: Efficacy, effectiveness, and patient progress. *American Psychologist, 51*, 1059–1064. doi:10.1037/0003-066X.51.10.1059

Hoyt, W. T. (1996). Antecedents and effects of perceived therapist credibility: A meta-analysis. *Journal of Counseling Psychology, 43*, 430–447. doi:10.1037/0022-0167.43.4.430

Iacoviello, B. M., McCarthy, K. S., Barrett, M. S., Rynn, M., Gallop, R., & Barber, J. P. (2007). Treatment preferences affect the therapeutic alliance: Implications for randomized controlled trials. *Journal of Consulting and Clinical Psychology, 75*, 194–198. doi:10.1037/0022-006X.75.1.194

Ilardi, S. S., & Craighead, W. E. (1994). The role of nonspecific factors in cognitive-behavior therapy for depression. *Clinical Psychology: Science and Practice, 1*, 138–156. doi:10.1111/j.1468-2850.1994.tb00016.x

Jacobson, N. S., Follette, W. C., & Resvenstorf, D. (1984). Psychotherapy outcome research: Methods for reporting variability and evaluating clinical significance. *Behavior Therapy, 15*, 336–352. doi:10.1016/S0005-7894(84)80002-7

Jacobson, N. S., & Truax, P. (1991). Clinical significance: A statistical approach to defining meaningful change in psychotherapy research. *Journal of Consulting and Clinical Psychology, 59*, 12–19. doi:10.1037/0022-006X.59.1.12

Kazantzis, N., & Deane, F. P. (1999). Psychologists' use of homework assignments in clinical practice. *Professional Psychology: Research and Practice, 30*, 581–585. doi:10.1037/0735-7028.30.6.581

Kazdin, A. E., & Krouse, R. (1983). The impact of variations in treatment rationales on expectancies for therapeutic change. *Behavior Therapy, 14*, 657–671. doi:10.1016/S0005-7894(83)80058-6

Kirsch, I., Moore, T. J., Scoboria, A., & Nicholls, S. S. (2002). The emperor's new drugs: An analysis of antidepressant medication data submitted to the U.S. Food and Drug Administration. *Prevention & Treatment, 5*, 23. doi:10.1037/1522-3736.5.1.523a

Klein, E. B., Stone, W. N., Hicks, M. W., & Pritchard, I. L. (2003). Understanding dropouts. *Journal of Mental Health Counseling, 25*, 89–100. Retrieved from http://amhca.metapress.com/link.asp?id=xhyreggxdcd0q4ny

Kludt, C. J., & Perlmuter, L. (1999). Effects of control and motivation on treatment outcome. *Journal of Psychoactive Drugs, 31*, 405–414. doi:10.1080/02791072.1999.10471770

Knox, S., Adrians, N., Everson, E., Hess, S., Hill, C., & Crook-Lyon, R. (2011). Clients' perspectives on therapy termination. *Psychotherapy Research, 21*, 154–167. doi:10.1080/10503307.2010.534509

Kocsis, J. H., Leon, A. C., Markowitz, J. C., Manber, R., Arnow, B., Klein, D. N., & Thase, M. E. (2009). Client preference as a moderator of outcome for chronic forms of major depressive disorder treated with nefazodone, cognitive behavioral analysis system of psychotherapy, or their combination. *Journal of Clinical Psychology, 70*, 354–361. doi:10.4088/JCP.08m04371

Kohut, H. (1984). Introspection, empathy, and semicircle of mental health. *Emotions & Behavior Monographs, 3*, 347–375.

Kokotovic, A. M., & Tracey, T. J. (1987). Premature termination at a university counseling center. *Journal of Counseling Psychology, 34*, 80–82. doi:10.1037/0022-0167.34.1.80

Lambert, M. J. (2001). Psychotherapy outcome and quality improvement: Introduction to the special section on client-focused research. *Journal of Consulting and Clinical Psychology, 69*, 147–149. doi:10.1037/0022-006X.69.2.147

Lambert, M. J. (2013). The efficacy and effectiveness of psychotherapy. In M. J. Lambert (Ed.), *Bergin and Garfield's handbook of psychotherapy and behavior change* (6th ed., 169–218). New York, NY: Wiley.

Lambert, M. J., Hansen, N. B., & Finch, A. E. (2001). Client-focused research: Using client outcome data to enhance treatment effects. *Journal of Consulting and Clinical Psychology, 69*, 159–172. doi:10.1037/0022-006X.69.2.159

Lambert, M. J., Morton, J. J., Hatfield, D., Harmon, C., Hamilton, S., Reid, R. C., . . . Burlingame, G. M. (2004). *Administration and scoring manual for the Outcome Questionnaire—45*. Salt Lake City, UT: OQ Measures.

Lambert, M. J., & Ogles, B. M. (2004). The efficacy and effectiveness of psychotherapy. In M. J. Lambert (Ed.), *Bergin and Garfield's handbook of psychotherapy and behavior change* (5th ed., pp. 139–193). New York, NY: Wiley.

Lambert, M. J., & Shimokawa, K. (2011). Collecting client feedback. In J. C. Norcross (Ed.), *Psychotherapy relationships that work* (2nd ed., pp. 203–223). New York, NY: Oxford University Press. doi:10.1093/acprof:oso/9780199737208.003.0010

Lampropoulos, G. K. (2010). Type of counseling termination and trainee therapist–client agreement about change. *Counselling Psychology Quarterly, 23*, 111–120. doi:10.1080/09515071003721552

Larimer, M. E., Palmer, R. S., & Marlatt, G. A. (1999). Relapse prevention: An overview of Marlatt's cognitive-behavioral model. *Alcohol Research & Health, 23*, 151–160. Retrieved from http://pubs.niaaa.nih.gov/publications/arh23-2/151-160.pdf

Lebow, J. (1982). Consumer satisfaction with mental health treatment. *Psychological Bulletin, 91*, 244–259. doi:10.1037/0033-2909.91.2.244

Leichsenring, F., & Rabung, S. (2008). Effectiveness of long-term psychodynamic psychotherapy: A meta-analysis. *JAMA, 300*, 1551–1565. doi:10.1001/jama.300.13.1551

Levensky, E. R. (2003). Motivational interviewing. In W. T. O'Donohue, J. E. Fisher, & S. C. Hayes (Eds.), *Cognitive behavior therapy: Applying empirically supported techniques in your practice* (pp. 252–260). Hoboken, NJ: Wiley.

Leykin, Y., DeRubeis, J., Gallop, R., Amsterdam, J. D., Shelton, R. C., & Hollon, S. D. (2007). The relation of patients' treatment preferences to outcome in a randomized clinical trial. *Behavior Therapy, 38*, 209–217. doi:10.1016/j.beth.2006.08.002

Lin, P., Campbell, D. G., Chaney, E. F., Liu, C. F., Heagerty, P., Felker, B. L., & Hedrick, S. C. (2005). The influence of client preference on depression treatment in primary care. *Annals of Behavioral Medicine, 30,* 164–173. doi:10.1207/s15324796abm3002_9

Lutz, W., Ehrlich, T., Rubel, J., Hallwachs, N., Rottger, M., Jorasz, C., . . . Tschitsaz-Stucki, A. (2013). The ups and downs of psychotherapy: Sudden gains and sudden losses identified with session reports. *Psychotherapy Research, 23,* 14–24. doi:10.1080/10503307.2012.693837

Macias, C., Barreira, P., Hargreaves, W., Bickman, L., Fisher, W., & Aronson, E. (2005). Impact of referral source and study applicants' preference for randomly assigned service on research enrollment, service engagement, and evaluative outcomes. *American Journal of Psychiatry, 162,* 781–787. doi:10.1176/appi.ajp.162.4.781

Manthei, R. J. (1995). A follow-up study of clients who fail to begin counseling or terminate after one session. *International Journal for the Advancement of Counseling, 18,* 115–128. doi:10.1007/BF01421563

Manthei, R. J., Vitalo, R. L., & Ivey, A. E. (1982). The effect of client choice of therapist on therapy outcome. *Community Mental Health Journal, 18,* 220–229. doi:10.1007/BF00754338

McKay, J. R., Alterman, A. I., McLellan, A. T., Boardman, C. R., Mulvaney, F. D., & O'Brien, C. P. (1998). Random versus nonrandom assignment in the evaluation of treatment for cocaine abusers. *Journal of Consulting and Clinical Psychology, 66,* 697–701. doi:10.1037/0022-006X.66.4.697

McKay, J. R., Alterman, A. I., McLellan, A. T., Snider, E. C., & O'Brien, C. P. (1995). Effect of random versus nonrandom assignment in a comparison of inpatient and day hospital rehabilitation for male alcoholics. *Journal of Consulting and Clinical Psychology, 63,* 70–78. doi:10.1037/0022-006X.63.1.70

Mellor-Clark, J., Barkham, M., Connell, J., & Evans, C. (1999). Practice-based evidence and standardized evaluation: Informing the design of the CORE system. *European Journal of Psychotherapy, Counselling and Health, 2,* 357–374. doi:10.1080/13642539908400818

Miller, M. R., & Rollnick, S. (2013). *Motivational interviewing: Helping people change* (3rd ed.). New York, NY: Guilford Press.

Miller, S. D., Duncan, B. L., Brown, J., Sparks, J. A., & Claud, D. A. (2003). The Outcome Rating Scale: A preliminary study of the reliability, validity, and feasibility of a brief visual analog measure. *Journal of Brief Therapy, 2,* 91–100. Retrieved from http://scottdmiller.com/wp-content/uploads/documents/OutcomeRatingScale-JBTv2n2.pdf

Miller, S. D., Duncan, B. L., Sorrell, R., & Brown, G. S. (2005). The Partners for Change Outcome Management System. *Journal of Clinical Psychology, 61,* 199–208. doi:10.1002/jclp.20111

Miller, W. R., & Rose, G. S. (2009). Toward a theory of motivational interviewing. *American Psychologist, 64,* 527–537. doi:10.1037/a0016830

Miller, W. R., & Tonigan, J. S. (1996). Assessing drinker's motivation for change: The Stages of Change Readiness and Treatment Eagerness Scale (SOCRATES). *Psychology of Addictive Behaviors, 10,* 81–89. doi:10.1037/0893-164X.10.2.81

Milton, S., Crino, R., Hunt, C., & Prosser, E. (2002). The effect of compliance-improving interventions on the cognitive-behavioural treatment of pathological gambling. *Journal of Gambling Studies, 18,* 207–229. doi:10.1023/A:1015580800028

Monks, G. M. (1996). A meta-analysis of role induction studies. *Dissertation Abstracts International: Section B. The Sciences and Engineering, 56,* 7051.

Mueller, M., & Pekarik, G. (2000). Treatment duration prediction: Client accuracy and its relationship to dropout, outcome, and satisfaction. *Psychotherapy: Theory, Research, Practice, Training, 37,* 117–123. doi:10.1037/h0087701

Muran, J. C., Safran, J. D., Gorman, B. S., Samstag, L. W., Eubanks-Carter, C., & Winston, A. (2009). The relationship of early alliance ruptures and their resolution to process and outcome in three time-limited psychotherapies for personality disorders. *Psychotherapy: Theory, Research, Practice, Training, 46,* 233–248. doi:10.1037/a0016085

Nock, M. K., & Kazdin, A. E. (2001). Parent expectancies for child therapy: Assessment and relation to participation in treatment. *Journal of Child and Family Studies, 10,* 155–180. doi:10.1023/A:1016699424731

Norberg, M. M., Wetterneck, C. T., Sass, D. A., & Kanter, J. W. (2011). Development and psychometric evaluation of the Milwaukee Psychotherapy Expectations Questionnaire. *Journal of Clinical Psychology, 67,* 574–590. doi:10.1002/jclp.20781

Norcross, J. C. (Ed.). (2011). *Psychotherapy relationships that work* (2nd ed.). New York, NY: Oxford University Press. doi:10.1093/acprof:oso/9780199737208.001.0001

Norcross, J. C., Krebs, P. M., & Prochaska, J. O. (2011). Stages of change. In J. C. Norcross (Ed.), *Psychotherapy relationships that work* (2nd ed., pp. 279–300). New York, NY: Oxford University Press. doi:10.1093/acprof:oso/9780199737208.003.0014

Norcross, J. C., & Lambert, M. J. (2011). Evidence-based therapy relationships. In J. C. Norcross (Ed.), *Psychotherapy relationships that work* (2nd ed., pp. 3–21). New York, NY: Oxford University Press. doi:10.1093/acprof:oso/9780199737208.003.0001

Ogrodniczuk, J. S., Joyce, A. S., & Piper, W. E. (2005). Strategies for reducing client-initiated premature termination in psychotherapy. *Harvard Review of Psychiatry, 13,* 57–70. doi:10.1080/10673220590956429

Oldham, M., Kellett, S., Miles, E., & Sheeran, P. (2012). Interventions to increase attendance at psychotherapy: A meta-analysis of randomized controlled trials. *Journal of Consulting and Clinical Psychology, 80,* 928–939. doi:10.1037/a0029630

Oliveau, D. C., Agras, W. S., Leitenberg, H., Moore, R. C., & Wright, D. E. (1969). Systematic desensitization, therapeutically oriented instructions and selective positive reinforcement. *Behaviour Research and Therapy, 7*, 27–33. doi:10.1016/ 0005-7967(69)90045-X

Orne, M. T., & Wender, P. H. (1968). Anticipatory socialization for psychotherapy: Method and rationale. *The American Journal of Psychiatry, 124*, 1202–1212.

Pai, S., & Kapur, R. L. (1982). Impact of treatment intervention on the relationship between dimensions of clinical psychopathology, social dysfunction and burden on the family of psychiatric clients. *Psychological Medicine, 12*, 651–658. doi:10.1017/S0033291700055756

Paul, G. L. (1967). Strategy of outcome research in psychotherapy. *Journal of Consulting Psychology, 31*, 109–118. doi:10.1037/h0024436

Pekarik, G. (1983). Follow-up adjustment of outpatient dropouts. *American Journal of Orthopsychiatry, 53*, 501–511. doi:10.1111/j.1939-0025.1983.tb03394.x

Pekarik, G. (1985). The effects of employing different termination classification criteria in dropout research. *Psychotherapy, 22*, 86–91. doi:10.1037/h0088531

Pekarik, G. (1991). Relationship of expected and actual treatment duration for adult and child clients. *Journal of Clinical Child Psychology, 20*, 121–125. doi:10.1207/ s15374424jccp2002_2

Pekarik, G. (1992a). Posttreatment adjustment of clients who drop out early vs. late in treatment. *Journal of Clinical Psychology, 48*, 379–387. doi:10.1002/1097-4679 (199205)48:3<379::AID-JCLP2270480317>3.0.CO;2-P

Pekarik, G. (1992b). Relationship of clients' reasons for dropping out of treatment to outcome and satisfaction. *Journal of Clinical Psychology, 48*, 91–98. doi:10.1002/1097-4679(199201)48:1<91::AID-JCLP2270480113>3.0.CO;2-W

Pekarik, G., & Wierzbicki, M. (1986). The relationship between clients' expected and actual treatment duration. *Psychotherapy: Theory, Research, Practice, Training, 23*, 532–534. doi:10.1037/h0085653

Perlis, R. H., Ostacher, M., Fava, M., Nierenberg, A. A., Sachs, G. S., & Rosenbaum, J. F. (2010). Assuring that double-blind is blind. *The American Journal of Psychiatry, 167*, 250–252. doi:10.1176/appi.ajp.2009.09060820

Piselli, A., Halgin, R. P., & MacEwan, G. H. (2011). What went wrong? Therapists' reflections on their role in premature termination. *Psychotherapy Research, 21*, 400–415. doi:10.1080/10503307.2011.573819

Prochaska, J. O., & DiClemente, C. C. (1983). Stages and processes of self-change of smoking: Toward an integrative model of change. *Journal of Consulting and Clinical Psychology, 51*, 390–395. doi:10.1037/0022-006X.51.3.390

Proctor, E. K., & Rosen, A. (1981). Expectations and preferences for counselor race and their relation to intermediate treatment outcomes. *Journal of Counseling Psychology, 28*, 40–46. doi:10.1037/0022-0167.28.1.40

Raue, P. J., Schulberg, H. C., Heo, M., Klimstra, S., & Bruce, M. L. (2009). Patients' depression treatment preferences and initiation, adherence, and outcome: A randomized primary care study. *Psychiatric Services, 60*, 337–343. doi:10.1176/ appi.ps.60.3.337

Reis, B. F., & Brown, L. G. (1999). Reducing psychotherapy dropouts: Maximizing perspective convergence in the psychotherapy dyad. *Psychotherapy: Theory, Research, Practice, Training, 36*, 123–136. doi:10.1037/h0087822

Reis, B. F., & Brown, L. G. (2006). Preventing therapy dropout in the real world: The clinical utility of videotape preparation and client estimate of treatment duration. *Professional Psychology: Research and Practice, 37*, 311–316. doi:10.1037/0735-7028.37.3.311

Renjilian, D. A., Nezu, A. M., Shermer, R. L., Perri, M. G., McKelvey, W. G., & Anton, S. D. (2001). Individual versus group therapy for obesity: Effects of matching participants to their treatment preferences. *Journal of Consulting and Clinical Psychology, 69*, 717–721. doi:10.1037/0022-006X.69.4.717

Resick, P. A., Nishith, P., Weaver, T. L., Astin, M. C., & Feuer, C. A. (2002). A comparison of cognitive-processing therapy with prolonged exposure and a waiting condition for the treatment of chronic posttraumatic stress disorder in female rape victims. *Journal of Consulting and Clinical Psychology, 70*, 867–879. doi:10.1037/0022-006X.70.4.867

Rhodes, R. H., Hill, C. E., Thompson, B. J., & Elliot, R. (1994). Client retrospective recall of resolved and unresolved misunderstanding events. *Journal of Counseling Psychology, 41*, 473–483. doi:10.1037/0022-0167.41.4.473

Rickers-Ovsiankina, M. A., Geller, J. D., Berzins, J. I., & Rogers, G. W. (1971). Patients' role-expectancies in psychotherapy: A theoretical and measurement approach. *Psychotherapy: Theory, Research and Practice, 8*, 124–126. doi:10.1037/h0086637

Rief, W., Nestoriuc, Y., Weiss, S., Welzel, E., Barsky, A. J., & Hofmann, S. G. (2009). Meta-analysis of the placebo response in antidepressant trials. *Journal of Affective Disorders, 118*, 1–8. doi:10.1016/j.jad.2009.01.029

Rogers, C. R. (1957). The necessary and sufficient conditions of therapeutic personality change. *Journal of Consulting Psychology, 21*, 95–103. doi:10.1037/h0045357

Rokke, P. D., Tomhave, J. A., & Jocic, Z. (1999). The role of client choice and target selection in self-management therapy for depression in older adults. *Psychology and Aging, 14*, 155–169. doi:10.1037/0882-7974.14.1.155

Rose, J. P., Geers, A. L., Rasinski, H. M., & Fowler, S. L. (2012). Choice and placebo expectation effects in the context of pain analgesia. *Journal of Behavioral Medicine, 35*, 462–470. doi:10.1007/s10865-011-9374-0

Rosenzweig, S. (1936). Some implicit common factors in diverse methods of psychotherapy. *American Journal of Orthopsychiatry, 6*, 412–415. doi:10.1111/j.1939-0025.1936.tb05248.x

Roth, A., & Fonagy, P. (2004). *What works for whom?: A critical review of psychotherapy research* (2nd ed.). New York, NY: Guilford Press.

Royal College of Psychiatrists. (2011). *National Audit of Psychological Therapies for Anxiety and Depression. National Report 2011*. Retrieved from http://www.rcpsych.ac.uk/pdf/NAPT%202011%20Report%20.pdf

Safran, J. D., Muran, J. C., & Eubanks-Carter, C. (2011). Repairing alliance ruptures. In J. C. Norcross (Ed.), *Psychotherapy relationships that work* (2nd ed., pp. 224–238). New York, NY: Oxford University Press. doi:10.1093/acprof:oso/9780199737208.003.0011

Sandell, R., Alfredsson, E., Berg, M., Crafoord, K., Lagerlof, A., Arkel, I., . . . Rugolska, A. (1993). Clinical significance of outcome in long-term follow-up of borderline clients at a day hospital. *Acta Psychiatrica Scandinavica, 87,* 405–413. doi:10.1111/j.1600-0447.1993.tb03396.x

Scamardo, M., Bobele, M., & Biever, J. L. (2004). A new perspective on client dropouts. *Journal of Systemic Therapies, 23,* 27–38. doi:10.1521/jsyt.23.2.27.36639

Scheel, M. J., Hanson, W. E., & Razzhavaikina, T. I. (2004). The process of recommending homework in psychotherapy: A review of therapist delivery methods, client acceptability, and factors that affect compliance. *Psychotherapy: Theory, Research, Practice, Training, 41,* 38–55. doi:10.1037/0033-3204.41.1.38

Shapiro, A. K., & Shapiro, E. (1997). *The powerful placebo: From ancient priest to modern physician.* Baltimore, MD: Johns Hopkins University Press.

Sharf, J., Primavera, L. H., & Diener, M. J. (2010). Dropout and therapeutic alliance: A meta-analysis of adult individual psychotherapy. *Psychotherapy: Theory, Research, Practice, Training, 47,* 637–645. doi:10.1037/a0021175

Shedler, J. (2010). The efficacy of psychodynamic psychotherapy. *American Psychologist, 65,* 98–109. doi:10.1037/a0018378

Sheeran, P., Aubrey, R., & Kellett, S. (2007). Increasing attendance for psychotherapy: Implementation intentions and the self-regulation of attendance-related negative affect. *Journal of Consulting and Clinical Psychology, 75,* 853–863. doi:10.1037/0022-006X.75.6.853

Sherman, R., & Anderson, C. A. (1987). Decreasing premature termination from psychotherapy. *Journal of Social and Clinical Psychology, 5,* 298–312. doi:10.1521/jscp.1987.5.3.298

Snyder, C. R. (1995). Conceptualizing, measuring, and nurturing hope. *Journal of Counseling & Development, 73,* 355–360. doi:10.1002/j.1556-6676.1995.tb01764.x

Sterling, R. C., Gottheil, E., Glassman, S. D., Weinstein, S. P., & Serota, R. D. (1997). Patient treatment choice and compliance: Data from a substance abuse treatment program. *The American Journal on Addictions, 6,* 168–176. doi:10.3109/10550499709137028

Stiles, W. B., Honos-Webb, L., & Surko, M. (1998). Responsiveness in psychotherapy. *Clinical Psychology: Science and Practice, 5,* 439–458. doi:10.1111/j.1468-2850.1998.tb00166.x

Strassle, C. G., Borckardt, J. J., Handler, L., & Nash, M. (2011). Video-tape role induction for psychotherapy: Moving forward. *Psychotherapy, 48,* 170–178. doi:10.1037/a0022702

Strong, S. R. (1968). Counseling: An interpersonal influence process. *Journal of Counseling Psychology, 15,* 215–224. doi:10.1037/h0020229

Stulz, N., & Lutz, W. (2007). Multidimensional patterns of change in outpatient psychotherapy: The phase model revisited. *Journal of Clinical Psychology, 63,* 817–833. doi:10.1002/jclp.20397

Swift, J., & Callahan, J. (2008). A delay-discounting measure of great expectations and the effectiveness of psychotherapy. *Professional Psychology: Research and Practice, 39,* 581–588. doi:10.1037/0735-7028.39.6.581

Swift, J., & Callahan, J. (2009). Early psychotherapy processes: An examination of client and trainee clinician perspective convergence. *Clinical Psychology & Psychotherapy, 16,* 228–236. doi:10.1002/cpp.617

Swift, J. K., & Callahan, J. L. (2010). A comparison of client preferences for intervention empirical support versus common therapy variables. *Journal of Clinical Psychology, 66,* 1217–1231. doi:10.1002/jclp.20720

Swift, J. K., & Callahan, J. L. (2011). Decreasing treatment dropout by addressing expectations for treatment length. *Psychotherapy Research, 21,* 193–200. doi:10.1080/10503307.2010.541294

Swift, J. K., & Callahan, J. L. (2013, August). *Preferences for therapist ethnicity, multicultural competence, and culturally adapted Treatments.* Paper presented at the 2013 Annual Convention of the American Psychological Association, Honolulu, HI.

Swift, J. K., Callahan, J. L., Ivanovic, M., & Kominiak, N. (2013). Further examination of the psychotherapy preference effect: A meta-regression analysis. *Journal of Psychotherapy Integration, 23,* 134–145. doi:10.1037/a0031423

Swift, J. K., Callahan, J. L., & Levine, J. C. (2009). Using clinically significant change to identify premature termination. *Psychotherapy: Theory, Research, Practice, Training, 46,* 328–335. doi:10.1037/a0017003

Swift, J. K., Callahan, J. L., & Vollmer, B. M. (2011). Preferences. In J. C. Norcross (Ed.), *Psychotherapy relationships that work* (2nd ed., pp. 301–315). New York, NY: Oxford University Press. doi:10.1093/acprof:oso/9780199737208.003.0015

Swift, J. K., & Greenberg, R. P. (2012). Premature discontinuation in adult psychotherapy: A meta-analysis. *Journal of Consulting and Clinical Psychology, 80,* 547–559. doi:10.1037/a0028226

Swift, J. K., Greenberg, R. P., Whipple, J. L., & Kominiak, N. (2012). Practice recommendations for reducing premature termination in therapy. *Professional Psychology: Research and Practice, 43,* 379–387. doi:10.1037/a0028291

Swift, J. K., Whipple, J. L., & Sandberg, P. (2012). A prediction of initial appointment attendance and initial outcome expectations. *Psychotherapy, 49,* 549–556. doi:10.1037/a0029441

Taft, C. T., Murphy, C. M., Elliott, J. D., & Morrel, T. M. (2001). Attendance-enhancing procedures in group counseling for domestic abusers. *Journal of Counseling Psychology, 48,* 51–60. doi:10.1037/0022-0167.48.1.51

Task Force on Promotion and Dissemination of Psychological Procedures. (1995). Training in and dissemination of empirically validated treatments: Report and recommendations. *Clinical Psychologist, 48*, 3–23.

Thunnissen, M., Remans, Y., & Trijsburg, W. (2006). Premature termination of short-term inpatient psychotherapy: Client's perspectives on causes and effects. *Therapeutic Communities, 27*, 265–273.

Tryon, G. S., Blackwell, S. C., & Hammel, E. F. (2007). A meta-analytic examination of client-therapist perspectives of the working alliance. *Psychotherapy Research, 17*, 629–642. doi:10.1080/10503300701320611

Tryon, G. S., & Winograd, G. (2011). Goal consensus and collaboration. In J. C. Norcross (Ed.), *Psychotherapy relationships that work* (2nd ed., pp. 153–167). New York, NY: Oxford University Press. doi:10.1093/acprof:oso/9780199737208. 003.0007

Van, H. L., Dekker, J., Koelen, J., Kool, S., Aalst, G. V., Hendriksen, M., . . . Schoevers, R. (2009). Patient preference compared with random allocation in short-term psychodynamic supportive psychotherapy with indicated addition of pharmacotherapy for depression. *Psychotherapy Research, 19*, 205–212. doi:10.1080/10503300802702097

Vollmer, B., Grote, J., Lange, R., & Walker, C. (2009). A therapy preferences interview: Empowering clients by offering choices. *Psychotherapy Bulletin, 44*, 33–37. Retrieved from http://www.divisionofpsychotherapy.org/publications/ psychotherapy-bulletin

Walsh, B. T., Seidman, S. N., Sysko, R., & Gould, M. (2002). Placebo response in studies of major depression: Variable, substantial, and growing. *JAMA, 287*, 1840–1847. doi:10.1001/jama.287.14.1840

Wampold, B. E. (2001). *The great psychotherapy debate: Models, methods, and findings*. Mahwah, NJ: Erlbaum.

Wampold, B. E., Minami, T., Tierney, S. C., Baskin, T. W., & Bhati, K. S. (2005). The placebo is powerful: Estimating placebo effects in medicine and psychotherapy from randomized clinical trials. *Journal of Clinical Psychology, 61*, 835–854. doi:10.1002/jclp.20129

Warren, N. C., & Rice, L. N. (1972). Structure and stabilizing of psychotherapy for low-prognosis clients. *Journal of Consulting and Clinical Psychology, 39*, 173–181. doi:10.1037/h0033430

Weaver, J. F. (1998). Treatment credibility and the outcome of psychotherapy. *Dissertation Abstracts International: Section B. The Sciences and Engineering, 58*(8-B), 4478.

Westra, H. A., & Dozois, D. J. A. (2006). Preparing clients for cognitive behavioral therapy: A randomized pilot study of motivational interviewing for anxiety. *Cognitive Therapy and Research, 30*, 481–498. doi:10.1007/s10608-006-9016-y

Wierzbicki, M., & Pekarik, G. (1993). A meta-analysis of psychotherapy dropout. *Professional Psychology: Research and Practice, 24*, 190–195. doi:10.1037/0735-7028.24.2.190

Winefield, H. R., & Harvey, E. J. (1994). Needs of family caregivers in chronic schizophrenia. *Schizophrenia Bulletin, 20*, 557–566. doi:10.1093/schbul/20.3.557

World Health Organization. (2001). *The world health report 2001—Mental health: New understanding, new hope*. Retrieved from http://www.who.int/whr/2001/en

Zane, N., Hall, G. C., Sue, S., Young, K., & Nunez, J. (2004). Research on psychotherapy with culturally diverse populations. In M. J. Lambert (Ed.), *Bergin and Garfield's handbook of psychotherapy and behavior change* (5th ed., pp. 767–804). New York, NY: Wiley.

Zanjani, F., Bush, H., & Oslin, D. (2010). Telephone-based psychiatric referral-care management intervention health outcomes. *Telemedicine and e-Health, 16*, 543–550. doi:10.1089/tmj.2009.0139

Zetzel, E. R. (1956). Current concepts of transference. *The International Journal of Psychoanalysis, 37*, 369–376.

Zlotnick, C., Elkin, I., & Shea, M. T. (1998). Does the gender of a patient or the gender of a therapist affect the treatment of patients with major depression? *Journal of Consulting and Clinical Psychology, 66*, 655–659. doi:10.1037/0022-006X.66.4.655

INDEX

and therapeutic alliance, 140
variables affecting, 171–172, 183
Dropouts
    definitions of, in Swift and Green-
        berg's meta-analysis, 42,
        57–58
    and dissatisfaction with treatment,
        14, 28–29, 183
    motivation of, 129
    reasons for termination given by,
        28–29
    treatment outcomes for, 14–15
Duration-based measurements, 18–20,
        23, 24, 26–27, 182
Duration expectations, 94–96, 173–174

"East Coker" (Eliot), 93
Eating disorders
    and premature termination, 171
    in Swift and Greenberg's meta-
        analysis, 45
    and treatment orientation, 51, 52, 55
Education level of clients, 34, 35, 37,
        41, 46, 47
Effect sizes, 43
Efficacy-type studies, 58–59, 172
Eliot, T. S., 93
Elliott, J. D., 130
Employment status, 41, 46, 47
Ethnicity, 28, 34, 35, 37, 46, 47
Eubanks-Carter, C., 139
Evans, L. A., 72
Expectations
    duration, 94–96, 173–174
    hope and outcome. See Hope and
        outcome expectations
    positive-outcome, 114
    role. See Role expectations
Experience level of providers
    and pacing of treatments, 179
    and premature termination, 171
    in Swift and Greenberg's meta-
        analysis, 42, 56–57
    therapist characteristics vs., 141–142
    and treatment settings, 50
Exposure
    and appropriate pacing of treatments,
        180
    for treating PTSD, 55
External difficulties, 28, 29

Failure to complete measurements,
        19–21, 182
Farber, B. A., 16
Feedback
    from clients, about progress, 161
    improving therapy with, 149
    provided to therapists, 155–156
    and reliable change, 156–157
Finch, A. E., 100
Fluckiger, C., 137–138
Forman, E. M., 58, 100
Format, of treatment, 41, 49–50
Fowler, S. L., 82
Frank, J. B., 115
Frank, J. D., 68, 115
Franklin, Benjamin, 105
Frayn, D. H., 129
Frued, S., 137–138

GAD (generalized anxiety disorder), 53
Gambling problems, 130
Garfield, S. L., 28, 34
Geers, A. L., 82
Gender, 34, 41, 42, 46, 47, 57
Generalized anxiety disorder (GAD), 53
Gibbons, M. B., 35
Goldman, E. D., 85
Greenberg, R. P., 17, 24, 39–61, 85, 98,
        121, 141
Grote, J., 87
Group therapy, 49–50

Halgin, R. P., 16
Hammel, E. F., 142
Hannan, C., 150–151, 154–155
Hansen, N. B., 58, 100
Hatchett, G. T., 24–25
Hedges, L. V., 42
Higgins, J. P. T., 42
Hoehn-Saric, R., 68
Homework, 110
Hope and outcome expectations,
        113–126, 174–175
    building, with client preferences,
        82–83
    in clinical examples, 124–126
    definition and description of, 114–116
    empirical research on, 116–120
    strengthening, 120–124
    and treatment outcomes, 70

Horvath, A. O., 137–138
Howard, K. I., 96, 100, 108, 150
Hoyt, W. T., 119–120
Hunt, C., 130

Ilardi, S. S., 70
Imagining attendance, 179
Imber, S. D., 68
Improvement, as reason for premature
    termination, 28
Individual therapy, 49–50
Initial appointment attendance, 177–178
Integrative approaches
    and rates of premature termination,
        55–56
    treating depression with, 51
    treating PTSD with, 51
Interviewing, motivational. *See*
    Motivational interviewing
IQ, 34
Ivanovic, M., 85–86
Ivey, A. E., 83

Jacobson, N. S., 23, 152
*Journal of Consulting and Clinical Psychol-
    ogy* (Swift and Greenberg), 39
A Journey to the Center of the Earth
    (Verne), 113–114
Joyce, A. S., 15–16
Julius Caesar (Shakespeare), 105

Kappa coeffecients, 24–26
Kazdin, A. E., 118
Kellett, S., 99, 130, 178
Kennedy, John F., 113
Kirsch, I., 116
Knox, S., 13–14
Kocsis, J. H., 83–84
Kokotovic, A. M., 14
Kominiak, N., 85–86
Krebs, P. M., 128

Lambert, M. J., 58, 97, 100, 156
Lampropoulos, G. K., 15
Lange, R., 87
Leitenberg, H., 70
Levine, J. C., 151–152
Linear progression, of therapy, 106, 107
Logistical information, 71

The Lord of the Rings (Tolkien), 65,
    127–128
Lundwall, L., 34
Lutz, W., 150

MacEwan, G. H., 16
Maintenance stage (of change), 128
Manthei, R. J., 28, 83
Manualization, of treatment, 42, 49,
    50, 171
Marital status, 41, 46, 47
Martinovich, Z., 150
McArthur, Douglas, 11
Median-split procedure, 20, 24–27
Miles, E., 130, 178
Miller, Arthur, 93
Miller, W. R., 131
Milton, S., 130
Milwaukee Psychotherapy Expectations
    Questionnaire (MPEQ), 74
Minami, T., 116
Missed appointments
    anxiety about, 179
    as measure of premature termination,
        19, 21–22, 24–27, 182
Monks, G. M., 69–70
Moore, R. C., 70
Moore, T. J., 116
Moras, K., 150
Morrel, T. M., 130
Moses, 13
Motivational interviewing
    addressing client motivation with, 131
    enhancing motivation in psycho-
        therapy with, 175
    treating anxiety problems with, 130
Motivation for psychotherapy, 127–135,
    175
    and client preferences, 82
    in clinical example, 133–135
    definition and description of, 128–129
    empirical research on, 129–130
    lack of, 34
    and pacing treatments, 179–180
    strategies for increasing, 130–133
MPEQ (Milwaukee Psychotherapy
    Expectations Questionnaire), 74
Muran, J. C., 139, 140
Murphy, C. M., 130

Narrative reviews, 34–35
Nash, E. H., 68
National Institute of Mental Health, 85, 118
Nicholls, S. S., 116
Nock, M. K., 118
Norcross, J. C., 87, 128–131
Norring, C., 14
Number of sessions. *See* Sessions, number of

Obsessive–compulsive disorder (OCD), 53
Office space, 177
Ogrodniczuk, J. S., 15–16
Oldham, M., 130, 178, 179
Oliveau, D. C., 70
OQ–45.2, 158
OQ (outcome questionnaires) system, 156, 158–159
Orne, M. T., 66–68, 72
ORS (Outcome Rating Scale), 159–160
Oslin, D., 130
Outcome expectations. *See* Hope and outcome expectations
Outcome questionnaires (OQ) system, 156, 158–159
Outcome Rating Scale (ORS), 159–160
Outcome studies, 38

Panic disorder, 53
Park, H. L., 24–25
Partially randomized preference trials (PRPTs), 84
Partners for Change Outcome Management System (PCOMS), 156, 159–160
Patient-focused research, 150
Patient predictors, 45–48
Patient profiling, 150
Patient trajectories, 158–160
Patterns of therapeutic change, 105–112, 174
    in clinical example, 110–112
    definition and description of, 106–107
    educating clients about, 108–110
    empirical research on, 107–108
Paul, Gordon, 50–51

PCOMS (Partners for Change Outcome Management System), 156, 159–160
Peale, Norman Vincent, 33
PEI–R (Psychotherapy Expectancy Inventory—Revised), 74, 87
Pekarik, G., 23–24, 28, 35–38, 44, 94
Pekarik, Gene, 14
Personality disorders
    and premature termination, 171
    in Swift and Greenberg's meta-analysis, 45
    and treatment orientation, 53
Phase model of psychotherapy, 96, 106–110, 174
Piper, W. E., 15–16
Piselli, A., 16
Placebos, 116–118
Placebo treatments, 116–118
Positive-outcome expectations, 114
Posttraumatic stress disorder (PTSD), 51, 54, 55
Precontemplation stage (of change), 128, 129, 131
Predictors of premature termination, 33–61
    narrative reviews of, 34–35
    patient predictors, 45–48
    provider predictors, 56–57
    study predictors, 57–59
    Swift and Greenberg's meta-analysis of, 37–61
    treatment-by-disorder effects, 50–56
    treatment predictors, 48–50
    Wierzbicki and Pekarik's meta-analysis of, 35–37
Premature termination, 11–31, 169–184
    conceptualizations of, 29–31, 170–171
    definition and description of, 17–18, 170
    empirical research on, 23–27
    ending with positive interaction, 181
    frequency of, 43–44
    future research on, 182–184
    lessening negative impact of, 180–182
    meta-analyses of, 35–61, 171–172
    narrative reviews of, 34–35
    operationalizations, 18–23
    other terms used for, 18

ABOUT THE AUTHORS

Joshua K. Swift, PhD, is an associate professor in the Department of Psychology at the University of Alaska Anchorage and a core faculty member in the Joint University of Alaska Fairbanks/University of Alaska Anchorage PhD program in clinical-community psychology, where he directs the Psychotherapy Process and Outcome Research Lab. He is also a licensed psychologist in the state of Alaska. As an early career psychologist he has authored or coauthored over 80 professional publications and presentations. He has also been recognized with a number of awards, including the American Psychological Association Division 29 Distinguished Publication of Psychotherapy Research Award, Division 29 President's Award for Psychotherapy Research, and University of Alaska Anchorage's Chancellor's Awards for Excellence in Teaching and Research.

Roger P. Greenberg, PhD, is Distinguished Professor and director of the Psychology Division at State University of New York (SUNY) Upstate Medical University in Syracuse. He is also the psychology internship training director at SUNY and a long-standing clinician in private practice. He has authored or coauthored about 250 publications and presentations, including *The*

Art and Science of Brief Psychotherapies: An Illustrated Guide (2012), *From Placebo to Panacea: Putting Psychiatric Drugs to the Test* (1997), and the award-winning *The Scientific Credibility of Freud's Theories and Therapy* (1985). He has received the National Register of Health Service Psychologists' Alfred B. Wellner Lifetime Achievement Award, the New York State Psychological Association's Joanne Lifshin Mentorship Award, the Association of Psychology Postdoctoral and Internship Centers' Excellence in Training Award, and the SUNY President's Award for Excellence in Teaching.